The Author

BREVARD S. CHILDS is Professor of Old Testament at Yale University and a member of the Departments of Religious Studies, Divinity School, and Near Eastern Languages and Literature. He is a graduate of the University of Michigan, Princeton Theological Seminary, and the University of Basel, Switzerland (Dr. Theol.). Recipient of a Guggenheim Fellowship, he has studied at the Hebrew University, Jerusalem.

Biblical
Theology
in Crisis

by BREVARD S. CHILDS

THE WESTMINSTER PRESS
Philadelphia

ISBN 0–664–20882–7

LIBRARY OF CONGRESS CATALOG CARD No. 74–96698

BOOK DESIGN BY
DOROTHY ALDEN SMITH

Published by The Westminster Press ®
Philadelphia, Pennsylvania

PRINTED IN THE UNITED STATES OF AMERICA

Contents

PART III
Testing a Method

Though a man had a precious and a rich jewel, yet if he knew not the value thereof, nor wherefore it served, he were neither the better nor richer of a straw. Even so though we read the scripture, and babble of it ever so much, yet if we know not the use of it, and wherefore it was given, and what is therein to be sought, it profits us nothing at all. It is not enough, therefore, to read and talk of it only, but we must also desire God, day and night, instantly, to open our eyes, and to make us understand and feel wherefore the scripture was given, that we may apply the medicine of the scripture, every man to his own sores. Unless we intend to be idle disputers, and brawlers about vain words, ever gnawing upon the bitter bark without, and never attaining unto the sweet pith within; and persecuting one another in defending of wicked imaginations, and phantasies of our own invention.

—William Tyndale; prefixed to the translation of the Pentateuch, 1530.

PREFACE

IT IS EVIDENT to most people who are engaged professionally in the teaching of theology that the discipline has recently passed through one phase and entered into another. Many lay people are also conscious of a shift in the winds. However, the exact nature of this change is not fully clear, and most of the reflections on the nature of the change remain impressionistic and often visceral. The layman senses the new emphasis on the secular side of Christian responsibility, and the focus of attention on contemporary social issues. The professional theologian speaks of the end of the theological consensus, often identified with "neo-orthodoxy," and the opening up of new theological fronts. He is also aware that the interest seems to have shifted away from Biblical studies to social action. But, above all, he is keenly aware of the fluid state of theological studies.

My purpose in writing this book is to attempt to understand one phase in the changing situation, specifically that which is related to Biblical studies. It is generally recognized that interest in the Bible has been characteristic of the period following the Second World War. I believe that one can go beyond this statement and even speak of a "Biblical Theology Movement." My initial concern is to describe this movement. Then I attempt to trace its rise, evaluate its strengths and weaknesses, and suggest why something new is emerging in its place. The second part of the book offers my own suggestions for a new approach in doing Biblical Theology which takes the canon of the Christian church more seriously. The final section provides four illustrations of the method that I am proposing.

I would like to thank my colleague S. Dean McBride for much incisive criticism. I am also grateful for the helpful response of the members of the New Haven Colloquium on Bible and Theology who heard parts of the first section and for permission to use material which I previously published in *Interpretation* XXIII (1969). Lastly, I am much indebted to my wife, Ann, who originally encouraged me to write this book and who discussed each chapter as it took shape.

PART I

Remembering a Past

1
THE BEGINNING
OF A MOVEMENT

INTRODUCTION

The initial purpose of this book is to describe the emergence of a distinctive American way of understanding theology in its relation to the Bible. In the period that followed the Second World War an approach to Biblical studies developed that can best be characterized as the "Biblical Theology Movement." The concept of the theological task was distinctive and clearly set apart from the theological trends which preceded the movement as well as from those which followed. Although the movement arose largely in response to certain European influences and continued to reflect a close relationship to the various theological currents from abroad, its peculiar American stamp gave the movement a significant shape that distinguished it from its foreign counterparts. The movement was strongly Protestant in its orientation and directed consciously toward the needs of the Christian church. Its influence spread widely beyond these borders, but the center of the movement remained concentrated in a limited area of the Protestant spectrum. The movement had a rather closely definable beginning and an approximate ending.

THE CHANGING CLIMATE IN BIBLICAL
AND THEOLOGICAL STUDIES

During the last years of the Second World War a number of books began to appear in England and in the United States within the field of Bible which represented a break with the dominant scholarly tradition of the thirties. In 1944 H. H. Rowley's book *The Relevance of the Bible* appeared, followed within a year by the *Rediscovery of the Old Testament*. Alan Richardson's *A Preface to Bible Study* (1943) and Archibald M. Hunter's *The Unity of the New Testament* were published within a few months of one another, and shortly appeared in American editions. In America, Floyd V. Filson's *One Lord, One Faith* appeared in 1944, to be followed by a steady stream of well-written, exciting books such as G. Ernest Wright's *The Challenge of Israel's Faith* (1944), Paul S. Minear's *Eyes of Faith* (1946),[1] and Bernhard W. Anderson's *Rediscovering the Bible* (1951).

Among the theological journals a flood of articles appeared with titles that frequently referred to the "rediscovery" or "rebirth" of Biblical Theology. In 1943, James D. Smart published two long articles with the title "The Death and Rebirth of Old Testament Theology." [2] In the following year *Theology Today* carried such lead articles as Paul Minear's "Wanted: A Biblical Theology" and Frederick Dillistone's "The Rediscovery of the Gospel." Then in 1946 the first of Otto Piper's four articles on the Bible in *The Christian Century* exploded into popular journalism and forced the issue out of the theological seminaries and into the churches. From every side there emerged a veritable flood of articles on the centrality of the Bible for the life of the church.[3] The recurrent theme was the beginning of a new understanding of the Bible for the life and service of the church. Another indication of the new spirit of Biblical-theological interest appeared with the inauguration of a rash of new periodicals, *Theology Today* (1944), *Interpretation* (1947), *Scottish Journal of Theology* (1948), all of which voiced the avowed purpose of combining the study of the Bible and theology in a new and creative way.[4]

In spite of the chorus of voices that were being heard, the one message kept coming through that something new and vital was being discovered in the Bible which had been lost. This discovery was consistently announced with great enthusiasm and zeal. Although it was directed to all levels of the theological world, particular emphasis was laid on its being directed to the members of the Christian church. The theme was constantly reiterated that the church, in particular, had suffered from its misunderstanding of the Bible and needed to hear its fresh notes in order to be awakened to its real task. Shortly this appeal began to resound from pulpits across the United States. The return to the Bible implied a return to Biblical proclamation. Although the challenge to recover the essential message of the Bible was often couched in polemical language, it was also clear that the basic assault was not directed against historical criticism as such. Rather, the point was continually being made that criticism had its rightful place which should not be contested. At this juncture, frequently a sharp polemic was delivered against Fundamentalism whose literalistic interpretation of the Bible was blamed for the prevailing apathy for the Bible. However, the major thrust was directed against the misuse of historical criticism by the theological liberals. Critical scholars were faulted for having lost themselves in the minutiae of literary, philological, and historical problems. As a result the Bible had been hopelessly fragmented and the essential unity of the gospel was distorted and forgotten. Biblical scholarship had deteriorated into an exercise in trivia, in which tragic process the profound theological dimensions were overlooked.

Up to this point in describing the emergence of the Biblical Theology Movement, the focus of attention has been on the effect of the new approach to Biblical studies. However, there was another side of the movement that was of equal importance, and in terms of historical sequence, preceded and strongly influenced the shape of the fresh Biblical interest. The reference is, of course, to the resurgence of theological interest that occurred in Europe following the First World War. This development in the twenties and thirties was primarily associated in the Anglo-Saxon world with the names of Karl Barth and Emil Brunner. Obviously the attempt to trace the full effect of this European theology on America lies beyond both the scope of the book and the competence of the author. Fortunately there has been sufficient study of this period to provide a reliable picture of the development at least in its broad lines.[5] This work is confined to those specific effects of the theological resurgence on the Biblical Theology Movement.

Of fundamental importance was the radical shift by certain systematic theologians respecting the place of the Bible in the formation of theology. Here the break with the dominant liberal tradition of American theology was dramatic. H. Richard Niebuhr's *The Meaning of Revelation* (1941) was an important beginning in the new direction. In the same year John A. Mackay's *A Preface to Christian Theology* introduced a whole new catalog of virtually new names to the American theological scene. Berdyaev, Dostoevsky, and Pascal suddenly became important theologians who were deeply rooted in the Biblical tradition. Of great significance was the translation into English of Søren Kierkegaard which had begun in the late thirties and which evoked an immediate response among American theologians. Similarly, the appearance of Martin Buber's *I and Thou* in English garb provided a new theological vocabulary for many theologians in successfully combining the language of the Bible with existentialism. The thunder of Reinhold Niebuhr's brilliant Gifford Lectures, *The Nature and Destiny of Man,* had penetrated even the most fortified strongholds of liberal theology, although it was generally recognized that his was an emphasis which was to be distinguished from the European.

However, perhaps more influential than all of these in the decade of the forties was the impact of Emil Brunner on American theology. Brunner had been brought to Union Seminary and Princeton Seminary in the late thirties and had learned to know the theological climate of America firsthand. While the name of Karl Barth had become a household word following the end of the Second World War, Brunner was the theologian whom Americans could understand! The impact of his *Divine-Human Encounter* (1943), followed by *Revelation and Reason* (1946)—both in unusually lucid English prose—can hardly be overestimated.[6] Here was a theology that was equally adamant in placing the Bible at the center of its work. Moreover, Brunner's sharp attack on the Fundamentalists to the right and on the Liberals to the left was highly compatible to the mood of the Biblical scholars. For the first time in many a generation the exciting possibility emerged that the new Biblical scholarship could join ranks with the new "neo-orthodox" theology to wage a common battle.

THE AMERICAN SETTING
FOR THE NEW BIBLICAL THEOLOGY

It is not obvious from the brief sketch of the renewed American interest in the Bible and theology during the forties that one can speak of a distinct Biblical Theology Movement. Would it not be more appropriate simply to describe America's reaction to European theology as an extension of a postwar movement which, for various reasons, had placed unusual emphasis on the role of the Bible? The major reason for defending the use of the term "Biblical Theology Movement" is not to deny its derivative character in respect to Europe, but rather to highlight the unusual shape that the American appropriation assumed. The usual treatment of the subject, which focuses its attention on Germany during the period of the twenties and sees American theology as simply a delayed reaction to the same historical catalyst, has failed to describe accurately the real historical forces at work in America. Moreover, this common approach to the subject neither has produced an adequate description of the peculiar shape of Biblical Theology that emerged in America nor has it successfully analyzed its inner dynamic.

The term "Biblical Theology Movement" suggests a distinction between the American development and the broad use of the term "Biblical Theology." This latter was a loosely defined European discipline that began in the post-Reformation period and was an attempt on the part of both rationalists and pietists to delineate a theology that was allegedly Biblically oriented in reaction to the confessional orthodoxy of the day. The history of this general Biblical Theology discipline has been frequently rehearsed in recent years.[7] As if now well known, the impact of historical critical scholarship in the late nineteenth century had the effect of seriously undercutting the older theological approaches to the Bible, and replaced the discipline with an allegedly objective science of the history of religions. Again for various reasons, particularly because of the changing *Zeitgeist* which followed the First World War, the interest in Biblical Theology revived, and within Germany culminated in several magnificent volumes of Biblical Theology associated with such giants in the field as Eichrodt, von Rad, and Bultmann. Although the Biblical Theology Movement in America was clearly dependent on this European revival, often mediated by British scholars, it is nevertheless our conviction that the American development was so distinctive as to demand a separate characterization.

The failure to take seriously the peculiarly conditioned historical background of American theology has led many to misunderstand the inner dynamic of the Biblical Theology Movement. Stendahl [8] may be generally correct in his analysis of the rise of modern Biblical Theology in Germany. He suggests that the radical criticism of scholars such as Wrede, Weiss, and Schweitzer destroyed the grounds of the older liberal position of Harnack, thus opening up the new possibility for a different understanding of Biblical Theology in Barth and Bultmann. However, to include the contemporary works of the American Biblical scholars within this framework is to misunderstand the American development. Even a casual examination of the literature of the period reveals the wholly different atmosphere.

What was this peculiar historical and sociological matrix of America which led to the Biblical Theology Movement? It is quite clear that one of the most important factors was the aftermath of the Fundamentalist-Modernist controversy which had been waged with such fury from 1910 through the late twenties. Most of the major Protestant denominations had remained sharply divided regarding this issue, even well into the thirties, and none was more bitter than the Presbyterian.[9] Even in those denominations which had effected a compromise, many of their members continued to be identified with one of the parties and retained a greater factional loyalty than denominational. By the middle of the thirties, if not before, it had become evident to the great majority of theologians that the Liberals had won the battle of historical criticism. The reorganization of Princeton Theological Seminary in 1929 took away the last stronghold of scholarly resistance within a major denomination.

Nevertheless, the theology of Liberalism remained incompatible to a whole segment of Protestantism that had reluctantly begun to accept the validity of Biblical criticism. During the period of the thirties there did not appear any major theological work that had even begun to effect a reconciliation between the liberal and conservative wings of the church. Conservative theologians concentrated by and large on polemics[10] or in a repristination of seventeenth-century dogmatics.[11] Reinhold Niebuhr's criticism of Liberalism was received with approval, but his double-edged attacks on conservatism as well prevented his being recognized as an ally. Elements of European theology had begun to trickle into America, starting with Douglas Horton's translation of Barth's *The Word of God and the Word of Man* (1928). It was at first cultivated and mediated to a large extent by German-speaking Reformed theologians. But its influence was not widespread in any of the major centers of theological education, and remained almost unknown in the local churches.

The contrast in theology between this American setting and the atmosphere in Germany in the twenties and thirties could hardly have been sharper. Within Germany the major battle over historical criticism had been fought at the end of the nineteenth century. The defeat and disillusionment following the First World War had shaken the assumptions of Liberal theology to the roots, and had given birth to an agonizing reappraisal of the Bible and theology which had begun to take a definite shape in the middle twenties. Within America the wounds that had been opened in the battle over the Bible were far from healed. To many, the polarities between liberals and conservatives seemed as unbridgeable as ever. Neither the First World War nor the Depression of the thirties had produced an intellectual shattering of ongoing Liberal theology or a drastic reappraisal of conservative theological tradition.

Looking back, one sees clearly that a ferment in American theology had indeed started in the late thirties, and had begun to grow in the early forties. During the war years the signs of a new theological maturity continued to multiply, even though the preoccupation of the war delayed their development. But with the end of the Second World War the new burst of theological life sprang forth as if in full bloom, ready and eager to meet the great influx of new theological students returning from the war. Now for the first time there emerged in

America a genuine opportunity to break out of the theological impasse inherited from the past. There was another alternative made available beyond that of the liberal-conservative syndrome. One was offered the possibility of accepting Biblical criticism without reservation as a valid tool while at the same time recovering a robust, confessionally oriented theology. This was the peculiar American setting which was so open to European theology, and yet which would use it to address a special American problem.

It is significant that the most aggressive leaders in the new movement were often Presbyterian in background or affiliation, and had experienced the effects of the older hassle and were intent on promoting a new alternative in theology. Theological and Biblical scholars such as G. Ernest Wright, Floyd V. Filson, James D. Smart, John Wick Bowman, John A. Mackay, Elmer G. Homrighausen, Joseph Haroutunian, Paul Lehmann, Otto Piper, Donald G. Miller, and Balmer H. Kelly were prominent in the movement. The Westminster Press, responding to the call for adequate literature in the field, published an American edition of the majority of English books on the subject of Biblical Theology, and, following the lead of the SCM Press, promoted translations of compatible German and Swiss theology. Of course, very shortly all the major Protestant denominations were influenced and many contributed their own first-rate scholars (Paul Minear, James Muilenburg, Bernhard Anderson). However, the real impetus of the movement continued to center in the Free Church wing of Protestantism which had been hardest hit by the Fundamentalist-Modernist controversy.

When one reviews the many articles of the late forties that served to introduce and promote the Biblical Theology Movement, one is impressed with the continual attempt either to overcome or to avoid the errors of the past generation. John A. Mackay writes in the first editorial of *Theology Today*: "If only Biblical scholars, both liberal and conservative, had re-

membered that the Bible . . . must be studied in terms of its
own central category of redemption, how much theological
confusion and bitter controversy would have been avoided." [12]

Again, G. Ernest Wright,[13] in defending the need for a
newer understanding of the Bible, can still refer in 1947 to the
Hodge-Warfield theory of Biblical inspiration which he contrasts with Calvin's less rigid view. Earlier, Wright had written: "My approach is neither liberal nor conservative. Such
terms have outlived much of their usefulness. We need to approach the Scripture with a point of view which transcends
such extremes." [14] Similarly, the editors of *Interpretation*
consistently issue the challenge for a fresh approach to the
Bible and theology against the background of the impasse
reached by the factions on both the left and the right.[15]

It is clear that from its inception certain English and European authors played an enormous role in the formation of the
American movement. Nevertheless, in our opinion there never
was a Biblical Theology Movement in Britain or Europe
which was similar to that in America. Indeed, the contrasting
forms that the revived interest in the Bible took in Britain and
in America are striking. American theologians saw in Biblical
Theology a chance to get beyond the frustrating Fundamentalist-Modernist deadlock. They proclaimed the dawn of a
new and better day. English scholars, in contrast, especially
those in the Church of England, usually welcomed the revived
interest in the Bible, but gave no hint that they thought of it
as a radical break with the scholarship of the past. One looks
in vain in such typical journals as *The Expository Times, Theology,* or *The Journal of Theological Studies* for any evidence
of an appeal similar to that being sounded in America in the
name of Biblical Theology.

A characteristic difference between England and America
was the consistent lack of enthusiasm in England for the theology of Brunner and Barth, which in America had become such
an integral part of the movement. Even those who welcomed

the growing interest in the use of the Bible found the so-called "theology of crisis" basically uncongenial.[16] Those aspects of the newer theology which were accepted were generally assimilated through English mediators such as Hoskyns. In typical English fashion the Anglican tradition of theology had managed to overcome the sharp polarities that had emerged in America between the left and the right. As a result, there was little need expressed even in the immediate postwar period for a completely new direction in theology.

Additional evidence of the contrasting concept of Biblical theology between England and America appears in the writers' attitude to the Biblical scholarship of the thirties. It was characteristic of the younger American Biblical theologians not only to see their work as offering something radically new but also as a protest against the prevailing type of scholarship in which most of them had been trained.[17] America had produced or acquired an impressive list of internationally recognized Biblical scholars during the thirties. In Old Testament, one thought, above all, of Pfeiffer, Waterman, Irwin, Meek, Montgomery, Barton, Morgenstern, Bewer, Burrows, and Albright. In New Testament, there was an equally impressive list of critical scholars: Bacon, Ropes, Lake, Torrey, Nock, Cadbury, Goodenough, Enslin, Case, Riddle, Kraeling, Goodspeed, Craig, Grant, Willoughby, and Moffatt. With the exception of Albright, the newer school of Biblical scholars was basically critical of the general theological position of these so-called liberal scholars. Significantly, great conservative Biblical scholars of the stature of Warfield, Machen, and A. T. Robertson had all but disappeared from the American scene.[18]

American Biblical scholars with theological interest, finding themselves unable to agree with the prevailing trends of American scholarship, turned to Britain and Europe for inspiration and guidance. The works of Hoskyns, Phythian-Adams, Rowley, Snaith, Richardson, Dodd, Hunter, Hebert, T. W.

Manson, and others occupied greatest attention. Among
pastors, William Barclay began to exert an enormous influence. But of equal importance, and perhaps even regarded as
the ultimate source for the newer insights, were the translated
works of the Europeans. Cullmann and Eichrodt headed the
list; Buber, Nygren, Aulén, Vischer, and de Dietrich were
highly treasured by others. Only somewhat later did the
names of Bultmann and von Rad begin to appear in any significant way.

If one turns to England, the sharp contrast between the
younger and older generations is not at all so apparent. The
leading Old Testament Biblical theologian, H. H. Rowley, understood his work to be in direct continuity with his mentor,
H. Wheeler Robinson.[19] Again, in the writings of Alan Richardson, who for many epitomized the New Testament theologian, one does not get the sense of a sharp polemical break
with the past, which was current in America.[20] When *The Expository Times* in 1946 requested a series of articles on the
"Unity of the New Testament," the large majority of scholars
selected were already well known in the thirties and simply
reasserted their previous interest in the subject (A. E. J. Raw-
linson, Vincent Taylor, T. W. Manson).

In 1946, C. H. Dodd's popular handbook of Biblical Theology, *The Bible Today*, appeared, but without any repudiation
of his earlier book, *The Authority of the Bible* (1928; revised
edition 1938), which was thoroughly liberal in its position.
Even in the works that best illustrated the newer trends in
British Biblical Theology, such as those of Archibald M. Hunter, A. G. Hebert, and Norman H. Snaith, one rarely found remarks that were characteristic of the American debate. In the
same way in Scotland, the leading Biblical scholars reflected
the newer interest in Biblical Theology without feeling the
need to repudiate the work of the previous generation. Norman Porteous, William Manson, and James Stewart, all of Edinburgh, were typical of the Scottish attitude. Of course, such

generalizations are dangerous if pushed too hard. Certainly in
Scotland the break in dogmatic theology was much more radical, and at this point there were elements that joined with the
American Biblical Theology Movement. The editors of the
newly constituted *Scottish Journal of Theology*, Torrance and
Reid, drank deeply from the theology of the Continent. Being
strongly influenced by Barth and seeking to recover their Reformation heritage, they found themselves at odds with the
dominant idealistic theology of John Baillie, A. E. Taylor, and
others. However, even in this area, the burning issues between
the Church of Scotland and the Church of England, particularly in the light of the vigorous challenge from the Anglo-
Catholic wing, gave the postwar debate in Scotland a different
structure from that being waged in America.

No clearer indication of the sharp polarity in the American
scene can be had than from the heated response that the appearance of the new Biblical theologians called forth from the
older—and some younger—liberal scholars. William Irwin[21]
complained that "through the specious appeal of 'the new orthodoxy,' the mood of the irrational again threatens us." Morton Enslin,[22] characterizing Otto Piper's position, wrote in
The Christian Century: "To my mind this whole thesis is not
only wrong, but wrongheaded and utterly out of place in the
modern world." Norman Pittenger[23] suggested: "Much of the
revived Biblical Theology is, in my belief, a return to a precritical position." In his inaugural address to the Society of
Biblical Literature in 1950, Robert Pfeiffer[24] attacked the revived theological approach to the Bible, particularly in the
form presented by Filson, and defended the purely historical
approach. Henry Cadbury warned: "This so-called biblical
theology seems particularly inappropriate in relation to the
Gospels." [25] Part of the explanation for the intensity of the
opposition to the Biblical Theology Movement certainly
stemmed from the haunting memory of specters returning
from the battles of the not-too-distant past. Cadbury made

specific reference to J. Gresham Machen in contesting the new
theological trends.[26] To be sure, the new emphases of Biblical
studies were not greeted with enthusiasm by every scholar in
England, but even those who represented the older position
appeared under no threat and were ready to argue calmly the
merits of the case.[27]

In a similar way the development of renewed interest in
Biblical theology in the Scandinavian countries, particularly in
Sweden, emerged with a form characteristically distinct from
that of the American movement. For example, there seemed to
be wide agreement among the contributors of the volume *The
Root of the Vine: Essays in Biblical Theology*, by Anton
Fridrichsen and other members of Uppsala University (1953),
that Biblical theology was primarily a historical, descriptive
task that was to be sharply distinguished from the later theological reflections. This is, of course, the position that Stendahl[28] developed at length in his well-known article. Without
arguing the merits of this position, it is a fact that this distinction was not widely held by American Biblical theologians. Indeed, the major polemic of such men as Smart, Filson, and Minear was directed to such a separation. Bible and theology
belong together, both on the descriptive and constructive
levels.

Of course, the emphasis on the discontinuity between the
American movement and the revival of Biblical interest in Europe should not obscure the genuine lines of continuity. There
were certainly significant groups within Britain—particularly
from the Free Churches—which shared many of the goals and
attitudes of the American Biblical Theology Movement even
though the general national pattern was distinct from that of
America. One thinks especially of the Student Christian Movement during this period, an organization that, significantly
enough, had experienced in an earlier decade strong polarities
between the liberal and conservative factions. Moreover, the
American movement in turn was able for a time to exercise

considerable influence on the direction of general Biblical theology in Britain. While the influence of the American movement appears to have been slight in Germany—American Biblical Theology works of this period were seldom quoted—the reverse effect on England was certainly discernible. The wide sale of the SCM Press series Studies in Biblical Theology, which carried many contributions from American scholars, would confirm this statement. On the continent it was especially in ecumenical circles that the American Biblical theologians left a significant impact.[29]

THE EFFECT OF THE MOVEMENT ON AMERICAN THEOLOGY

A good barometer for measuring the force of a movement is the degree to which its impact is felt on the existing institutions that come under its influence. The concern to change the theological climate of America was characteristic of the Biblical Theology Movement from the outset. It was the evangelical fervor of the American theologians to get the message to the seminaries and the churches which transformed a theological trend into a movement. Within a very short time the Biblical Theology Movement had managed to effect major transformations in several fundamental structures of the Protestant Church. The role of The Westminster Press in popularizing the movement has already been mentioned. The new *Christian Faith and Life* Curriculum of the Presbyterian Church U.S.A., under the aggressive leadership of James D. Smart, was the first creative venture in bringing the newer insights of Biblical Theology down to the grass roots of Christian education.[30] The widespread use of the Presbyterian material by many other denominations resulted in the revision of church school curricula by most of the major denominations within a decade. The effect was to popularize Biblical Theology throughout the entire spectrum of Protestantism.

The impact of the new movement on the American seminaries was dramatic. Some indication of the influence is found in the rash of new courses in Biblical Theology, which, in typical American fashion, provided means of entering the subject matter without the need of Greek or Hebrew. The Niebuhr report of seminary education which began in 1954 and published its second volume in 1957 endorsed with considerable enthusiasm the new approach to the Bible. Quoting Bernhard W. Anderson, the report applauded the blending together of the historical and critical disciplines in order to reach to the theological heart of the Bible.[31]

The emphasis on Biblical preaching for the church was another major stress of the movement. Countless books and articles urged the minister to recover the heritage of the Reformation by "proclaiming the Word." [32] Topical preaching was frequently blamed for the shallowness of the American pulpit. Ministers were urged to return to the exposition of the Bible and begin with a text. At least for a time, one gains the impression that many pastors tried to put the suggestion into practice, while holding on to a typical American homiletical style.

Again, the effect of the Biblical Theology Movement on the ecumenical movement was far-reaching. The changing approach to the Bible was already reflected in the two ecumenical studies of London in 1946 and Bossey in 1947.[33] Following the Amsterdam Assembly of 1948, the World Council requested its Study Department to pursue the question of "The Bible and the Church's Message to the World." The volume that reported the results of the study appeared in 1951 with the title *Biblical Authority for Today* and represented in many of its sections a classic statement of the emphases of Biblical Theology.[34] Several of the finest statements were developed by American Biblical theologians. Amazingly enough, some fifteen leading Biblical scholars were then able to agree on the guiding principles for the interpretation of the Bible. A study document on Faith and Order in preparation for the Third World Conference in Lund in 1952 commented on the profound effect that Biblical Theology had already made on the ecumenical movement. "It has led to the refurbishing of traditional Christian words, like *redemption, sacrifice, faith, grace,* etc. Above all, it has led to a common rediscovery of the biblical idea of the Church." [35] In the ecumenical discussions of this period the forces that had arisen from the general European revival of theology joined ranks with the American movement. It is not possible to distinguish clearly between the various influences at work. The significant factor is that the ecumenical movement provided an arena in which the American form of Biblical scholarship received a warm reception and was prized for its contribution.

Finally, the influence of the Biblical Theology Movement on the American Roman Catholic Church calls for notice. Although the subject is too broad to analyze properly in a brief treatment, a few observations are in order. In 1947 a volume appeared under the editorship of Harold R. Willoughby, entitled *The Study of the Bible Today and Tomorrow.*[36] Among the essays was one by James H. Cobb on the topic "Current Trends in Catholic Biblical Research." The author began his survey of Catholic scholarship by sharply distinguishing the "world view" of Catholic scholars from that of "liberal scholars" (i.e., Protestant). The Liberals regard the Bible as differing in "no essential ways from other literature." In contrast, the Catholic scholar regards Scripture and tradition as the "total deposit of faith as, and only as, this is officially interpreted by the living *magisterium* of the church." [37] In essence, the point was made that there could be no real dialogue on the Bible between Catholics and Protestants.

Cobb's article, which represented an extremely conservative Catholic position even for the forties, is significant to the extent to which it shows the dramatic and open shift in the Catholic stance regarding the interpretation of the Bible. In the immediate postwar period there seemed to be little stirring among American Catholic Biblical scholars. But by 1956, when John L. McKenzie published *The Two-edged Sword: An Interpretation of the Old Testament,* the Biblical Theology Movement had deeply penetrated into Catholic scholarship, and interest in the Bible was at a high pitch among both scholars and laity.[38] Again, there were obviously many other factors involved, particularly the role of the papal encyclical of 1943, *Divino Afflante Spiritu.* But beginning in the middle fifties a stream of excellent popular treatments began to appear that attempted to convey a new approach to the Bible. Along with this came a flood of translations of European books on the Bible.[39] Characteristic of the newer type of book was the frequent reference to the work of the Protestant Biblical theologians. It was fully obvious that the Catholic scholars now conceived of their work in interpreting the Bible as participating in a common enterprise with their Protestant counterparts.

In spite of these common elements, there remained characteristic differences in the doing of Biblical Theology by Catholics. Much of the difference lay in the focus and stress that was placed on the various Biblical themes rather than in specific interpretations. McKenzie's general understanding of the Old Testament was not too far removed from that of Anderson or Wright; nevertheless, certain issues, such as revelation in history, were played down and given a different context. A similar observation holds true for the introduction to the Gospels of Bruce Vawter,[40] or the standard European New Testament introduction of Robert-Feuillet. The difference in approach, which can no longer be classified in terms of doctrinal positions, may well stem from the varying historical experience of the Catholic Church in respect to the use of the Bible. The Catholic Church also faced a problem of Modernism, but in a form which, at least for American scholars, differed widely from the issue among Protestants. Again, the strong French influence distinguished the American Catholics from the Protestants who continued to be primarily oriented toward Germany and Britain.

To summarize: Following the Second World War there emerged in America a particular way of doing theology in relation to Biblical studies that has been characterized as the Biblical Theology Movement. Although American Biblical theologians made much use of British and European writers, the shape of this theology received a specific American stamp which justifies its designation as a movement.

2
MAJOR ELEMENTS
OF THE CONSENSUS

To speak of a Biblical Theology Movement is to suggest a unified position regarding the role of the Bible and theology. However, there was never an attempt among its adherents to formulate a "position." At the outset it is important to recognize the great variety within the movement. While there were certain common characteristics that gave the movement coherence, much freedom was allowed for differences in formulation. Little attempt was ever made to bring the different lines into a closely knit theology. There was a sense of sharing common goals, indeed of fighting on a common front, which could overlook whole areas of diversity. So, for example, Paul Minear's early writings could reflect the existential influence of Kierkegaard. H. H. Rowley, in contrast, still moved within the idealistic categories of values and ideas, whereas G. Ernest Wright attempted to combine a conservative view of the Old Testament inherited from Albright with a strong Calvinistic background in theology. Particularly in America during the early phase of the movement, so much energy was expended in attacking the older positions of liberal theology that seldom does one encounter much criticism directed against members with the newer emphases.

However, in spite of the variety within the movement, the fact remains that there was a remarkable similarity in some major themes that began to be emphasized. Very shortly certain themes became characteristic of the Biblical Theology Movement, and gave it a coherence because of this broad consensus. An attempt shall now be made to sketch the characteristic elements of the movement.

The Rediscovery of the Theological Dimension

Above all, the Biblical Theology Movement was a challenge to recover a theological dimension of the Bible. The concern was neither with a new doctrinal statement nor with a return to a theological system, but rather to penetrate to the heart of the Bible which was, in some way, thought to be theological. The use of such vague terms as "dimension" or "levels" seemed to indicate that much of the initial concern was visceral and intuitive. It was a groping after something that was only dimly perceived. One sensed with Barth that there was a "strange new world" within the Bible. Occasionally one caught a glimpse of the mystery and profundity of the Biblical message. There was the growing sense of frustration with the traditional critical way of reading the Bible. In spite of the tremendous energy that had been expended in the study of the Bible, the central theological role of the Scriptures had not become clearer. What did it mean to hear in the Bible the "word of God"? Could an interpreter any longer hear God speaking through these pages? In what sense was the goal of exegesis a "divine-human encounter"? Was there a divine process at work over and above the human forces which gave it its shape?

The younger scholars sensed a sterility and narrowness in the critical work of the preceding generation. Not only was there an obvious blind spot for theological problems, but an amazing superficiality which viewed the Bible from a typically American perspective. Value judgments that reflected modern culture were leveled against the Bible in a completely uncritical and naïve manner. For example, James Smart[1] was devastating in his attack on William Irwin for subsuming the Biblical understanding of divine revelation of a transcendent God under the rubrics of "human processes" and "empirical reason." Or again, Donald G. Miller, in reviewing Goodspeed's book, remained puzzled as to how the "dean of New Testament scholars in America should be so lacking in religious content and so devoid of the biblical point of view while writing about the Bible. Has not the day come when American biblical scholarship should end the process . . . of judging the Bible by the shallow canons of 20th century complacent American liberal thought?"[2] In a vicarious way the younger American scholars began to speak of "civilization shaken to its foundations by a world war and dazed men wandering about in the rubble of shattered dreams,"[3] and sought themselves to experience a new urgency in the Biblical message.

Of course, lying at the center of the new concern for a theologically oriented study of the Bible was the conviction that the Scriptures were highly relevant for modern man. This relevance was phrased in a variety of ways. Rowley[4] could speak of the Bible's "abiding significance—particularly for this generation." Haroutunian wrote: "We have discovered a new kinship between us and the Biblical people."[5] Others characterized it as a book that "carries upon it the name and address of every people and person to whom it comes."[6] Again, one heard the need for understanding one's present history in the light of the past. But most often one spoke of an encounter with the God of the Bible, an event in which God broke through the barriers of time to lay claim on modern man.

Right at the outset, those who were suggesting the need for a theological dimension in interpretation made it absolutely clear that this appeal was not a repudiation of the historicocritical method. If the Liberals were to be blamed for the loss of theological perspective, so also were the Fundamentalists at fault for their denial of valid Biblical criticism.

The movement rejected categorically a return to the pre-critical era of Biblical study, unless, of course, it was to Calvin and Luther, who somehow became models for theological interpretation without the onus of being precritical. The challenge was to get beyond criticism. "We have not entered the temple of Holy Scripture . . . when the critical process has done its work. We have merely stood at the door and looked in," [7] wrote the editors of *Interpretation*.

Again, John A. Mackay, in calling for a modern rediscovery of the Bible that would parallel the Reformation, was quick to add: "Bibliolatry we must, of course, eschew. Intellectual integrity and the Bible demand that the rights of Biblical criticism be safeguarded." [8] Rowley, Richardson, and Muilenburg —to name but a few—never tired of commending "honest" or "valid" criticism as a handmaiden to Biblical Theology, rather than an opponent. Only infrequently, such as in the writings of Otto Piper and Paul Minear, was there more fundamental questioning of presuppositions underlying the historicocritical method.

In general, the impression was given that the historico-critical method was sound. Its failure to produce theological fruits lay either in its misuse or in its overconcentration on peripheral matters. Even when major corrections were offered to the prevailing critical understanding of the Old Testament— Wellhausen's evolutionary development was to be repudiated —it was done in the name of a more objective, scientific understanding of the documents. [9] Because the critical tools were effective when correctly employed, the call was issued to press beyond prolegomena to theological matters. The new direction must not be "less scholarly than we have known but more profoundly theological." [10]

Wright envisioned that "one of the most important tasks of the Church today is to lay hold upon a Biblically centered theology" and regretted the fact that "it is difficult to find a leading graduate school in the world where a student can profitably specialize in Biblical theology." [11] At least for a time it looked as though a new direction was being charted.

THE UNITY OF THE WHOLE BIBLE

The circle of scholars who were identified with the revived interest in Biblical Theology were convinced of the need to overcome the sharp cleavage that had arisen within Biblical studies between the disciplines of Old Testament and New. This concern was not simply a theoretical one. From the beginning it expressed itself in a practical way. There was a newfound freedom which allowed, and indeed demanded, that New Testament scholars work in the Old Testament and Old Testament scholars in the New. Thus, Rowley's books in the forties invariably included a discussion of New Testament topics, and Minear's *Eyes of Faith* occupied itself equally with both Testaments. One of the great appeals of Cullmann's *Christ and Time* was its embracing of both Testaments. Even when the two fields were divided among specialists, a single title reflected the unified approach to the whole Bible as, for example, in Wright and Fuller's *The Book of the Acts of God.*

The attempt to deal with both Testaments in a unified way came as a protest against the tendency of increased specialization which had characterized American and British scholarship in the preceding generation. For America it was a sign that scholarship had come of age and was technical enough to debate with Germany on an equal footing. The younger Biblical theologians were convinced that something important in Biblical studies had been lost by this overspecialization. At times the complaint was of "not seeing the woods because of the trees." As early as 1936, Dodd had called for a "centripetal movement to succeed the centrifugal." [12] Or again, it focused on the fragmentation and splintering of the Biblical message into countless sources, traditions, and redactions.[13] Others complained that too much energy was being used for peripheral issues with the result that more important issues—particularly the theological—were being neglected. Finally, some felt that the Bible had become a private bailiwick of the scholar who had lost sight of the needs of the church to hear the word of God. It is interesting to note in the early period how often the criticism fell on two books that seemed to epitomize the problem, I. G. Matthews, *The Religious Pilgrimage of Israel* (1947), and E. F. Scott, *Varieties of New Testament Religion* (1943).

The call for a unified approach to the Bible was so widespread among the adherents of the newer direction that countless books and articles with similar-sounding titles appeared. Several periodicals devoted a series of articles to the subject, or even whole issues.[14] Moreover, there was an immediate broad consensus in respect to some of the main lines of the argument. First of all, there was a common rejection of certain methods of achieving a unity. The old allegorical method was eschewed as invalid. Some writers also included in their disavowal the use of typology as well, although there was disagreement here. While the term "typology" was often avoided, one began to hear of "finding the same pattern of revelation in the Old Testament and the New Testament." [15]

It is indicative of this reaction that the writings of Wilhelm Vischer[16] and Father Hebert,[17] which shared most of the concerns of the Biblical Theology Movement, were never fully recognized by American and British Biblical scholars. Again, there was an agreement that the Old Testament not be Christianized, and the specter of a so-called "Christomonism" [18] called forth and summarily dismissed. Finally, one heard that the unity dare not be "static," but dynamic. It must be a unity without uniformity.[19]

The most frequently used rubric by which to describe in a positive way the unity of the Bible was "unity in diversity." [20] This approach appeared to allow the Biblical theologian to affirm the detailed analytical work of his predecessors, while at the same time maintaining a unity. Once it was recognized that unity was not in contradiction to diversity, the manner by which this relationship was spelled out by the various Biblical theologians differed enormously. Rowley was particularly concerned to avoid two extremes: the one of seeing the unity merely as a line of human religious development that left out God's role; the other of seeing a history of revelation that minimized the place of human personality. His own formulation was that of a "unity of the Divine revelation given in the context of history and through the medium of human personality." [21] While Rowley's position seldom received a frontal attack, it was obvious that others found it less than satisfactory by the variety of other formulations offered.

James Muilenburg, in *Biblical Authority for Today*,[22] chose to delineate three categories of Biblical unity: the unity of the divine purpose, the covenant relation, and the continuity of the divine revelation. In a real sense Muilenburg's essay was an attempt to combine several emphases of European theologians without allowing anyone an exclusive right. He accepted Eichrodt's covenant emphasis, but modified it by stressing the eschatological movement from promise to fulfillment in an ongoing continuity of revelation which is closer to von Rad's position. Muilenburg stressed the need to use the Bible's own categories, but in his stating that "Christ is the final meaning of Israel," it remained difficult to see on what level he could affirm this statement. Robert C. Dentan[23] also remained somewhat vague in speaking of a "higher unity" that bound New Testament and Old Testament together.

A good many other models were used to explicate the unity of the Bible. Some scholars emphasized the need to recover the "one message which the makers of the Canon were sure was present." [24] Still others spoke of a "kerygmatic unity" which seemed to suggest reading the Old Testament from a New Testament vantage point in order to clarify the Old Testament's real intention.[25] H. R. Niebuhr spoke of "a single drama of divine and human action." [26] Finally, there were always those who found the fundamental unity in history, by which a history of revelation was usually meant along with the obvious historical lines that join the Old and the New Testament. Surprisingly enough, the role of the canon in creating and maintaining the unity of the Bible was seldom discussed. Often one got the impression that the concept of canon was part of the static, dogmatic unity that was being rejected for a new dynamic interpretation.

THE REVELATION OF GOD IN HISTORY

Few tenets lay closer to the heart of the Biblical Theology Movement than the conviction that revelation was mediated through history. It provided the key to unlock the Bible for a modern generation and at the same time to understand it theologically. Invariably one could expect to find among the major expositions of the new theological emphasis at least one chapter on the subject of "revelation in history." Obviously the idea was not a new one. It had been stressed in different ways earlier in the history of theology, and had even become the central characteristic of the Erlangen Theology of the mid-nineteenth century. Nevertheless, its use by the newer Biblical theologians did mark a decided break with traditional Anglo-Saxon theology.

First of all, it was employed as a polemical weapon against certain alternative views of how revelation was mediated that had been widely espoused in the preceding era. The emphasis on history as a vehicle for revelation was set over against seeing the Bible as a reflection of eternal truths, or a deposit of right doctrine, or particularly a process of evolving religious discovery. By emphasizing history the Biblical theologians were attacking positions both to the left and to the right of theirs. Again, there was a marked difference in the concept of

God's using history from the emphasis in the thirties. William Temple had written: "The meaning of History is found in the development of an ever wider fellowship of ever richer personalities. The goal of History is the Commonwealth of Value." [27] Again, in the writings of Millar Burrows[28] and C. R. North[29]—neither of whom were associated with the Biblical Theology Movement—the stress was on the experience of revelation in which no real tension was envisioned between divine revelation and human discovery. North was somewhat more guarded in his discussion of "progressive revelation," but basically his position was liberal. Even in the posthumous work of H. Wheeler Robinson,[30] who in many ways prepared the ground in England for the awakened theological interest in the Bible, the concept of history had not become an overarching category for the entire Bible, but was set alongside of revelation through the priest and the sage.

The stress on revelation in history seemed to solve many problems that had plagued Biblical studies in the preceding period. First, it allowed the modern critical scholar to recover objective events as related to the activity of God, which emphasis had been lost in seeing the Bible as a history of human development. Yet at the same time, it allowed the critic to bring in the subjective, human element in a way that did not destroy the concept of revelation. It appeared to offer a way around the theological impasse which centered in "inspiration and revelation." Again, the emphasis upon revelation as an event of divine self-disclosure shifted the content away from doctrine and propositional formulations concerning God to an encounter, the exact content of which was considered secondary or inferential from the event. Moreover, by stressing history, the fragmentation of the Bible which was associated with literary criticism was overcome. Behind all the sources and redactions was the one continuing line that joins the Old and the New Testament. Again, history as the vehicle for revelation provided an easy means to bridge the gap between the past and the present. Israel's history became the church's history, and subsequently our history. The church's liturgy was a participation in the selfsame redemptive events. Biblical Theology had become recital. Finally, the emphasis on history provided a theological rationale for doing the scientific archaeological work in which Americans had always excelled. The often-used phrase "taking history seriously" justified the concentration on excavating as another side of doing Biblical Theology.

In spite of the consensus regarding the importance of God in history, the various attempts of the Biblical theologians to explain with precision its meaning proved much more difficult. Very shortly a wide range of interpretations of the one rubric appeared. For H. H. Rowley the study of history was essential because it allowed one to see the authority of the Bible in "the totality of the concrete fact and its significance . . . to grasp the whole process through which the ideas were revealed." [31] The concept of history has become almost equated with the cultural background. The historical emphasis was set in opposition to seeing the Bible in a vacuum or on a "flat level of inspiration." [32] History was a medium of revelation. God limited himself by filtering his self-disclosure through finite human personality.[33] Rowley accepted the term "progressive revelation" so long as it did not reduce revelation to discovery.[34]

G. Ernest Wright shared a number of Rowley's concerns. He was also much opposed to static propositional truths but insisted on keeping Biblical theology in its concrete historical setting. However, there were important differences in the concept of history. For Wright the rubric of "progressive revelation" was anathema.[35] It distorted the essential element of the Biblical revelation which saw in history the objective and primary self-revelation of God toward Israel's redemption. Only in a secondary and inferential manner did human interpretation enter. "It is . . . the objectivity of God's historical acts which are the focus of attention, not the subjectivity of inner, emotional, diffuse and mystical experience."[36] Essentially the logic of Wright's position was simple:[37] God has revealed himself in the real events of human life which are found in the Bible. The theologian who seeks this knowledge of God must therefore study history. Since archaeology is the best tool for the study of ancient history, Biblical theology and Biblical archaeology belong together. Along with this theological move Wright added a relatively conservative interpretation of historical research. "We today possess a greater confidence in the basic reliability of Biblical history . . . than was possible before the historical criticism and archaeological research of the past century." [38]

Bernhard W. Anderson agreed with the broad consensus regarding history as revelation shared by Rowley and Wright, but focused his attention on another problem. History has ambivalent quality. "As a matter of fact, the history of Israel, when viewed by a purely secular historian, would not be substantially different from the histories of other people. What makes biblical history different is the *unique perspective* which the prophets had upon 'the normal course of human affairs.'" [39] It is not the mighty acts in themselves which are revelatory, but the perspective from which they are viewed. One's eyes must be opened "to perceive in a historical crisis a depth of meaning that is not obvious to everyone." [40] Still Anderson continued to resist the dogma of historicism in which historical events are bound to an unbreakable nexus of immanental cause and effect.[41]

A position far removed from those which have been discussed is found in Otto Piper. His being a New Testament scholar does not account for the difference of approach, since a good number of New Testament scholars can be found who agreed with Wright and Anderson.[42] Rather, Piper's position was a development of certain European influences that had played little role in America, particularly the *heilsgeschichtliche Schule* from Hofmann to Kaehler. "Within the historical life of mankind there is a special process of 'holy history' going on and converging toward us." [43] This special history is the entering of the "presence of the ever coming God" which transforms the church into the organizing center of all history. The fact that this "holy history" was not discerned by the world only confirms the New Testament's witness to the blindness of this age to the mystery of the Kingdom of God. Oscar Cullmann's[44] position followed a similar pattern. However, certain refinements were made. "Redemptive history" (*Geschichte*) was distinct from verifiable historical events (*Historie*) although the two were not to be divorced. Cullmann's concern lay in describing the nature of redemptive history which he found to be in its linear quality with Christ at its midpoint.

Although there was a certain formal parallelism between the *Geschichte-Historie* dialectic and H. Richard Niebuhr's "outer and inner history," once again the theological dynamic of Niebuhr's understanding was different. Niebuhr contrasted two different ways of looking at history. There was the scientific, objective, noncommitted point of view of outer history which dealt with objects in the past in an "I/it" relation, and the inner history which was the "story of our life," whose concern was with subjects within the category of personality.[45] "External history is the medium in which internal history exists and comes to life." [46] But Niebuhr found the key to the inner history of the Christian community in a common memory which provides the continuity and perspective to move the outer to inner history, from the past to the present.

Paul Minear also reflected the consensus in writing: "The distinguished mark of Biblical faith is its character as history and as revelation." [47] But what a vastly different understanding of history from those positions which have been sketched. From the start Minear had been consistent in radically calling into question the adequacy of the scientific historical method in the study of the Bible. It was false confidence in historical understanding which felt constrained to invoke the category of myth. Fundamental to his attack was the essential eschatological perspective of the New Testament.[48]

Historical time has been transformed by the appearance within time of an event that is ultimate. The entrance of the Kingdom of God brings a new quality of time but with a beginning and end marked by God's time. Minear's major point was that a historical method that has been constructed to deal with events in the "old age" according to the operation of its laws was fully incapable of understanding Biblical history. The task of the Biblical theologian is to study the "Biblical point of view" with the "eyes of faith," and to be addressed by God himself in a "final, ever-repeated act of creation, judgment and redemption." [49]

Finally, there is the position of Will Herberg which for many became a classic expression of Biblical Theology's concern for history. In the previous discussion of positions, there had frequently appeared existential terminology, but in Herberg this element has provided the major category of interpretation. "Biblical faith is faith enacted as history, or it is nothing at all." [50] It understands human existence in irreducibly historical terms. Faith is *Heilsgeschichte* in the sense that by examining the structure of our existence we see that each of us is a self who strives after history in its totality. "Redemptive history to be truly redemptive must be existential, appropriated in inwardness in personal existence as a demand and a responsibility." [51]

To summarize: Although there was the widest possible agreement among the Biblical theologians in regard to revelation in history, there was an equally wide spectrum of differing interpretations respecting the nature of history, revelation, and their relationship.

THE DISTINCTIVE BIBLICAL MENTALITY

It was generally agreed that the Bible had a "distinct" approach to matters of faith. This was not always a claim for uniqueness, but rather for a peculiar Biblical perspective that had often been neglected. Once again this rediscovery of the Biblical point of view was used polemically against both liberals and conservatives whose approach was criticized as being rationalistic, abstract, or fragmentary. The required position for understanding the Bible—and no distinction was made between the Testaments—was to stand at the Bible's "point of standing," [52] "to put ourselves within the world of the Bible," [53] to understand it "in its own categories." [54]

Very early in the Biblical Theology Movement the distinctive Biblical perspective became identified with "Hebrew mentality," [55] which was contrasted with Greek thought patterns. Since the latter were considered to be abstract, rationalistic, and theoretical, the term "Greek" epitomized the false perspective that had beclouded the understanding of the Bible. The issue, of course, was not one between the two Testaments, because it was felt that Hebrew mentality underlay both Testaments in spite of the use of the Greek language in the New Testament.[56] For many authors the dichotomy between Greek and Hebrew simply denoted succinctly the need for a distinct perspective, and afforded an easy way of making value judgments.[57]

However, for others more was involved than a peculiar perspective. The contrast between Greek and Hebrew suggested that a different thought process was at work. There was evidence of a different approach to reality which had arisen by virtue of peculiar categories of thought. Conversely these categories had received their shape by a genuine encounter with reality itself. Had not Brunner spoken of "truth as encounter" in which the subject-object polarity had been overcome? Buber and Kierkegaard had also suggested that more than an angle of vision was involved. In the course of his argument Brunner had even drawn on linguistic evidence in claiming a semantic distinction. "The decisive word-form in the language of the Bible is not the substantive, as in Greek, but the verb, the word of action. The thought of the Bible is not substantival, neuter and abstract, but verbal, historical and personal." [58]

It remained, however, for Biblical scholars to provide the full evidence to buttress the distinction in thought categories between the Greek and the Hebrew. A full study of this historical development in Britain and America has not yet been made,[59] but some of the broad lines are clear. Matthew Arnold had made a sharp distinction between "Hebraism and Hellenism" and had seen here two different approaches to life.[60] In the late twenties scholars such as George Adam Smith[61] had attempted to define the nature of the "Hebrew genius" as reflected in their peculiar use of language. By the thirties the new direction began to assume a clear shape and again the influence of H. Wheeler Robinson was enormous. Robinson had moved from the traditional word study method of his teachers, S. R. Driver and G. B. Gray, to a new concept that extended far beyond the area of grammar and syntax. The impact of his brilliant essay on "Corporate Personality" was immediate and widespread, affecting even German scholarship.[62] Some of the possibilities for this new type of study were seen in the several monographs of J. Aubrey Johnson.[63] The decisive influence, however, was the work of Johannes Pedersen.[64] This monumental work, written at first in Danish, was virtually unknown until the translation of Vols. I-II in 1926. Pedersen's work when seen from a European perspective was the continuation and application to the Old Testament of the work of Grønbech, Lévy-Bruhl, and others. But from the perspective of Biblical studies—particularly in Britain and America—the work proved extraordinarily illuminating. In spite of the fact that Pedersen's work was not theologically oriented, nor did it contrast Greek and Hebrew mentality in terms of value judgments, nevertheless it provided the material needed by the Biblical theologians. In Thorleif Boman's book *Hebrew Thought Compared with Greek*[65] some of the implications were drawn out for Biblical studies. Particularly, Cullmann's lucid book had great influence in illustrating the difference between the two concepts of time.[66]

Moreover, the contrast of mentality was exploited homiletically in a manner which went beyond that of the Biblical scholars. In countless articles and seminary lectures students were counseled "to think Hebraically," to abandon Athens for Jerusalem, and to penetrate to the substructure of Semitic thought.[67] Finally Biblical scholars had an effective tool with which to combat the "speculation of dogmatic theology." When any logical discrepancy was discovered by these theologians, the Biblical scholar could always appeal to Hebrew mentality to justify his line of argument.

The word study method became the most immediate avenue to the center of the Biblical mentality. Some spoke of the "new divine language" [68] of the Bible; others of a "semantic theology" which was especially conceived to overcome the difficulty that "plain words are forced to carry the heavy freight of transcendental meaning." [69] It was not by chance that the enormous task of translating Kittel's *Wörterbuch* was begun at the height of the Biblical Theology Movement. One of the interesting features to observe in the widely used *A Theological Word Book of the Bible* (ed. by Alan Richardson) is how some of the articles reflect the method of "semantic theology," while the work of others is quite uninfluenced by the newer trends.[70]

THE CONTRAST OF THE BIBLE
TO ITS ENVIRONMENT

A special feature of the American form of doing Biblical Theology was its great interest in the study of the background of the Bible. For Old Testament studies this meant a concentration on the Ancient Near Eastern setting with a particular focus on the role of archaeology. It was not accidental that the high-water mark of the Biblical Theology Movement coin-

cided with an awakened interest in "Biblical archaeology."
There are several obvious reasons why the historical, archaeological approach to the Bible found a fertile soil in America in
which to flourish. First, there was a native capacity and confidence in empirical study. It struck a happy note for Americans
to be told: "Objective contemporary data are worth far more
for the critical student of the Hebrew biblical text than any
amount of deduction from subjectively constructed premises
(sic German)." [71] Again, the impact of the religionsgeschichtliche Schule had been by and large blunted by the
early forties, and was mediated in its defeated form as an invalid application of evolution to history. Finally, the influence
of Albright, particularly as he was popularized by his students, was enormous. Archaeology, if scientifically executed,
was an ally, not an opponent, of Biblical Theology.

The thesis that was developed by the Biblical Theology
Movement respecting the relation of the Bible to its environment was as follows: The Bible reflects the influence of its
environment both in terms of its form and content, and therefore cannot be understood apart from the study of its common
Near Eastern background. Yet in spite of its appropriations
the Bible has used these common elements in a way that is totally distinct and unique from its environment. "Even when
we have noted all the similarities, the borrowing, and the syncretism, the differences between the literature of Israel and
that of Canaan are far more remarkable and significant than
the affinities." [72] At this point the Biblical theologian usually
listed those elements within the Old Testament which were
regarded as sui generis: monotheism, the "aniconic" character
of God, nonmythological, but historical.[73] It is clear that by
the term "Bible" originally the Old Testament was being referred to. However, the thesis of the Old Testament's distinctiveness was soon extended to include the New Testament as
well, although there never developed the same consensus.[74]

The point that kept coming through with forcefulness was

that the distinctiveness of the Bible could be scientifically demonstrated. It was not simply a matter of faith, but objective, historical study could prove the unique features of the Bible. The massive scholarship of Albright sought to demolish Wellhausen's reconstruction of Israel's religion by means of archaeological data and replace it with Mosaic monotheism "which was incomparably more qualified to move mankind than the selfish sentimentalism of Amarna."[75] At the same time unexpected help came from within the field of Oriental studies. In 1946 the famous book appeared from the Chicago Oriental Institute, *The Intellectual Adventure of Ancient Man.* Almost immediately it became a sort of Strack-Billerbeck to the field of the Ancient Near East. The leading scholars in Egyptian and Mesopotamian research—and indeed giants in the field—agreed that the Old Testament was utterly distinct. "It is possible to detect the reflection of Egyptian and Mesopotamian beliefs in many episodes of the Old Testament, but the overwhelming impression left by that document is one, not of derivation, but of originality."[76] Finally, Walther Eichrodt's masterful *Theology of the Old Testament*[77] provided an exhaustive and systematic demonstration that Israel had consistently transformed its common Near Eastern heritage into a unique expression of faith. Particularly in the writings of G. Ernest Wright, one sees how this material was developed into a hard-hitting, impressive new form of apologetic for Biblical religion.

It is remarkable to observe the extent to which the consensus reached regarding the distinctive quality of the Bible. Adherents of this position extended far beyond the borders of the Biblical Theology Movement. Among liberal Old Testament scholars, even William Irwin, who most often served as a convenient foil for the movement, could agree on the "supremacy of Israel's thinking in the ancient East."[78] On this issue Alt and Albright, Noth and Bright, found their positions akin. Nelson Glueck[79] and Harry Orlinsky[80] were equally confident that nothing comparable to the Bible had been produced by antiquity. For Hezekiel Kaufmann[81] the distinctiveness of Israel reflected itself in a Mosaic monotheism that had so broken with its environment that it could no longer even comprehend paganism. Among Roman Catholic writers Roland de Vaux[82] and John L. McKenzie[83]—to name but two—participated in the consensus, while at the same time expressing themselves in characteristically different form than did their Protestant and Jewish counterparts. Only occasionally were dissident notes sounded, but seldom heard. J. J. Finkelstein's[84] penetrating essay that raised the question as to whether the claim for Israel's superiority rested on a prior assumption rather than on objective evidence evoked only a momentary flutter. Occasionally one heard of Ivan Engnell [85] and the British "Myth and Ritual" [86] school, but their resistance hardly appeared as a major threat to trouble the quiet waters.

Of course, there remained certain ambiguities in the formulation of the distinctiveness of the Bible. Occasionally one sensed that the argument had moved out of the area of objective proof to a confessional stance. Filson[87] defended supplementing the historical scholarship with "personal response" once the question of truth claims arose. Again, Albright[88] was convinced that archaeology "cannot explain the basic miracle of Israel's faith, which remains a unique factor in world history. However, archeology can help enormously in making the miracle rationally plausible to an intelligent person." In any case, the argument for Biblical distinctiveness had moved in quite a different direction from the sort of question which Hoskyns[89] had raised as the riddle of Scripture and for which historicocritical research had not been able to supply an answer.

3
UNRESOLVED PROBLEMS

Before we turn to trace the historical developments that led to the breakdown of the movement, it might be helpful to reflect a bit on the problems that remained unsolved. It is ironical that many of the issues that the Biblical Theology Movement were most confident to have solved, in actuality were either glossed over or avoided. The decade of the fifties witnessed the return to the theological arena of problems which then increasingly began to cut away at the foundation blocks of the movement. Again, it is interesting to notice how positions that Biblical theologians had apparently destroyed in their battle with the older liberal scholars were revived in a slightly altered form, to be then championed by a younger generation in revolt against the Biblical theologians.

The Problem of the Bible

No problem had occupied the Biblical theologians more than that of the Bible. Failure to understand the Bible as a fully human book and yet as the vehicle for the Divine Word was held to blame for the sterility of the earlier period. Yet once this generalization had been made, its detailed implementation remained a vexing enterprise. By and large, Barth's own use of the Bible was rejected by the Biblical theologians

as "not taking historical criticism seriously." In its place appeared a variety of methods that claimed to be both theological and critical. Barth had objected to the critical attempt "to
go behind the text." However, the Biblical theologians were
agreed that something more important than the actual text
lay behind it. For some it was "the event . . . not the account," [1] and the purpose of exegesis was to recover the event.
Again others spoke of the "word behind the words," [2] or the
"original meaning," [3] of a passage as normative. The Biblical
theologians had attempted to modify the liberal insistence that
the historical context was the only legitimate perspective for
modern objective exegesis. But the result was that no clear alternative had emerged either, regarding the question of context or the subject matter of the interpretation. The confusion
was never dispelled as to whether the element of revelation
claimed for the Bible lay in the text, in some positivity behind
the text, or in a combination of text and event or mode of consciousness. This lack of clarity is best seen in the tortuous answers that were constructed in an effort to unite historical criticism and theological exegesis. Alan Richardson is typical,
when writing: "We must exercise our critical and historical
faculties in respect to the detail of each particular miracle-
story." Yet "the question whether the miracles really happened is not within the competence of the historian to decide.
Only those who came in faith understood the meaning of the
acts of power." [4]

Again, the perennial problem of relating the two Testaments
failed to elicit from the Biblical theologians a consistent or
unified answer. Christological exegesis such as practiced by
Luther and Calvin, among the Reformers, or by Barth, Bonhoeffer, or Vischer, among contemporaries, was almost universally eschewed. Yet one continued to talk about Christ to
whom the Old Testament pointed, or of a dimension with the
divine self-revelation which later theology designated as the
second Person of the Trinity, etc. Some even spoke of the

New Testament Christ as being the measure of Old Testament truth.[5] There was also a growing suspicion that this answer was dominated by Old Testament questions. Some New Testament scholars fell in line, but one missed a major new Christological development that would have thrown new light on this central issue of Biblical Theology.

In spite of the steady stream of books on the authority[6] of the Bible, the lack of a central thrust increased rather than diminished. One gained the impression that the fundamental authority of Scripture had somehow been assumed by the several writers, and this prior commitment allowed for the great lack of precision in explaining it. For some the authority lay in the encounter with God through Scripture. Others stressed elements of continuity with the body of normative tradition in which the Christian community participated, while for others there was a structure of Biblical teaching. The World Council study reports in the late forties could conclude its findings with a list of guiding principles for the interpretation of the Bible which reflected the high-water mark in the consensus of the Biblical Theology Movement.[7] Yet these guiding principles were prefaced by a series of articles on the authority of the Bible which simply served to emphasize how great the differences were regarding the authority of the Bible. Biblical theologians bent over backward to specify that the authority of the Bible lay in its relation to other factors, such as tradition, Holy Spirit, church, lest the emphasis on Biblical authority be taken as a return to Fundamentalism. Naturally, warrant was found for this move in the writings of the church fathers and Reformers. However, the clear, sharp notes that had once stirred Protestants often sounded like a distant echo reverberating in a muffled tone across rough mountain terrain. In all the writings of the Biblical theologians one seldom heard expressions of sheer joy or spontaneous adoration for Scripture which abounded in the pages of Calvin, Luther, Bunyan, Wesley, and others. Somehow this side of Biblical interpretation had become identified with pietism and rejected. For the movement as a whole the sentiment of Bishop How's famous hymn: "O Word of God Incarnate, O Wisdom from on high, O Truth unchanged, unchanging, O Light of our dark sky" remained as foreign as it had been to the Liberals of the thirties.

At the beginning of the Biblical Theology Movement the commentary of Edwyn C. Hoskyns on *The Fourth Gospel* (1940) was frequently held up as a model of sensitive theological exegesis which also served as an example of historicocritical rigor. The disappointing fact was that the new emphasis on Biblical Theology did not result in producing commentaries of this quality. One searches long and hard to find any commentary of this genre in either Old or New Testament which emerged from the Anglo-Saxon world during this period. It remains a puzzlement that Biblical Theology and exegesis did not establish a better union. In 1952 the long-awaited *Interpreter's Bible* began to appear. It was designed to meet the awakened interest in Biblical studies and sought to channel critical exegesis to the needs of the parish. The results are too well known to belabor. In many instances the introductory articles are classic expressions of the Biblical Theology Movement, particularly when dealing with topics relating to theology, authority, and the significance of the Bible. But once one passes through this thin veneer, the technical introductory articles on history and literature, and above all the exegesis of the Biblical books are in direct continuity with the critical methodology of the thirties. Some of the Biblical theologians are represented—Wright and Muilenburg in particular are impressive—but in general the major exegetical work is done by men not in any way associated with the newer movement. The section on "Exposition" is even more amazing because the effect of the newer emphases on the homiletical reflection is minimal or nonexistent. The majority of these expositors—many were of the older generation—appear totally untouched by the changing approach to the Bible in the postwar era. For whatever reason, the effect of the movement had not penetrated very deeply when it actually came to writing a Biblical commentary. Indeed, there was a rash of popular commentaries directed toward edification and instruction, but nothing approached the devotional quality of Adolf Schlatter or G. Campbell Morgan of the former era.

Finally, one was left with the growing suspicion that the Biblical Theology Movement's use of the Bible was usually confined to a limited number of books. The emphases on event, history, revelation, and eschatology seemed to work best when discussing Genesis and Exodus, John and the letters of Paul, while interest seemed to flag when discussing Leviticus and the Wisdom books, James and the Pastorals. Particularly in discussions with Jewish scholars one sensed a growing uneasiness as to whether a strong principle of selectivity[8] was at work among Christians which limited as effectively as any explicit "canon within the canon" the scope of the normative Biblical witnesses.

THE BIBLE IN THE SEMINARY

The impact of the Biblical Theology Movement had been strong on the seminaries during the immediate postwar period. Particularly in the Presbyterian schools where the tradition of Biblical studies had hung on, if in somewhat moribund form, the newer emphases were greeted as a refreshing wind across parched land. Soon the excitement had spread far beyond the conservatively oriented schools. In 1956 the Niebuhr report[9] could still discern a general enthusiasm for Biblical studies, and note especially the influence of certain charismatic Old Testament teachers. Of course, this did not mean a radical change toward the significance of the Biblical languages. There is evidence for some revived interest here, but the fundamental control remained the denominational requirements rather than the impact of the Biblical Theology Movement.

It seems quite clear in retrospect that the excitement that the newer theology had been able to generate seldom was translated into educational policy. Very infrequently did Biblical Theology become an integrating factor that provided a focus for the other disciplines. By and large, the centrifugal forces of the newer social sciences continued to multiply courses in American seminaries. Of course, the new Biblical approach had some effect on the other disciplines. Books appeared that attempted to relate Biblical Theology to Christian education,[10] pastoral care,[11] ethics,[12] and other disciplines. But it remained a question as to how profound a relationship had been established. Increasingly one had the impression that the basic theological stance which had characterized Christian education, psychology of religion, and social ethics in the period of the thirties continued to be retained and shared little in common with the major tenets of the Biblical theologians. Biblical Theology had succeeded for a time in revitalizing Biblical studies, but its own expectation to provide the foundation and critical norms for all theology began to appear more and more illusionary.

Biblical Theology had exerted its greatest influence when supported by the theology of Brunner and the other so-called "neo-orthodox." For many American seminarians interest in the Bible was mediated through the channel of systematic theology. What would the effect be when the inevitable disaffection set in with this one way of doing theology? The fact could not long be overlooked that another very live alternative for theology was being sounded by Paul Tillich, and one that represented a radically different position regarding the Bible. It also was becoming apparent that Americans could get excited with the theology of Rudolf Bultmann without feeling a necessity for entering into a detailed study of the Bible itself.[13] One began to wonder just how solid the marriage had been between systematic theology and Biblical theology. Barth had spoken of his need to do his own Biblical exegesis because of the inadequacies of the modern commentaries.[14] Was it possible that Biblical theologians would soon again find themselves also moving out alone into systematics?

Interest in hermeneutical questions had been part of the Biblical Theology Movement from the start. Opposition to the older liberal exegesis had often taken the form of a criticism regarding hermeneutics. But what would the effect be if a new form of hermeneutics would begin to attack rather than support the Biblical Theology Movement? What role would Biblical Theology play in the so-called "Post-Bultmannian era" which began to be heralded in the *avant-garde* university circles? By the early sixties, even in such an organ of the movement as *Interpretation,* there began to appear articles that were pointing in a different direction.[15]

BIBLICAL THEOLOGY AND THE MODERN WORLD

The Biblical Theology Movement had directed its message from its inception outside the walls of the seminary. It had been an initial concern that the study of the Bible in the preceding generations had tended to widen the gap between the scholar and the layman rather than to bridge it. In the early years of the movement the ability to communicate to the church and the world was held up as test of a truly Biblical theology and certainly some of the new enthusiasm of Bible study was transferred into the local churches. The excitement that surrounded the discovery of the Dead Sea Scrolls convinced many that something new and important was happening in respect to the study of the Bible. Of course, the impact of the Scrolls was not fully supportive of the movement, since the popular press often hinted that traditional Christianity might be endangered by the discovery.

It remained a more difficult question to determine how this

type of archaeological and travelogue interest in the Bible related to the major new theological emphases of the movement. The suggestion that the Bible had a particular perspective that demanded an adjustment on the part of modern man could be interpreted as a trend in a diametrically opposed direction. Rather than to suggest that the Bible was now being opened up for the first time in a new way by means of modern empirical study, the Biblical theologians were advocating the reverse. Only by returning to an ancient perspective could one understand the Bible. But the crucial issue at stake went even a step farther than this. Only by sharing the Biblical perspective could modern faith be genuinely Christian. Modern men must be retaught the language of the Bible because this was the language of faith. Of course, no one was advocating the old "what would Jesus do?" question. But the challenge to think as the Hebrews did seemed to demand the same archaizing stance, even when presented in a more sophisticated way.

There was another emphasis of the movement which contained inherent problems when communicated to the modern world. The new Biblical Theology had insisted that God was to be known in his great acts to the people of God, not in ideas or values that could be detached from the Biblical record. But what did this imply for the modern church? How would this God who acts in history be construed in a contemporary context? It is clear from reading the literature of the period that many different theological moves were suggested. However, it is also quite apparent that increasingly one major position began to emerge as the dominant one. The God of the Bible, who had acted redemptively in the history of his people, was still at work in the church. Indeed, in the ongoing life of the institutional church, particularly in the preaching of the Word and the Sacraments, redemptive history (Heilsgeschichte) continued. Christian education literature soon detected a correspondence between the sacred history in the rhythm of the Christian year and the pattern of human growth cycles.[16] Still one wondered how long this taming of the God who acts would go unnoticed. Could the conventional church life of a typical American suburban congregation carried on between eleven and twelve o'clock on Sundays provide even the faintest memory of the thunder and majesty of Israel at Sinai? Was it indeed the case that the church was the locus of the contemporary action of God? Many still thought so in the mid-fifties.

The major vehicle through which the congregation confronted the Bible remained the sermon. While the importance of the liturgy could be repeatedly affirmed, especially in high-level ecumenical circles, for most free churches the centrality of the sermon passed unchallenged. How deeply was preaching affected by the Biblical Theology Movement? The impact is difficult to determine from reading the periodicals. As one would expect, the older and well-known ministers who were publishing sermons hardly reflected the new point of view. Nor is it easy to assess the significance of the selection of sermons that appeared in the national preaching journals. However, it does seem clear that no new genre of Biblical preaching emerged. In fact, signs of a sharp break with the prewar period seemed even less noticeable than in any other of the theological disciplines. What changes did occur in the sermon style appeared to reflect much more strongly other forces, such as the widespread use of psychological language.

Finally, it remained a disturbing fact that the traditionally strong and aggressive interest of Americans in social ethics continued to thrive, and indeed attract the most promising of the theological students, without being seriously influenced from the side of Biblical studies. Paul Ramsey's *Basic Christian Ethics*[17] had made a promising start in the early fifties, but his interest in the Biblical approach did not catch fire. When the Bible was used in ethical discussions, it was a question whether it was those elements close to the heart of the Biblical Theology Movement which attracted attention. It would rather seem that the continuity with Biblical studies in the thirties was basically maintained. The emphasis on the prophets and social justice, or the Kingdom of God in the teaching of Jesus, were hardly distinctive to the Biblical Theology Movement. In an important journal such as *Christianity and Crisis* one discovered only occasional references to the Bible, but when it came to the wrestling with hard issues of local politics, international relations, and social change, appeals to the Bible for any kind of significant warrant became minimal. At best, a rather vague recognition of "the mind of Christ," which Reinhold Niebuhr had once popularized, continued to be invoked. There was the growing suspicion that an integral relation between Biblical studies and the theory and practice of social ethics was extremely nebulous. In fact, the Biblical Theology Movement's attack on the naïveté of the Social Gospel's use of the Bible only increased the hesitation in suggesting a closer relation between the two disciplines.

As we look backward with all the advantages of hindsight, it is now obvious that a whole nest of thorny problems remained partially hidden just under the surface. Before all too long the issues were to erupt with a vengeance that would shake not only the Biblical theologians but the whole structure of the seminary and church as well.

4
THE CRACKING OF THE WALLS

We are probably still much too close to the events we are describing to be able to achieve the required level of historical objectivity. It would seem that suddenly the barometers that measure the theological change in climate began to plummet. Soon it became obvious to nearly everyone involved in the discipline that a stormy, unsettled period had moved in. As we reflect on what has happened, it is now possible to see clear signs of the beginning of a breaking up of the older theological alliances that constituted the Biblical Theology Movement in America. In a real sense the collapse of the movement as a dominant and cohesive force in American theology resulted from the impact of an erosion from within as well as from pressures from without.

The Erosion from Within

Part of the real strength of the Biblical Theology Movement from the outset was its ability to grow and incorporate the results of new research into its bloodstream, often by scholars who were in no way associated with its main objectives. It is interesting to notice an almost imperceptible change in the influence of certain major scholars whose dominant role was gradually assumed by another group of scholars. In the late

62 BIBLICAL THEOLOGY IN CRISIS

forties and early fifties Eichrodt was, by all odds, the most important European Old Testament scholar who was cited by the members of the Biblical Theology Movement.[1] By the end of the fifties his authoritative position had been more and more assumed by von Rad, especially following the appearance of the latter's *Theologie des Alten Testaments* in 1957. In a similar manner Cullmann's influence in New Testament circles was enormous following the Second World War and well into the mid-fifties, but here again the name of Bultmann and his disciples began increasingly to be regarded as providing the real cutting edge of New Testament studies.[2] For a time it appeared as if members of the Biblical Theology Movement were continuing to pursue their method of doing Biblical studies by simply adjusting the footnotes to take notice of the latest continental research. Only gradually did it become apparent that a radically different concept of historical method separated von Rad from Eichrodt, and an enormous gap both historical and philosophical divided Bultmann from Cullmann. The growing recognition of basic divergencies in approach added increasingly to the difficulty of regarding Biblical Theology as representing a unified movement. Ironically enough, it was precisely in those areas in which the Biblical theologians had felt most confident in having established a solid consensus that the erosion of positions began.

Revelation in History

The first signs of serious disagreement came with the attempt to define the nature of history, through which it was agreed revelation was mediated. The complexity of the problem of history had long been recognized in Germany,[3] but this did not at first emerge as a threat among the Biblical theologians. A more vocal opposition to the newer emphasis on history continued to be heard from the older liberal wing in the name of scientific history. This was an old position against which the Biblical theologians had always waged battle and which raised no new fears.[4] In Old Testament, Eichrodt had taken a cautious position that held firmly together scientific history and redemptive history (*Historie* and *Geschichte*) as being two sides of the same coin.[5] This point of view for a brief time seemed to satisfy both advanced German scholarship with its literary emphasis and the American archaeologically oriented school of Albright. However, with von Rad a totally different concept of history emerged, one in which a tremendous tension developed that threatened to pull completely apart the two aspects of history.

In the field of New Testament the implications of Bultmann's program of demythologization slowly began to have an effect on an increasing number of scholars and their students, in spite of the sustained polemic against Bultmann on the part of the Biblical theologians within the movement. Bultmann again seemed to be operating with two kinds of history, but in a polarity that was entirely different from that used in Old Testament circles. To the average Anglo-Saxon reader it was not at all clear how kerygmatic history, which was being existentially interpreted, was related to the Biblical presentation of historical events, which were being regarded frequently as mythical. In spite of the eager attempt of some American scholars to educate their constituency in the intricacies of existentialism, there was a growing sense of uneasiness among those who had been confidently championing the historical quality of Biblical revelation. The much-heralded "event" of revelation was becoming increasingly difficult to pin down. Bultmann's followers were still speaking of revelation and history. But it was obvious to all that a totally different concept was operative from that current within the Biblical Theology Movement. The effect was that the theological device which at first seemed to be a way around the difficulties of seeing the Bible as revelation had backfired. The more deeply one probed into the subject, the more bogged down and unilluminating the discussion appeared.

In America recognition of the complexity of the concept of history began to be voiced, often in a polemical setting, and directed against the emphases of the Biblical Theological Movement. James M. Robinson's much-heralded "new quest," which envisioned the goal of the historian to "encounter Jesus' selfhood by an insight into the understanding of existence presupposed in his intention," only compounded the confusion.[6] In 1956 *Religion in Life* offered a symposium to assess the present situation in Biblical Theology. The lead article by James Branton[7] was a broadside attack on the major tenets of the movement, above all, that Biblical Theology had lost "its real rootage in history." Basically Branton's position was uninformed by any of the new developments and represented the older American liberal position which still had a visceral reaction to Barth and Brunner.

A year later Winston King[8] mounted a much more incisive attack on certain ambiguities in the use of history, particularly in confusing the relation between fact and interpretation. King objected that Biblical theologians, i.e., Wright and Anderson, admitted in principle the legitimacy of the distinction, but at the crucial points various modifications were introduced. Moses' calling, for example, was understood as a historical event, but the burning bush accompanying the call was only a figure of speech. Or again, whenever historical events were in historical doubt, the interpretation of the sacred history was said to carry the theological meaning. When an event had historical support, the historically real quality of the Biblical history was passionately affirmed. Unquestionably King was probing weaknesses in historical and theological method which were becoming more and more obvious. However, his arguments appeared to many as only a slightly revised form of American historicism, and the article made little impression on the adherents of the movement itself.

In many ways Langdon Gilkey's famous article[9] in the summer of 1961 was only an extension of earlier criticism of Bran-

ton and King. It was also thoroughly American in orientation
and certainly not a reflection of the contemporary European
debate on history. Yet the article carried a tremendous force.
First of all, it placed the problem of history within the larger
framework of systematic theology, and pursued the theological inconsistencies of various popular positions with a relent-
less logic. Here was an attack that could not be categorized as
"old American Liberalism." It came from the side of one who
understood the inner dynamics of the movement, but who re-
gretfully found the approach to be fundamentally inadequate.
Gilkey's major point was that Biblical theologians—the attack
was again directed toward Wright and Anderson—had tried
"to have their cake and eat it too." They used Biblical and orthodox language to speak of divine activity in history, but at
the same time continued to speak of the same events in purely
naturalistic terms. "Thus they repudiate all the concrete elements that in the biblical account made the event itself unique
and so gave content to their theological concept of a special
divine deed." [10] Gilkey's criticism was particularly painful because it raised the fundamental question of whether the recourse of the Biblical theologians to history had in fact
succeeded at all in solving the old crux between the Conservatives and the Liberals.

James Barr's inaugural lecture in 1962, followed by his
book,[11] can well be regarded as the final blow. Not only did
Barr continue Gilkey's line of argument, but he incorporated
in his attack the full weight of the whole European debate. He
spoke from the perspective of the post-Bultmannian–von
Radian age. Barr argued that the concept of history was in danger of becoming "a construct which is supposed to be related
to the biblical material but which is ambiguous in the degree
in which it affirms the actual form of the biblical material." [12]
His fundamental criticism was not that the Biblical theologians failed to take historical criticism seriously, but that they
failed to take the Biblical text seriously! The emphasis on his-

tory had distorted the Biblical narrative by introducing a form
of abstraction which at best worked on only a small portion of
the Bible. Barr's criticism was of major importance because it
not only summarized the weaknesses of the "main line" theologians of the movement, but also served to raise the question as
to whether the more sophisticated substitutes for Biblical Theology, particularly the so-called "new hermeneutic," had not
also entered the same cul-de-sac.

The Unity of the Bible

From the beginning of the movement a group of scholars
had always resisted Biblical Theology's emphasis on the unity
of the Bible. Usually they saw the stress on the unity as a conservative reaction to critical scholarship, often dictated by
dogmatic presuppositions. They argued that Biblical Theology had returned to an illegitimate form of precritical harmonization. Therefore, when Branton raised this same objection in 1956, it was not a new attack, nor did it make a
fresh impact.[13] The Biblical theologians defended themselves
by admitting a wide divergence within the Bible, but continued to stress the centripetal forces that pulled it all together.

Eichrodt's attempt to see in the idea of the covenant the
basic unifying center continued to be highly regarded through
the early fifties by a large number of American Old Testament
scholars. Usually it was commended by the Biblical theologians, but again some criticism was often registered which
suggested its one-sidedness. Few seemed completely convinced by Eichrodt's position on the covenant. Particularly as
the concept was extended to cover wider areas in volumes II
and III, a sameness in the treatment emerged that reflected
more of Eichrodt's systematic categories than the Biblical material itself. The achievement of Eichrodt, however, should not
be underestimated. Following Mendenhall's discovery of the
parallels between Old Testament covenant forms and the
Hittite treaties, there was a renewed interest in Eichrodt's em-

phasis on the covenant. Even if the concept was not the all-encompassing category envisioned by Eichrodt, there remained little doubt that Eichrodt had described accurately a major element of Old Testament theology. Interestingly enough, although Mendenhall's discovery helped to support Eichrodt's position and damaged von Rad's in the eyes of many, the lines along which the subsequent debate unfolded moved more in the direction sketched by Alt and von Rad than by Eichrodt. This is to say, the interest in the covenant as a theological idea fell into the background, and the interest focused rather on establishing the institutional roots of the covenant in the life of Ancient Israel. Even among the American scholars the form critical and historical methodologies employed stood in direct continuity with von Rad rather than Eichrodt.[14] The result was that the covenant emphasis of Eichrodt retained its significance, but its systematic use as a means of supporting the unity of the Old Testament gained little new support.

Von Rad was also very much interested in establishing the unity of the Bible, but he employed a method that differed fundamentally from that employed by Eichrodt as well as from the "unity in diversity" approach that was so popular in Biblical Theology circles. Already in 1951 von Rad had argued for a revised form of typological exegesis,[15] a suggestion that met with more enthusiasm in Europe than in the Anglo-Saxon world. In the second volume of his *Theology* the full significance of the argument emerged.[16] Pursuing a rigorous form critical method von Rad argued that the Old Testament revealed no one unifying center. Rather, what gave it a unity was Israel's process of continual reinterpretation of sacred tradition that resulted from her sense of the great divine acts of redemption done on her behalf. The warrant for typological exegesis was found in the tradition-building process which continually projected the future hope in the form of analogies of the past. Then von Rad proposed that the New Testament should be seen as the final result of Israel's interpretation of her tradition in which the whole process climaxed and from which a fresh sense of divine intervention in Israel's future-oriented history arose.

In spite of the brilliance of the presentation and the moving testimony to the author's own Christian faith, this theological move presented some major difficulties from the outset. First of all, from the standpoint of Old Testament scholarship the question could be raised whether von Rad had extended the form critical method beyond its legitimate descriptive role to become a new type of systematic category. To see a direct line of continuity between the Old Testament history of tradition and the New Testament seemed to be dictated more by a dogmatic principle of selectivity than by strictly literary evidence. Could it actually be demonstrated that the "Old Testament leans toward the New," or was this a New Testament perspective which in turn provided a principle of selection? Secondly, von Rad's use of the New Testament received a less than enthusiastic reaction from many New Testament scholars.[17] It suddenly became clear in what a different direction European New Testament scholarship had moved in the postwar period. If, in the late forties, Cullmann's interpretation of the New Testament had supported a use of *heilsgeschichtliche* categories to link the Old Testament with the New, the ensuing attacks on his position would now seem to apply to von Rad's New Testament interpretation as well. One missed the precise and sensitive hearing of the New Testament with its whole chorus of voices which was so characteristic of von Rad's understanding of the Old. As a result, his theology succeeded admirably in showing the lack of any one center in the Old Testament, but did not succeed in restoring the unity within the Old Testament, much less in relation to the New Testament.

As we turn now to the New Testament, because of almost fortuitous reasons stemming from the disasters of the Second

World War, Bultmann emerged in the postwar period as the one dominant figure in New Testament without a rival in Europe. Very shortly his group of brilliant students dominated the major New Testament centers with a few exceptions (notably Jeremias). In the early fifties, while Americans were just beginning to wrestle with the implications of Bultmann's demythologizing program, it was hardly noticed that German New Testament scholarship had moved beyond the form criticism of the pre-Second World War type with its emphasis on the common tradition and turned its attention to studying the nature of gospel individuality in the history of redaction. The name of the method was new but the principles involved were not, and interest turned again to problems once discussed by Wellhausen and Wrede, Bacon and Cadbury. Conzelmann's dissertation[18] appeared in 1954 and described a theology of redaction used by Luke which was in striking contrast to that of Matthew and Mark. Of particular significance was that the *heilsgeschichtliche* categories that Cullmann had employed to establish the unity of the New Testament could at most be related to only one school within the New Testament.

There followed a series of studies in the fifties that strove to recover the individuality and particular redactional stamp of each evangelist.[19] Obviously, this new interest did not for a moment negate the solid contributions of the earlier form critics. But it was evident that the interest in discovering the common elements had been replaced by one moving in the opposite direction. In terms of the history of research the two approaches were complementary, but in measuring the temper of the times, the new approach had little interest in supporting a major thesis of the Biblical Theology Movement, namely, the essential unity of the Bible.

In the essays of Ernst Käsemann[20] the essential unity of the New Testament received an even more aggressive challenge. Käsemann was not interested in merely showing sharp redactional differences within the New Testament corpus.

Rather, he argued that in several instances, particularly in respect to Paul, the polemic attack of one writer was directed against an opponent whose position was represented within the New Testament canon. So, for example, the tendency to blunt the gospel through the institutional "early Catholicism" of Luke-Acts emerged soon in the development of early Christianity. Käsemann drew the theological implications that the modern Biblical theologian would have to operate with some form of canon within the canon, which in his own practice reflected a Pauline center. Without entering into the debate which Käsemann's essays have provoked in New Testament studies, it is sufficient to suggest that the direction for much of the *avant-garde* scholarship has taken a very sharp turn away from the emphasis on Biblical unity. Käsemann is also typical of post-Bultmannian New Testament scholarship in having little sustained interest in relating the Old Testament to the New. Here Bultmann's legacy, which had never supported the movement's concern for discovering some sort of unity within the canon, can be recognized.

The Distinctive Biblical Mentality

Already in the early fifties there had been some scholars who watched the developing consensus regarding Hebrew mentality with considerable suspicion. Millar Burrows[21] had attacked the interpretation of Biblical time as reflecting a peculiar category, particularly as it was presented by John Marsh. Again, the appearance of Boman's book had met with some critical reviews which raised a number of questions regarding the validity of Boman's distinctions.[22]

A different sort of criticism was offered in a highly perceptive article by Henry Cadbury which bore the characteristic title "The Peril of Archaizing Ourselves." [23] Cadbury contrasted the older liberal attempt to modernize the Bible, especially the figure of Jesus to fit in with modern religious disposition, with the Biblical Theology Movement's opposite reaction in which the Bible's unusual categories and distinct message must be fully respected and preserved. However, to make the transition from the Biblical approach to the modern age required that modern man return to the Bible's way of thinking and acting. Cadbury argued that this resulted in a use of the Bible which often appeared as a call to archaize. He then questioned whether the time-conditioned, culturally stamped elements of the ancient Semitic world were being absolutized as an unchanging part of the Biblical content. Was not some sort of critical evaluation necessary for a modern theologian before an appropriation from a past religious document could be taken? In his article Cadbury did not defend any particular form of critical analysis, but raised the fundamental question whether it was simplistic to suggest that nothing of this sort was required.

Although such types of criticism clearly raised some important questions, the attack caused, by and large, little major impact.[24] These appeared to be perennial problems of which the Biblical theologians had been fully cognizant and to which they often replied with forceful arguments. Attention to Bultmann's program had forced these theologians to face at an early date the problem of the actualization of the past as well as the problem of mythological patterns of language and culture. They insisted that the Biblical message must be retained in its historical form and continued to fight hard against any separating of form from content whether by means of idealistic, existential, or psychological maneuvers. For these reasons the Biblical Theology Movement did not really feel a new threat from these persistent attacks calling for critical translations of ancient thought patterns.

The onslaught of James Barr's famous book *The Semantics of Biblical Language* (1961) was of a totally different sort. Suddenly an attack was launched which struck with such incisive and devastating criticism that the defenses appeared like a Maginot line facing a new form of blitzkrieg. Barr launched

his barrage against a rather loosely defined group of Biblical
theologians (Torrance, Hebert, and Cullmann came in for an
undue proportion of criticism), but the force of the argument
was anything but imprecise. The major thrust of his book is
too familiar to require a detailed review. Barr's major point
was that Biblical Theology had been guilty of a fundamental
erroneous approach to the semantics of language. By iso-
lating the study of Hebrew from the cognate disciplines, the
Biblical theologians had developed a line of linguistic argument in support of a Hebrew mentality that rested on a faulty
method of selective lexicography and lexical stocks. The
method most frequently employed failed to treat either Hebrew or Greek as a true language. As a result of an illegitimate
semantic transfer, differences in semantic range were interpreted as reflecting differences in thought patterns, which in
turn were afforded a positive theological value judgment. Hebrew thinking was something essentially good in contrast to
Greek which was considered bad.

In reflecting on the effect of Barr's book, one cannot help
being impressed with the success of his attack. Seldom has one
book brought down so much superstructure with such effec-
tiveness. Barr's argument seemed to most English scholars and
a majority of Americans to be fully convincing. When reserva-
tions did come, it was in terms of an overly negative style of
argument, and in regards to the outer limits of his criticism.
But even among those Biblical theologians who remained un-
convinced, there was agreement that the emphasis of the
Biblical Theology Movement on a distinctive mentality could
never be carried on without a major revision. There even fell a
shadow across the mighty Kittel's *Wörterbuch*, which had
begun to appear in English translation in the hope of revitalizing American Biblical scholarship. One began to sense that the
future of this sort of theological analysis of words had moved
into a period of much uncertainty.

The Contrast of the Bible to Its Environment

In the period of the thirties the criticism was voiced that theology had been replaced by the history of religions. By the end of the fifties one could well ask whether the reverse tendency had taken place. This generalization seems particularly to be true in the field of Old Testament.

Several of the classic presentations of the religion of Israel in this period were hard to distinguish from theologies of the Old Testament.[25] Characteristically, Muilenburg[26] began his article of the "History of the Religion of Israel" with a discussion of "faith and history," "Bible and Church," and "the Biblical Perspective."

In the field of New Testament the break with the classic discipline of history of religion was never carried through so thoroughly. Certainly the influence of Bultmann was important in this regard. Bultmann stood in a direct scholarly line with some of the greatest advocates of the *religionsgeschichtliche Schule,* and never broke with the direction established by Bousset and Reitzenstein. Even though the Biblical Theology Movement ignored to a great extent this whole side of New Testament research, the continuity survived in many of Bultmann's students (e.g., Bornkamm, the early Käsemann, Braun, etc.). Among Anglo-Saxon New Testament scholars Dodd's interest in the Hellenistic, Gnostic background of the New Testament continued unabated even during the height of his popularity with the Biblical theologians. It is also clear that Dodd presented it in a way which did not seem to be in any violent conflict with the current theological interpretation. In America the History of Religions approach to the New Testament continued to be represented in a brilliant way by Arthur Darby Nock.[27]

Again, in the work of Erwin Goodenough, who spanned the field of New Testament and Judaism, the issue of Biblical distinctiveness emerged with a sharpness that could not be avoided. George F. Moore, in his monumental interpretation

of Judaism, had argued for a "normative Judaism" which was
not only distinct from its Hellenistic environment, but from
the Jewish sectarians of the period. Beginning with his work
on Philo[28] and culminating in his multivolume set on *Jewish
Symbolism*,[29] Goodenough was able seriously to erode the
distinction and in the minds of many to destroy it as a useful
scholarly category. If early Judaism showed the effects of
syncretism throughout its development, the implications for
many claims of New Testament distinctiveness were obviously
damaging. Increasingly in the writings of Samuel Sandmel
and Morton Smith and others, an opposition was voiced
against the separating of the New Testament from its cultural
environment.

Significantly the discovery of the Dead Sea Scrolls played
an important role—if somewhat indirect—in shifting the emphasis away from the contrast between the Bible and its environment which it had received in the Biblical Theology Movement. After the initial suspicions voiced by Edmund Wilson
that the Scrolls might overturn Christian theology were
proved ill-founded, scholars of all sorts of theological back-
grounds began to study the documents seriously. Ironically
enough, even conservative scholars who would have found the
method of Reitzenstein and Bousset totally unacceptable
when used on the New Testament began to employ techniques on the Scrolls which had a close resemblance. While no
serious scholar wanted to identify early Christianity with the
Qumran sect the fact that there were many strong lines of religious continuity became soon apparent. Again, if the impetus
for comparative studies from Qumran was great, the impact of
the recently discovered Gnostic material of Nag Hammadi
began to be even greater. Already the call for technically
trained Coptic scholars has been sounded, and it seems clear
that for many New Testament scholars the major occupation
during the next decades will be with comparative studies of
these fresh extra-Biblical sources.

One of the most interesting developments in marking the changing times came from an unexpected area of Old Testament studies. As a student of W. F. Albright and G. Ernest Wright, Frank M. Cross, Jr., had early achieved an international reputation on the basis of his brilliant articles (usually with David Noel Freedman) and his work on the Dead Sea Scrolls. In the early sixties[30] there began to appear a series of articles that moved in a direction not usually associated with Albright's position. Cross argued that the research on the history of Israel's early religion had reached an impasse between the English-Scandinavian "Myth and Ritual" school and the German "History of Redemption" (*Heilsgeschichte*) school. The former defended the position that the Ancient Near Eastern mythical pattern of kingship and creation in cosmogonic struggle were primary in the formulation of Israel's religion and were only later progressively historicized. The latter argued that the early Israelite cult served to reenact the historical acts of redemption in sharp distinction from the Near Eastern pattern, and only used mythopoeic language to enrich historical tradition. Cross began to develop a new synthesis that would take advantage of the strengths of each position. He did it be agreeing, first of all, with the "Myth and Ritual" school that Israel's early cult did emerge from a mythopoeic past that shared completely the patterns of the Canaanite world. But he also agreed with the "History of Redemption" school that it was the force of the historical traditions which transformed the mythological pattern.

At this juncture the concern is not to follow the details of Cross's thesis nor evaluate its validity. Many of the crucial points of his abbreviated presentation continue to be sketchy and tentative. Rather, interest focuses on seeing some of the implications in Cross's approach for the future direction of Old Testament studies in America. The shift in understanding Israel's relation to the myth comes out clearly in contrasting Cross's two articles on Ex., ch. 15. In 1955 (with Freedman)[31]

Cross argued forcefully against seeing in the poem a mythological conflict that had been historicized. The poem contained
no cosmic element of conflict, even though "certain clichés
may be derived secondarily from mythical cycles." [32] The
enemy is historical and "there is not the slightest hint that he
is the Enemy, the symbol of cosmic chaos, dissolution or
death." [33] In his article of 1968 Cross again defends the view
in a brief sentence that "there is no question here of a mythological combat between two gods. Yahweh defeats historical
enemies," [34] but now he argues that the poem preserves Canaanite patterns of the combat of the Divine Warrior, the
building of a cosmic sanctuary, and the deity's manifestation
of eternal kingship. Although the Song of the Sea reflects
historical memories, the enormous power of the mythical patterns now shapes the form of the tradition.[35]

Although Cross continues to use Albright's concept of "historical memory"—often it appears as a vestige from the earlier
position—the dialectic which he suggests between myth and
history is clearly distinct from the traditional emphasis on
monotheism and historical reality found in Albright[36] and
Wright. Equally important in Cross's work are the signs of a
basically different focus of interest from the original lines of
the Biblical Theology Movement. Now the weight of the research falls on describing the elements of commonality with
the Ancient Near East, not on making precise that which is
distinct. The older approach of the "Bible against its environment" has been replaced by one that talks of accommodation
rather than opposition. In an amazing way Engnell and Hooke
had been pushed out of the front door only to return through
the back!

If one can still use the term "distinctiveness" in reference to
Israel's religion—for Cross it has actually become irrelevant—
it is now restricted to a later stage of religious development. It
is also a question whether the change from the "re-enactment
of primordial events of cosmogonic myth" into "festivals re-

enacting epic events" is really a difference in quality such as would be able to bear the theological weight that has been attached to the category of distinctiveness. While Cross has been willing for the time being to allow the approach of the "redemptive history" school to go unchallenged for the period that followed Israel's emergence from her mythopoeic past, others among the Scandinavians have questioned even here the distinctiveness of Israel's historical consciousness. Is it really the case that a concept of redemptive history is unique to Israel? Bertil Albrektson has argued that the contrast has been greatly overemphasized, and that the difference between Israel and her Ancient Near Eastern background is, at most, one of degree. He writes: "The Old Testament idea of historical events as divine revelation must be counted among the similarities, not among the distinctive traits." [37]

In the light of the changing emphasis, Barr[38] has summarized the issue at stake for Biblical Theology when he points out the dangers for a theology that tries to correlate patterns of cultural distinctiveness with differences between revelation and nonrevelation. One can hardly avoid the impression that the concentration on the elements of demonstrable distinctiveness was basically a form of modern apologetic, which like the medieval proofs for the existence of God, maintains its validity only among those who had already assumed its truth.

The Theological Dimension

There had always existed in America a number of Biblical scholars who tended to resist the emphasis on Biblical Theology at the expense of historical study. James Smart[39] recalled attending a meeting of Biblical scholars in which the speaker, referring to himself as a historian and not a theologian, brought forth enthusiastic applause. Such an experience is a typically American reaction which would scarcely have been paralleled in either England or Germany. But more important to observe is that a new type of resistance to the theological emphasis arose which began to be felt in the middle fifties and which was in no sense simply a recrudescence of American Liberalism.

First of all, the breakdown of the theological consensus that had been held together within the amorphous category of "neo-orthodoxy" came more quickly than anyone could have imagined. As we look back, it is difficult to imagine much theological consistency, in either method or content, within a grouping that included Barth, Brunner, the Niebuhrs, and Tillich. The main element of commonality lay in their criticism of the extreme forms of Liberalism which had somehow survived in America into the thirties. The loss of a theological center had a debilitating effect on the Biblical Theology Movement. No one person or even a group of theologians rose to lend support to the concerns of the movement. H. Richard Niebuhr, whose influence continued to grow until his untimely death in 1962, moved more and more away from his affinity with Barth. His book *The Meaning of Revelation* had marked his farthest swing toward Barth's direction. In his later books he returned to many of the formulations of his earliest books, *Social Sources* and *The Kingdom of God in America*. Although Bonhoeffer's popularity grew through the fifties and into the sixties, the interest focused, not on his exegesis nor on those emphases compatible to the doing of Biblical Theology, but rather on his fresh approach to secularity in a "world come of age." In America and beyond, Tillich's influence continued to make impressive inroads and provided a theological grounding for those who wanted to work theologically and philosophically without a close relation to the Bible. Tillich dealt seriously with a set of questions, such as art and aesthetics, theology and culture, which were of vital interest to Americans, but which had been given a minor role in the height of the neo-orthodoxy period. The effect of the breakdown of one dominant theological position was increasingly to isolate the Biblical theologians from the active support of the systematic theologians. Biblical theologians were forced to do their own theology. This often ended up as an eclectic picking and choosing of bits from a wide variety of theologians.

Another important trend that had a serious effect on the movement's approach to the theological dimension of the Bible was the effort to distinguish sharply between the legitimate areas of work of the historian and the theologian. The early force of the movement had arisen by means of the successful combining of Bible and theology. This approach received a major challenge in the brilliant article of Stendahl.[40] Stendahl argued that the descriptive task of Biblical studies should be radically separated from the constructive task of the theologian. He claimed for both a legitimate function, but the major task of Biblical studies lay in historical description that could be objectively controlled by scientific investigation. Theologians of the Bible were then allowed to make value judgments or homiletical applications, just as long as they were fully aware that such disciplines were subjective and outside the pale of objective verification. Without debating the validity of Stendahl's position at this point, it seems quite clear that it struck a blow at the very heart of the movement, as it was originally conceived. The wedge between the Biblical and theological disciplines that the movement had sought to remove was again being slipped into place.

Of course, it remains a question as to what extent the movement had ever really succeeded in overcoming the gap between exegesis and theology. Stendahl's article received such a ready response because he advocated what was, in fact, happening. Certainly *The Interpreter's Bible* dramatically illustrated in its format the austere separation of descriptive exegesis and theology. Above the sharp black line one could expect scientific exegesis according to the canons of historical interpretation; below the line there was room for theology, homiletics, old sermons, and poems! Little wonder that The Anchor Bible project decided to drop the "Exposition" in providing a commentary for the sixties and seventies.

Perhaps an even more important change from the climate of

the late forties which was concerned with recovering the theological dimension of the Bible was the new emphasis in America on hermeneutics. The term of course had been retained in conservative circles through the period that preceded the Biblical Theology Movement in the classical sense of the theory of interpretation in distinction from exegesis which was its practice. During the first years of the movement interest continued in hermeneutics but often as a polemical tool directed against the restrictions of historicism. Barth's Introduction in his *Romans* commentary had demonstrated how a new hermeneutical approach could be effectively used against the tyranny of historical criticism. By and large, interest in the subject was limited to only certain aspects of the subject, such as "faith and history," and little contribution was made by the movement to the theoretical side of the discipline. Bultmann's hermeneutical essays were frequently misunderstood, but more often treated with impatience by Anglo-Saxon Biblical scholars as typical German speculation having little to do with the text. The situation was, of course, different in Germany. One of the chief characteristics of the so-called "post-Bultmannian" period, which began in the early fifties, was its concentration on hermeneutical questions. Particularly under the impetus of Fuchs and Ebeling, who attempted to exploit the work of Dilthey and Heidegger in pushing beyond Bultmann, a new phase of the debate was ushered in. The term "hermeneutic" was introduced in distinction from hermeneutics to designate the "process of interpretation" which imposed upon man historical and ontological concerns. In a series of brilliant essays James Robinson[41] introduced the new hermeneutic to American theology, and hailed it as the wave of the future, and the cutting edge of future work in theology and Bible.

However one may judge the claims of the new hermeneutic—already a vast literature has accumulated of a positive and negative character—it is clear that the direction of this school

had little in common with that of the theological concerns of
the Biblical Theology Movement. Primarily it is an inner
scholarly debate rather than being focused on the needs of the
church. Again it is dominated by German theologians whose
philosophical concepts are rendered into English often with
tortuous results. The fundamental esoteric quality of much of
the discussion has made the possibility of any new consensus
between Bible and theology highly unlikely. There is the growing impression that this new way of unifying Bible and theology has had the very opposite effect. Except for a small
group of devotees who have found a center in the new hermeneutic, the vast bulk of American theologians and Biblical
scholars seem to be moving in a different direction.

The change in the theological climate has left its impact on
the ecumenical movement. In 1949 the study department of
the Commission on Faith and Order could report a tremendous sense of agreement that was expressed in a list of "guiding principles" by which to interpret the Bible. In 1967 the
chairman of a study project of the same ecumenical commission, Erich Dinckler, reluctantly reported his disappointment
at the lack of agreement that had emerged in a series of confer-
ences on Biblical Hermeneutics and the Ecumenical Movement. The report to the Commission on Faith and Order in
June of 1967 concluded as follows:

> When the World Council of Churches was founded,
> there was a strong hope, confirmed by facts, that in the
> different churches and theological schools the Bible
> would be read more and more along the same lines, pro-
> vided by the development of the so-called "biblical the-
> ology" of that period. . . . Now, two decades later, at-
> tention is increasingly drawn to the diversity amongst or
> even contradiction between biblical writers. . . . As a
> consequence the hope that the churches would find them-
> selves to have in the near future the basis of a common
> understanding of the one biblical message has been fad-

ing, even to such an extent that in the eyes of some the
new exegetical developments seem to undermine the
raison d'être of the ecumenical movement.[42]

The report tried to end on a confident note and spoke of
"deeper understanding" which might grow out of the divi-
sions, but in point of fact, the report serves to mark the end of
an epoch rather than to point to the beginning of anything
new.

Finally, and of great significance, is the growing polarity between Biblical studies and dogmatic theology. At many centers of theology so little has remained of the older consensus
that the students have difficulty in even conceiving of a common front between the disciplines. The old concern for the
"theological dimension of the Bible" has been rejected as inadequate. Unfortunately, nothing has yet arisen to fill the
vacuum.[43]

THE PRESSURES FROM WITHOUT

Alongside of the forces of deterioration from within, the
Biblical Theology Movement had another set of pressures that
could be felt from outside. No attempt can be made here to
describe all the recent economic, social, and political developments which have resulted in such significant changes in the
spirit of American culture in the sixties. Enough has been
written on the subject that the reader can find adequate cover-
age elsewhere. Rather, the concern is to describe various reactions within the church that have responded to the changing
contemporary scene in a manner that has a bearing on the
Biblical Theology Movement.

One can hardly read a modern church publication without
sensing immediately the impact of a new era in American life
which is as dramatically different from the preceding age as
was the post-Second World War period from the prewar.

Hardly an issue passes without some article on problems of automation, population explosion, or international health. The modern challenge to the church has come, not in abstract intellectual formulations, but in terms of an urban crisis, a black revolution, birth control programs, new sexual mores, unrest in education, and political revolution.

If the theologians of the Victorian age found the discoveries in natural science to be a major source of alarm, the modern theologian has felt the shock of scientific advance as it has been mediated through the social sciences. He has become sensitized to the various uses of power that control and transform the lives of people. The prevailing spirit of acute secularity has convinced many that whatever religion has to offer in this age, it must be in terms of immediate relevance that is translatable into concrete action. The intensity of American social problems has accelerated the search for improving the common good within a pluralistic religious climate. It is obvious that a generation of theologians who have imbibed deeply this new *Zeitgeist* would find the emphases of the Biblical Theology Movement increasingly foreign.

The disillusionment with Biblical Theology on the part of theologians, which appeared in the early sixties, expressed itself in a variety of ways, but invariably reflected the impact of the changing cultural climate. Langdon Gilkey spoke for a whole group of younger theologians when he wrote: "The trans-natural reality that neo-orthodoxy proclaimed—the transcendent God, his mighty acts and his Word of revelation— became more and more unreal and incredible to those who had learned to speak this language. Younger enthusiasts began to wonder if they were talking about anything they themselves knew about when they spoke of God, of encounter, of the eschatological event and of faith." [44] Like the crowds in Hans Christian Andersen's tale, they suddenly agreed that they were unable to see the king's invisible clothing. The language of Biblical faith that had been rediscovered in Europe following the agony of the First World War no longer corresponded to any religious experience for a new generation of Americans. The discrepancy between theological formulation and religious belief had become intolerable. One way out of the dilemma was to discard the formulation.

During the height of the popularity of the Biblical Theology Movement considerable effort had been expended to relate the theology of the acts of God to the contemporary life of the church. It was universally affirmed that the God who had once acted so powerfully in the redemption of Israel at the Reed Sea (sic) was still at work. To the query as to where this new action was manifest, the answer was given in terms of the ongoing life of the institutional church. In the church's liturgy, in the proclamation of the Word and the Sacraments, in the administering of social services and in the other aspects of the ministry, God was acting. The insistence on the unbroken continuity between ancient Israel and the modern church grew out of a theology of sharing a common *Heilsgeschichte*. For a while the oft-repeated slogan "Let the church be the church" seemed to quiet any misgivings that the church really did play only this role in the divine economy. One of the earliest in a series of books that pointed out the precariousness of this ecclesiastical posture was the sociological critique of Peter Berger.[45] In spite of the host of rejoinders the book undoubtedly struck a sensitive nerve. The inability of applying to the average American church the vocabulary of "the acts of God" became increasingly obvious, particularly in the main-line denominations which eschewed religious fervor as fanaticism. The negative criticism of Berger and others certainly prepared the ground for the major shift of attitude toward the church and the world.

Bonhoeffer had coined the term "religionless Christianity." Whatever it might have meant for its original author, it proved to be immediately attractive to a new breed of secular-oriented Christian. Emphasis on Biblical tradition and the mission of the church gave way to a new call for social action based on common humanity, appeal to conscience, human dignity, and the natural rights of self-expression for the new theology. God had abandoned the sanctuary and gone out into the streets. Perhaps even more damaging to the influence of the Biblical Theology Movement was a growing sense in America of the inadequacy of this older way of relating Bible and theology to provide answers for the pressing problems that suddenly faced the church in the world. Many pastors who continued to hold the major tenets of the movement struggled unsuccessfully to apply the theology to concrete issues. Neither the concept of a Biblical mentality nor redemptive history of the people of God provided the needed insights or carried the required authority for the issues of the day. Suddenly the familiar approach to the Bible began to seem as outdated as had Harry Emerson Fosdick's theology to the Biblical theologians of the forties. The growing uncertainty regarding the place of the Bible reflected itself again in the form of the sermon. Whatever criticisms one could aim at the older Liberals in respect to its content, one had to admit that the preaching of Fosdick, Luccock, and Sockman had been at least interesting, lucid, and relevant. These qualities appeared to many modern preachers again to claim top priority.

If one were to attempt to mark a date for the end of the Biblical Theology Movement as a dominant force in American theology, it probably should be done in reference to important publications that served both to renounce the past and to announce a new direction. J. A. T. Robinson's *Honest to God,* which appeared in May of 1963, arose from a peculiarly English context. Nevertheless, it carried an enormous impact far beyond its original audience. Robinson had been well-known as a New Testament scholar, who had chosen to write mainly in the field of Biblical Theology, rather than in the technical areas of historical or philological problems of the New Testament. Robinson was the first to admit that his new approach to theology was dependent on a combination of insights obtained from other theologians, particularly Tillich, Bonhoeffer, and Bultmann. Nevertheless, his own form of appropriation was highly significant in marking his dramatic reversal of theological positions. If the Biblical theologians had spoken of the God of history, Robinson turned instead to Tillich's ontological category of the "ground of being." If the Biblical theologians had focused on the mission of Israel and the church by means of a unique tradition, Robinson spoke to the world as a thoroughly secular modern man who reflected on problems of universal human existence. Finally, in the place of a theocentric message of redemption, Robinson chose a man-centered model of human concern with, of course, some Christological overtones. In Robinson's case the impact of the book was derived chiefly from the fundamental honesty of the author in breaking sharply with traditional Christianity in spite of his ecclesiastical commitments.

Harvey Cox's *The Secular City* (1965) was a genuinely American phenomenon. Its massive impact stemmed from its brilliant use of sociological categories coupled with an incisive use of empirical data by which he successfully illuminated a whole range of modern problems. It is quite apparent that Cox was educated during the Biblical Theology Movement. He frequently makes use of its vocabulary and concepts. In fact, nowhere in the book does Cox explicitly repudiate his past as did Robinson. Rather, Cox's book is of particular significance in being an extension of the Biblical Theology Movement as well as its radical metamorphosis. On the one hand, Cox still speaks of God's acting in history, of the unity of the Bible, even of Greek vs. Hebrew mentality. Yet on the other hand, the focus has shifted from a theology of history in the past to a theology of history in the present which means politics. Once this shift has been made then God is at work in the world "wherever the action is." The church becomes the agent for social change and functions as a partner with God in ushering in the Kingdom of God, pictured by means of the model of the secular city. Cox's achievement lay in his making the older categories of the Biblical Theology Movement bend to accommodate a new theology that has a dynamic totally its own.

Finally, the writings of Langdon Gilkey are important barometers of the changing climate within the world of American theology.[46] He has served an important function as incisive critic both of the Biblical Theology Movement and the newer theological alternatives that have been proposed. In contrast to Robinson and Cox, Gilkey has been frank to admit his inability to see clearly the direction which theology will take in the future. Still he is concerned to face the modern issues and to ask the right questions. For Gilkey the fundamental theological question of the age concerns the reality of God. But indicative of his break with the past is Gilkey's confidence that this question must first be solved apart from and prior to a reference to the Bible. "In such a situation these questions must be settled before we can treat the Bible as the source of truth and therefore of theological truth." [47] One will have to wait to see whether Gilkey's ultimate answer to the problem he poses as being central for the future of theology will take a radically new shape or will simply reflect a retooling of the older philosophical categories. Regardless of the outcome, it is clear that Gilkey had struck out in search for a newer path because he was convinced the older paths could no longer be trusted as guides to ultimate truth.

To summarize: The Biblical Theology Movement underwent a period of slow dissolution beginning in the late fifties. The breakdown resulted from pressure from inside and outside the movement that brought it to a virtual end as a major force in American theology in the early sixties.

PART II

Seeking a Future

5

THE NEED FOR A NEW
BIBLICAL THEOLOGY

There will be some theologians in America who upon hearing of the demise of the Biblical Theology Movement will surely rejoice. They will sigh in relief that this "bout with the Bible" is now passed and that theology can direct its full attention to the solid social issues of the day. Surely it is only a small minority, however, who will think that the clock can be turned back. In our opinion, the majority of theologians are rather asking, Where do we go from here in the use of the Bible? Again, there is the same uncertainty among Biblical scholars. Probably the majority would agree that the old-style Biblical Theology proved in the end to be inadequate. Yet only a small group would suppose that the way was now clear for returning to the minutiae of historicocritical scholarship without any continuing concern for the theological dimensions of the Bible or responsibility for the life of the church.

Not only are the seventies different from the thirties, but the movement has left an impact on the American scene—in its moments of both success and failure—which cannot be overlooked. It should not be forgotten that many of the present leaders in American theology not only were trained in the period of the movement but caught their first enthusiasm for theology through the impact of these Biblical theologians. The present health and tremendous vitality of Biblical studies in America is due, at least in part, to the reawakening of the discipline through the energy of the movement. It is highly significant that many of the leading Biblical scholars of the present generation, while at times critical of the older theological positions, still identify with the long-range goals of the movement and share in gratitude a strong sense of solidarity with this generation of church-oriented scholars. The majority of these scholars are likewise concerned that the ground won by the last generation not be abandoned by the present. This can only be accomplished if the discipline is not renounced but pursued with new rigor, insight, and enthusiasm.

There are a number of reasons that suggest that the need for Biblical Theology in some form is greater than ever. First of all, the shape of the disciplines of Old Testament and New Testament in America for the next decade at least gives the impression of being basically oriented toward historical, philological, and literary problems, with priority being given to highly technical competence. This direction can be explained and justified in the light of the new areas that have been opened up through Ugarit, Qumran, Nag Hammadi, etc. There is no doubt that a descriptive task of importance needs to be done that will serve to break new ground and critically to test the older foundations. However, with such a concentration on detailed description the danger is acute that the Biblical disciplines will again be fragmented. There is need for a discipline that will attempt to retain and develop a picture of the whole, and that will have a responsibility to synthesize as well as analyze.

It is equally important to raise the question as to how the Biblical material is to be used in the constructive theological and homiletical disciplines of theology if the emphasis of Old Testament and New Testament is primarily descriptive. To suggest that the responsibility lies with the theologians is fully inadequate because the material is not in any form that can be appropriated. This is not to suggest that Biblical Theology serve merely as a packaging process, but that a constructive use of the material of the separate Biblical disciplines must be done first by a Biblical scholar. The task lies not primarily in sifting, simplifying, and ordering, but in approaching the material in a theologically significant way and addressing questions that not only are compatible to the Biblical material but relate to the theological task as well. There is little hope of the Biblical and theological disciplines interacting in a beneficial way unless Biblical scholars are working constructively in theology, and conversely challenging the theologians to come to grips with the material described by the Biblical disciplines. The proposal is not implying that the traditional division between Biblical and Dogmatic Theology be abandoned, but rather suggesting that to have an area of overlap can aid in creating a genuine dialogue. It simply will not do to limit Biblical Theology to the descriptive task.

One of the soft spots of the Biblical Theology Movement lay in the failure to develop the area of Biblical Theology as a rigorous discipline. It tended to be considered an avocation by men whose primary competence lay in some other area. It remained unclear how the constructive and descriptive tasks related. Often one gained the impression that what distinguished Biblical Theology from the disciplined study of the Old and New Testaments was a homiletical topping. One obvious reaction to the lack of rigor is to reject Biblical Theology *in toto*. A far more responsible reaction is to establish the discipline on a solid foundation while resisting the challenge of those denying the right of constructive theology to relate Bible and theology.

There is another important aspect of the problem that would support the need for developing the area of Biblical Theology in our time. The United States has entered a period of tremendous political and social change. A series of crises have produced a turmoil and soul-searching restlessness which is unparalleled since the Civil War. And yet it is a period with enormous potential for creativity in every area of our culture. Certainly this is no time for Biblical studies to turn its back on the burning issues of the day. The church needs the guidance of the Bible as never before in its own struggle for understanding and faithful response. It simply cannot afford to enter a barren period in which its life is fragmented into activist and traditionalist factions, or one in which the intellectuals are at odds with the devout. To be relevant without being faithful or to be faithful without being relevant are both errors that the church must seek to avoid. The threat of a new American theological liberalism that finds its warrant for social action in a vague reference to "making human the structures of society" has already made strong inroads into the life of the church. Biblical Theology would seem to have a decisive role to play in meeting this challenge at this time.

Again, a good case could be made that some of the major impetus for the new left in theology has come from the Bible even though the influence has been largely indirect. The majority of clichés that one associates with radical theology have roots within the Biblical tradition: a "prophetic" ministry against the religious establishment, social justice for all men, the idolatry of nationalism, the freedom to live and love boldly in the present moment, radical secularity as the grounds for recovering one's full humanity, the search for authenticity, the humanizing of society, etc. It is of great importance that these concepts be filled with a content that is informed by the study of the Bible. Nothing would be more unfortunate for theology if these concepts were distorted and misunderstood in order to serve a totally alien function from their original intent. One only has to recall the tragedy of the Marxist discovery of Christian eschatology at a time in which the church had largely forgotten it, or Christian Science's use of a Biblical emphasis on wholeness of body and soul when the Christian church had, by and large, ignored it.

The reverse is also true. If Biblical studies are to remain vi-

brant for theology, they must benefit from active confrontation
with the new questions of the age, and not be allowed to slip
back into a state of scholarly antiquarianism. Because of the
changing context of our society, even when one simply passes
along established scholarly contributions of the past, this task
must be done in a fresh way. The future has a way of robbing
the past of its meaning unless the heritage is rethought and
reevaluated.

Then again, there is a very practical reason why Biblical
Theology should be pursued in a fresh and disciplined way.
Christian pastors continue to do their own Biblical Theology.
Whether consciously or unconsciously the working minister
must come to some understanding of theology in its relation to
the Biblical tradition. The real question is not whether to do
Biblical Theology or not, but rather what kind of Biblical Theology does one have! By the very nature of his office a Christian pastor must have arrived at some level of theological
reflection that informs his work. The fact that in practice a
minister's theological synthesis may be fragmentary, incoher-
ent, or even irrational does not vitiate his having made some
sort of personal appropriation of tradition that affects his ministry at various levels.

During the Biblical Theology Movement many pastors
found the current emphases of great aid. To one group whose
Biblical training had seemed totally irrelevant to the Christian
ministry, the movement provided ways of making the Bible a
central focus to its ministry. To another group that came from
a Bible-oriented tradition, the movement often served to buttress and update this heritage. With the slow breakdown in
the movement the confusion has spread among these pastors.
Is it really true that modern Biblical studies have repudiated
Biblical Theology? Have we been misled? Where does one go
from here? It is imperative that direction be given to these
pastors and that substantial help be offered in making the
Bible again a tool of fundamental importance. The tragic part

of the Biblical Theology Movement lies not only in the defeats it suffered because of its inadequate scholarship and conceptual confusion but also in the impression that has been left that the Bible has no significant role to play in the coming age. The ultimate judgment on the Biblical Theology Movement will depend, in large measure, to what extent interest in Biblical Theology can survive and flourish in a new form rather than leading to a total disaffection with the subject.

As Biblical scholarship enters a new period it is important to be reminded that the scholar has the important function to perform in attempting to control the rise of new fads within the discipline. While it is highly unlikely that the "new hermeneutic" will ever make a lasting impression on the Anglo-Saxon world because of its heavy-footed prose, it certainly does add to the present confusion of the parish to have such turgidity heralded as the hope of the future. It is a disheartening experience to be asked to advise a church board on a new educational curriculum and be forced to characterize the proposed "new approach" as a passing curiosity that has already been bypassed by current Biblical research. Surely a major responsibility of the theologians of the church is to caution against such pitfalls and seek to distinguish between creative scholarship and enervating fads.

It might also be refreshing for the pastor to be told that the interaction between the university and the parish is not a one-way street. It may well be that some of the direction for the new Biblical Theology of the future will come from the experiences of pastors on the front lines of the church's confrontation with the world. It was not by accident that a working pastor in the forgotten Swiss village of Safenwil first discovered what Romans could mean to a congregation before dropping his theological bomb on the scholarly community. Fortunately God still has a way of making use of the Bible which is not synchronized to the publication schedule of the religious press.

6
THE SHAPE OF A NEW
BIBLICAL THEOLOGY

THE PROBLEM OF CONTEXT

The first step in laying a foundation for a new Biblical Theology, in our opinion, is to establish the proper context for interpreting the Bible theologically. By "context" more is meant than simply "perspective" which focuses on the angle of vision of the interpreter. Rather, context refers to the environment of that which is being interpreted. As a literary term, context denotes the parts of a composition that constitute the texture of the narrative. To interpret a sentence "out of context" is to disregard its place in its larger literary design. In a broader sense the term "context" includes both the formal and the material elements of design that belong to a historical period. Thus one speaks of the necessity of understanding the Puritan emphasis on prudence as a religious virtue within the context of England's political and economic developments in the early seventeenth century.

Now it is apparent that there are many different and fully legitimate contexts from which to interpret the Bible. The Old Testament can be seen within the context of Ancient Near Eastern literature. Within this larger context one can study a limited area such as Hebrew grammar as a part of the larger family of Semitic languages. Or one can describe the various literary genres within the Old Testament to show the elements

of commonality and distinctiveness in relation to parallel literary types in Egypt and Babylon, or one can investigate the
growth and development of Israel's institutions. In the same
way, the New Testament can be analyzed as an example of
Hellenistic literature that has appropriated and refashioned
Jewish religious traditions in a particular way. Its language
can be also examined in tracing the development of Greek di-
alects. Its religious vocabulary can be studied in relation to
the piety of the classical world, the mystery religions, and
Gnostic speculation.

The interpretation of the material will vary in relation to the
particular context in which it is placed. Because there is often
an interrelation between different contexts, one can expect to
find areas that reflect a common design for several different
contexts. The search to discover the original historical contexts
for the various parts of the Old and New Testaments is essential for a number of historicocritical disciplines, such as literary,
historical, and comparative religion analysis. However, it is
also true, as the adherents to the school of "newer criticism"
in the field of English literature have continued to point out,
that an interpreter can approach the same material and use
only the final stage of the literature as a legitimate context.
The results will vary greatly depending on whether the context includes or excludes the diachronistic dimension.

A great confusion persisted throughout the period of the
Biblical Theology Movement in regard to the proper context
for the doing of Biblical Theology. Some scholars felt that the
Biblical material in its original historical context contained
theological elements, which when "objectively" described
formed theological patterns that could then be directly appropriated by modern Christian theology. "God's revelation in
history" or "the unity of the Bible" was thought to reflect, not
the bias of the interpreter, but objective results of solid historicocritical scholarship. Others worked on the assumption that
there was a common context for the descriptive task to which

one added the perspective of Christian theology to make a
bridge to the modern age. Finally, a few Biblical theologians
defended the view that, when doing theology, there was no
common ground. The interpreter's stance, whether within or
without the faith, determined what he found in the Biblical
material. We have already traced the disastrous effect of this
fundamental ambiguity respecting context within the movement.

THE CANON AS THE CONTEXT
FOR BIBLICAL THEOLOGY

As a fresh alternative, we would like to defend the thesis
that the canon of the Christian church is the most appropriate
context from which to do Biblical Theology. What does this
mean? First of all, implied in the thesis is the basic Christian
confession, shared by all branches of historic Christianity, that
the Old and New Testaments together constitute Sacred Scripture for the Christian church.[1] The status of canonicity is not
an objectively demonstrable claim but a statement of Christian belief. In its original sense, canon does not simply perform the formal function of separating the books that are
authoritative from others that are not, but is the rule that de-
lineates the area in which the church hears the word of God.[2]
The fundamental theological issue at stake is not the extent of
the canon, which has remained in some flux within Christianity, but the claim for a normative body of tradition contained
in a set of books.

Again, to speak of the canon as a context implies that these
Scriptures must be interpreted in relation to their function
within the community of faith that treasured them. The Scriptures of the church are not archives of the past but a channel
of life for the continuing church, through which God instructs
and admonishes his people. Implied in the use of the canon as
a context for interpreting Scripture is a rejection of the

method that would imprison the Bible within a context of the historical past. Rather, the appeal to the canon understands Scripture as a vehicle of a divine reality, which indeed encountered an ancient people in the historical past, but which continues to confront the church through the pages of Scripture. The church's prayer for illumination by the Holy Spirit when interpreting Scripture is not a meaningless vestige from a forgotten age of piety, but an acknowledgment of the continuing need for God to make himself known through Scripture to an expectant people. Because the church uses the text as a medium of revelation the interrelation of Bible and theology is constitutive in the context of the canon. The descriptive and constructive aspects of interpretation may well be distinguished, but never separated when doing Biblical Theology according to this model.

To do Biblical Theology within the context of the canon involves acknowledgment of the *normative* quality of the Biblical tradition. The Scriptures of the church provide the authoritative and definitive word that continues to shape and enliven the church.[3] The full force of this claim should not be missed. Many are willing to use the Bible as a helpful illustration of how men once tried to be faithful to God. Accordingly, the Bible affords at most a guide. It is illustrative and not binding in any sense. Then the modern Christian functions in a way that is parallel to the tradition, rather than derivative. This concept of the place of the Biblical tradition usually lies behind the popular cliché of the "prophetic ministry." Just as Amos testified with a divine word of judgment to Amaziah in the eighth century B.C., so I am called up to testify to the political structures of my day with a word from God. Certainly the appeal of this analogy is clear. God is just as alive today as then. If the word of God is to be anything, it must speak to a concrete situation in the present. Indeed the Christian minister must submit the pride and folly of human society to the divine judgment. Thus, Reinhold Niebuhr was to the thirties as Jeremiah was to the seventh century B.C.!

In spite of the widespread appeal, particularly to the radical wing of the church, there is a fundamental error involved that is rejected by those who take the canon seriously. The Bible must function normatively and not merely illustratively for the church. If one reflects a bit on the popular appeal of a "prophetic ministry," the implications of this theology for the use of the Bible are all too clear. First of all, the modern appropriation of the term "prophet" only functions on the assumption of a radical demythologization of the Bible. As a modern minister I do not hear the word of God in the same way as the Biblical prophets confess to doing. I cannot say, "Hear the word of God," in the same way that Amos did. Therefore, one argues that neither did Amos. The formula "Hear the word of God" is only an idiom for saying: "This is what I as a sensitive religious person think." The effect is that the analogy of a "prophetic ministry" is maintained by reducing the prophets in size. Rather than the Biblical tradition serving as a norm, the reverse is true. Modern human experience becomes the norm for what is of value in the tradition.

The acknowledgment of the canon as the context for interpreting the Bible offers another alternative toward understanding the "prophetic ministry." The responsibility of proclaiming the Word of God in word and deed remains the same from the past until the present. The responsibility to address the contemporary issues in the light of divine judgment and redemption has not changed. But the medium through which revelation is transmitted has changed. This conclusion is constitutive to the concept of a canon. The revelation of God to his people is now mediated through the witness of the prophets and apostles. In the context of a normative body of tradition the minister as pastor, priest, and prophet seeks to discern the will of God in pursuit of the obedient life. The Bible does not function in its role as canon to provide a collection of eternal ideas, nor is it a handbook of right doctrine, nor a mirror of man's religious aspirations. Rather the canon marks the area in which the modern issues of life and death are defined in

terms of what God has done and is doing, and what he demands as a response from his people.

Again, the attempt to do Biblical Theology in the context
of the canon has important hermeneutical implications for the
approach to the Biblical text. One of the persistently weak
points of the Biblical Theology Movement was its failure to
take the Biblical text seriously in its canonical form. It accepted uncritically the liberal hermeneutical presupposition
that one came to the Biblical text from a vantage point outside
the text. For some it was the basic historicity of the Bible; for
others, the intention of Jesus, or the gospel kerygma. At times
theologians attempted to apply some form of "canon within
the canon" to isolate what was basically Christian. But at other
times, a decision, which was grounded in ontology, general
ethical theory, or secular humanism, determined what was
normative within Scripture. Because the Biblical Theology
Movement shared this hermeneutical uncertainty, it was vulnerable to every shifting wind that blew, from Cullmann's
"salvation-history" to Bultmann's "self-understanding" to Ebe-
ling-Fuchs's "linguisticality of being." In conscious opposition
to this approach to hermeneutics, the confession of the Christian canon as the context for Biblical theology makes the claim
that the "theological data" of the Bible does not lie in some
form of positivity behind the text, such as *Heilsgeschichte*,[4]
language phenomenology,[5] or in a mode of consciousness illustrated by the text, such as authentic existence or the like.[6]
Even though there is an obvious history of development that
lies behind the formation of the canon, and even though there
are a variety of modes of consciousness involved at various
levels and periods, the confession of a canon holds this context
to be normative for the Christian faith.

The insistence that Biblical Theology work with Scripture
in its canonical book form does not, of course, imply that the
Bible as a book is to be isolated from the community that
treasured it. The Bible is the Scriptures of the church. It is

precisely this false dichotomy between the book and the community which is rejected by speaking of its canonical context. Scripture does not exist as a book of truth in itself, yet there is no church tradition independent of the Biblical text. The relation of Scripture to tradition receives its normative form in the acknowledgment of a canon. Again, to speak of taking the Bible as a canonical text seriously does not imply that one is forced to read the text "on the flat." Already in its early controversy with the synagogue, the church insisted on relating the text to the reality to which the text pointed. The Christian church has never been text-bound in the sense that the text has an authority separated from the reality of which it speaks. However, in the modern debate the acute danger has come from the reverse side, namely, in trying to separate the reality from the text. The confession of a canon opposes both attempts at separating text from reality. The text of Scripture points faithfully to the divine reality of Christ while, at the same time, our understanding of Jesus Christ leads us back to the Scripture, rather than away from it.

During the period of the Biblical Theology Movement the theology of the inspiration of Scripture was generally replaced by a theology of Scripture as revelation. This was understandable as an effort to break the impasse that had developed in the debate with Fundamentalism. The reflex to defend or dismiss a theory of inerrancy that had become attached to discussions of inspiration brought the doctrine into general disrepute. Nor did the Liberal's attempt to detach inspiration from Scripture and reinterpret it as a quality of imagination within the writer offer a solid theological alternative. One of the major factors in the breakdown of the Biblical Theology Movement was its total failure to come to grips with the inspiration of Scripture. The strain of using orthodox Biblical language for the constructive part of the theology, but at the same time approaching the Bible with all the assumptions of Liberalism, proved in the end to cause an impossible tension.

Once again, the effort to take seriously the confession of a canon offers another alternative in respect to the inspiration of Scripture. The doctrine of inspiration is an attempt to deal adequately with the medium of revelation. The mistake of employing such a concept as inerrancy, among other things, was in its defining of the medium apart from its canonical context. In our opinion, the claim for the inspiration of Scripture is the claim for the uniqueness of the canonical context of the church through which the Holy Spirit works. Although there are innumerable other contexts in which to place the Bible—this is part of the humanity of the witness—divine inspiration is a way of claiming a special prerogative for this one context. The Bible, when understood as the Scriptures of the church, functions as the vehicle for God's special communicating of himself to his church and the world. This understanding of the Scripture's uniqueness remains a statement of faith. It neither requires a hidden apologetic nor must it be reformulated to accommodate itself to every new phase of the scholarly debate.

Yet the concept of canon remains to many an offense, not only in its assigning such an exclusive role to the Bible as the medium of revelation, but by insisting that it be understood within a particular context, if it is to function as the Word of God. Why is the canon anything more than a historical accident with which the church was burdened for many centuries? How can one place any significance on the canon when, from a critical point of view, the criteria used in its compilation are no longer accepted as valid? If the decisions on canon were historically conditioned, why should we be limited to them in our contemporary theological work?

First of all, one must not confuse the historical question of the development of the canon with the theological issue that is at stake. It is certainly true that the process of canonization by the church reflects a complex and often confusing picture. Under the pressure of Marcion's challenge the concept of a New Testament Scripture arose which began to function in conjunction with the ancient Scriptures to combat heresy. In the struggles of the third and fourth centuries different criteria for determining canonicity were used, various motivations played a role, and inner-church conflicts were at work. Such a book as that of Hans von Campenhausen offers a thorough examination and fresh evaluation of the variety of forces involved in this history.

However, in full knowledge of this history, the church has rightly insisted that no ecclesiastical body can ever "make a book canonical." Rather, the concept of canon was an attempt to *acknowledge* the divine authority of its writings and collections.[7] The church as a fully human institution bore witness to the effect that certain writings had had on its faith and life. In speaking of canon the church testified that the authority of its Scriptures stemmed from God, not from human sanction. Canonicity as the "rule of faith" was a confession of the divine origin of the gospel that had called the church into being.

The concept of canon as it developed was a testimony to the belief that faith in Jesus Christ was grounded upon the witness of both prophets and apostles. God had revealed his will, not in timeless universal truths, but in concrete manifestations of himself, restricted in time and space, and testified to by particular witnesses. Scripture served not as interesting "sources" of historical information about Jesus of Nazareth, but as a testimony that the salvation and faith of the old covenant was one with that revealed in Jesus Christ.

There is an analogy between the human and divine side of the Bible and the historical and theological aspects of the canon. The fact that the church confessed its faith in the divine origin of its Scripture in a thoroughly time-conditioned fashion can be readily acknowledged. But the theological issue at stake is the rightness of the claim for divine authority to which the church responded in setting apart certain writings as Scripture. The church today continues to bear witness to these Scriptures as from God, while at the same time seeking

new ways of understanding them and being open to new formulations, regarding both the scope and the character of the
Scripture's authority.

The appeal to the Christian canon is an attempt to find a
hermeneutical analogy for doing modern Biblical Theology.
Although the New Testament's use of the Old Testament is a
process separate and distinct from the development of canonization proper, the New Testament's approach to the Old
Testament provided a warrant for the later development. The
New Testament writers accepted the Scriptures of the synagogue as authoritative—some defined the scope more strictly
than others—and yet at the same time subjected them to a
critical reinterpretation in the light of their understanding of
Jesus Christ. The process of critical reinterpretation was not
the same for Paul, Luke, or John,[8] but the framework of their
message, namely, the faith of Israel confronting the gospel,
was held in common.

Likewise, the later church sought to understand the faith it
confessed by means of various dialectical moves between the
Old and the New. The church employed different exegetical
skills; allegory and typology replaced midrash. In turn, the
Reformation criticized medieval exegesis, while still sharing
much of it, and sought to unleash the power of Scripture by
calling for a new emphasis on the literal sense of the Bible,
Christologically understood. A major break in the church's approach to Scripture came with the development of the historicocritical method, which perfected a whole set of new tools
for understanding the historical and theological setting of the
Bible.

Now the appeal to the canon does not restrict the interpreter
to any one particular exegetical method. Obviously, the tools
of interpretation will change and vary according to each age.
Certainly the historicocritical approach has become a hallmark
of the modern period, and is an impressive contribution, above
all, of modern Protestant scholarship. But the theological is-

sue at stake is the context for doing one's exegesis. By taking seriously the canon, one confesses along with the church to the unique function that these writings have had in its life and faith as Sacred Scripture. Then each new generation of interpreters seeks to be faithful in searching these Scriptures for renewed illumination while exploiting to the fullest the best tools available for opening the texts. Ultimately, to stand within the tradition of the church is a stance not made in the spirit of dogmatic restriction of the revelation of God, but in joyful wonder and even surprise as the Scripture becomes the bread of life for another generation.

THE RELATION OF THE CONTEXT OF THE CANON TO OTHER CONTEXTS

Up to this point we have argued for the theological integrity of a Biblical interpretation that functions within the context of the canon of Sacred Scripture. However, there remains a multitude of problems to be explored. How does the alleged context of the canon relate to the other contexts in which the Bible can be read? Or to put this same question in another form, what is the role of the historicocritical method for the doing of Biblical Theology? Is not the method that has been outlined really a return to the precritical period of Biblical study? Although these questions are all related, it will be necessary to sort them out and deal with them in order.

First, it is significant to recall that a similar problem emerged early in the history of the church. A controversy arose between Jerome and Augustine that resulted from Jerome's attempt to translate the Old Testament directly from the Hebrew text.[9] Augustine questioned the wisdom of using the Hebrew as a means of correcting the Greek text. Although Augustine was primarily concerned from a practical point of view that the church not be split over the different translations, his arguments against Jerome are of great significance.

Augustine reasoned that the Greek translation of the Old Testament had become the Scriptures of the Christian church, as was already apparent in the New Testament. Any changes that the Greek reveals over against the Hebrew could therefore only be attributed to the work of the Holy Spirit. To return to the Hebrew text was to return to the pre-Christian stage of revelation. In his response Jerome abruptly rejected Augustine's arguments. Among other things he argued for the necessity for clarifying uncertain passages in the Septuagint on the basis of a better understanding of the Hebrew. He insisted that the task of translating from the Hebrew served the same purpose of supporting the faith as had the translation from the Greek.

While it would be a mistake to identify Augustine with the traditionalist and Jerome with the modern Biblical critic, there is a certain analogy to be drawn for the purposes of this discussion. To employ our own modern terminology, Augustine was arguing that the canonical context vitiated the need for making any reference to early settings. Jerome, in contrast, defended the need for understanding the original context of the Old Testament. While we would fully agree with Augustine's position that a new context had emerged in terms of the canon, it is apparent that Augustine drew some false inferences from the fact of the canon. Certainly in the end Jerome got the best of the argument. Whatever is meant by the canon as a setting in which the Christian church read its Scripture, it cannot imply that the original setting in which God addressed his people is irrelevant for the later generations. It remains a question whether Jerome fully understood the force of Augustine's argument, and certainly his own theological position was unimpressive in seeking to harmonize the Greek and the Hebrew. Notwithstanding, Jerome's defense of the Hebrew text is incontrovertible. The fact of a canon does not destroy the individual parts of the whole.

The same hermeneutical problem becomes acute in attempting to understand the relation of the Old Testament to the New. Does the confession of a theological context necessitate the rejection of the earlier historical settings? Because the church sought to read the Old Testament in the light of the New Testament, does this mean that the Old Testament has no theological significance in its own right?

First of all, the confession of the canon as a context is a claim that the juxtaposition of the two Testaments in a particular order and form creates a context that is different from either of the two Testaments alone. Moreover, the whole is more than the sum of its two parts. A theological context has been formed that makes use of both Testaments, but results in something new. The fact of a new context that differs from the original historical setting of the various books is easily demonstrated. Even in its arrangement of the Old Testament books, the Christian church has accepted a form that differs from the "Torah, Prophets, Writings" division of the Hebrew Bible and that has obvious theological implications.[10] In the same way, the grouping of the four Gospels together, which divided Luke from its sequel in Acts, reflects a peculiar canonical order. The arrangement of the Pauline corpus that precedes the letters of Peter and John is also not without significance.

Of far more importance, however, than these rather formal matters is the whole context into which the various parts now fit. While an interpretation of the New Testament in the light of the Old Testament background can be readily defended because of the historical dependence of the New on the Old, the reverse move, namely, an interpretation of the Old in the light of the New, is not at all obvious. Far more than historical continuity of background is being claimed. This latter move obviously has no historical rationale, but rests on the confession of a theological context in which the two parts are seen in a particular relationship. It was a recognition of this theological context that prompted the

Reformers to speak of "interpreting Scripture from Scripture" (*Scriptura sui ipsius interpres*) in an analogy of faith.

Calvin's interpretation of the Old Testament has been frequently misunderstood by modern scholars.[11] On the one hand, Calvin inveighed against the fourfold use of Scripture that had been practiced by the fathers because it destroyed the certainty and clarity of Scripture (cf. Gal. 2:8, cited by Wolf). He renounced allegory and demanded that the literal sense of Scripture (*sensus literalis*) be normative. Yet on the other hand, his own interpretation of the Old Testament frequently spoke of Jesus Christ and the life of the church. The usual explanation of this dual aspect as a sign of Calvin's inconsistency completely misses the point. For Calvin the literal sense of the Old Testament spoke of Jesus Christ. Once the term "literal sense" became identified with the historical sense, which happened in the eighteenth century, Calvin's position became unintelligible. To use another terminology, Calvin's literal sense refers to the plain sense of the text, but when interpreted within the canonical context of the church.

Again, one of the curious things about the whole Biblical Theology Movement was its misunderstanding of Karl Barth's exegesis. Although Barth's dogmatic theology—usually in mediated form—had exerted an influence on the Biblical theologians, very seldom was much serious attention paid to his exegesis. Usually it was dismissed by the Biblical theologians as well as by the older Liberals as "precritical," and at best tolerated as an unfortunate reaction against his past. Yet amazingly enough, Barth remained invulnerable to the weaknesses that beset the Biblical Theology Movement. He would have nothing to do with *Heilsgeschichte*,[12] Hebrew mentality, or unity in diversity of the Bible. His formulation of the Bible against its environment took a totally different shape from that which was defended by the movement.

James Barr's criticism is typical of a whole generation when he describes as "painful" the "great theologian's alienation from the world of Biblical scholarship," [13] and speaks of his "embarrassment with historical criticism." But Barr has failed to recognize that Barth has consistently worked from an avowed theological context, namely, from the context of the Christian canon.[14] Therefore, the work of the historical critics remained for him only prolegomena to the real theological task of exegesis within the discipline of Church Dogmatics.

But what is the nature of this relation between the Testaments within the context of the canon? It is important to recognize that most of the classical formulations of this relationship within Christian theology succeeded mainly in delineating certain proposals as erroneous. The parallel with the Christological formulation of the creeds is apparent. On the one hand, the two Testaments cannot be identified in their relationship because they speak of Christ in decidedly different ways. The two Testaments retain their separate identity as Old and New. Yet, on the other hand, the two Testaments cannot be separated, as if the New no longer needed the Old. Again, the relation of the Testaments is such that one cannot be subordinated to the other by categories of either history or theology. The Old Testament within the context of the canon is not a witness to a primitive level of faith, nor does it need to be Christianized. Within its historical context it is a witness to Jesus Christ. Such attempts as the Epistle of Barnabas to obliterate the Old Testament's own witness by allegory or typology must be rejected as a mistaken understanding of the function of the canon.

The reference to the canon as a context does not define in advance a theological system in which the two Testaments are placed. It does not prescribe a particular content. Rather it describes a context within which a dialectical relationship between the two Testaments is envisioned. It remains the exegetical task of the interpreter to study the exact relation of a given passage within this context. The context does not determine in advance what the relation must be. Two passages might be identical in their witness, or complement one another, or stand in sharp tension.

Fundamental to the exegetical task is the assumption with which we have already dealt that these texts as Scripture of the church are witnesses to a divine reality. The exegetical activity of tracing the dialectical movement between the two Testaments has as its goal, neither the harmonizing of different concepts of God nor the constructing of a set of right doctrine, but testifying to God in his redemptive work. The acknowledgment of a canon is a confession that both Testaments are testifying to the same God at work. How he worked must be heard from the text itself. The juxtaposing of the two Testaments to form a new context rests on a faith claim. Its validity cannot be demonstrated. Nevertheless, the truth claim of this assertion has not been abandoned. The interpreter is anxious to show the nature of the logic of faith. The joining of the two Testaments does not result in an arbitrary construct such as emerges from the joining of the Old Testament with Humpty Dumpty, but there is a compatibility between witnesses. This reveals itself in characteristic approaches to divine reality, commensurate imperatives, and a sustained level of seriousness respecting the major questions of life and death.

The fact that the canon continues to maintain the distinct entities of the Old and New Testaments within its new theological form has important implications for the problem of understanding the relationship of the canonical contexts to the original historical contexts of the individual Testaments. The witnesses of the Bible bear all the marks of their historical conditioning. To be correctly understood they must be heard in their particular period of history, through the culture-formed vehicles of language and thought patterns, and mediated through the individual and corporate personalities of authors and redactors. This characteristic of Biblical revelation offers a warrant for the historicocritical study of the Bible. There

is the full necessity for taking seriously the original context
of every Biblical passage. For this reason Jerome was justified
in defending against Augustine the necessity for translating
the Hebrew text. Nevertheless, the exegetical task of Biblical
Theology cannot stop with this step. The confession of a
canonical context seeks to relate these historical witnesses to
another set of time-conditioned, historical testimonies. It was
the recognition of this need that prompted Augustine to seek
to set the Old Testament in relation to its function within the
New Testament.

The use of the dialectic between the Old and New Testaments in the context of the canon prevents the interpreter
from the error of thinking that the movement between the
Testaments proceeds in one direction only, namely, from the
Old to the New. It is a widespread error to recognize the
historical conditioning of the Old Testament, but to conceive
of the New Testament as "the timeless interpretation" that has
transcended historical limitations. The modern Biblical theologian cannot share uncritically the witness of the New
Testament any more than he can that of the Old. His context
is just as different from that of the New as it is from that of
the Old. The formation of a canon of Scriptures is a recognition
of the need for a context, different from both Testaments,
in which the Christian church continues to wrestle in every
new age with the living God who continues to confront his
people through the ancient testimony of the prophets and
apostles.

Up to this point we have been defending the need for
understanding the original contexts of each Biblical passage
within a dialectical process of interpretation made possible
by the concept of a canon. By stressing the need for taking
seriously the original historical context, one implies a criticism
against the older system of doing Biblical Theology that as-
sembled proof texts, often out of context, in order to construct
a doctrine (the *dicta probantia* method). Again, a criticism

is also directed against doing a Biblical Theology of the two Testaments that works primarily with themes and motifs. The primary objection to motif study as part of the theological discipline is its methodological indifference to the bearers of traditions as well as to the historical contexts in which the material functioned. Motif study often focuses on such problems as the interaction of themes or the laws of motif transformation without feeling the need to relate the witnesses to a theological reality. This makes it an inappropriate method for doing Biblical Theology according to the model which is being outlined. Finally, it should be obvious that the method proposed moves in a different direction from that suggested by Roman Catholic scholars under the rubric of *sensus plenior*.[15]

CATEGORIES FOR BIBLICAL THEOLOGY

How then can the interpreter relate the Testaments in a dialectic process without falling victim to either proof texting or motif study, both of which methods have been faulted for not dealing seriously with original historical context of Biblical passages? No one method is being proposed as a final solution. Any sensitive reading of the Bible reveals that seldom does the Bible move within broad abstract categories such as the doctrine of man, sin, or the "last things." Rather, the psalms reflect on man in his created glory, and man in his insignificance within the world (Ps. 8). Or Deuteronomy speaks of the covenant as the arena of the obedient life, or Paul can testify to the law as both the medium of life and the vehicle of death. In all these illustrations there is a quality of theological specificity that cannot be overlooked without losing something essential to the various witnesses.

One approach for avoiding the dangers of abstraction in Biblical Theology—and the point should be stressed that this is only one of the alternatives—is to begin with specific Old

Testament passages which are quoted within the New Testament. The method has several clear advantages. First of all, a warrant for doing Biblical Theology in this way is already provided by the New Testament, which dealt exegetically with the text of the Old Testament rather than with some aspect of history or theology apart from the witness itself.[16] Secondly, by beginning with a text one is provided with a genuinely Biblical category from the outset. The familiar axes along which the Biblical witnesses move emerge with great clarity in the use of quotations. For example, "There is only one God, maker and preserver of all that exists" (I Cor., ch. 8, quoting Deut., ch. 6, etc.); "God as creator and redeemer of the world" (II Cor., ch. 4, quoting Gen., ch. 1, etc.); "God's demand for justice and mercy precedes sacrifice" (Matt., ch. 12, quoting Hos., ch. 6, etc.); "The kingship of God's anointed calls forth human opposition" (Acts, ch. 4, quoting Ps. 2, etc.). Thirdly, the use of quotations reveals with great clarity the different ways in which a text can function depending on its context. So, for example, the use of Ps. 8 serves an entirely different function in Heb., ch. 2, from its original one.[17] Moreover, its occurrence in I Cor., ch. 15, offers still another usage that differs from Hebrews. The variation in usage is a constant reminder of the historical conditioning of the Biblical texts and offers a resistance to the temptation of moving into abstract and timeless motif studies. Lastly, the theological task of reflecting on the different Biblical witnesses from the canonical contexts is made easier by having the same text in common. One easily gains a clear impression of the scope of the Biblical witness in its use of one passage, as well as the inner dynamic of a text in relation to the larger Biblical units.

Of course, there are several obvious objections to this proposed method of using quotations to determine the rubrics of Biblical Theology. First of all, the New Testament's use of the Old Testament is limited to only a portion of the Old Testament. Secondly, the New Testament's use of the Old

Testament reflects a great diversity in approach which includes examples of serious exegesis and also examples of
merely incidental and even curious application.

In respect to the first objection several points should be
made by way of response. The references to the Old Testament in the New, particularly when allusions are included,
are far more numerous than has generally been recognized.
The evidence for this assertion can be easily tested by examining the indices in such a reference book as Wilhelm
Dittmar's *Vetus Testamentum in Novo*.[18] Even more important, the various ways by which the Old Testament is employed in the New make it clear that a wider reference is
often intended beyond the citation or allusion. C. H. Dodd [19]
has argued convincingly that a verse citation serves as an
index to the whole context of the passage. Again, the use of a
verse often refers to a type of Old Testament material of
which only one example is given. The frequent citation of
Ps. 22 includes an interpretation of the whole class of "individual complaint" psalms which treat of the "suffering righteous I" of the Psalter. Further, the common New Testament
practice of composing a catena of citations gives evidence of
being a condensed way of including the entire background
of Scripture which is presupposed in the joining of particular
texts.[20] Similarly, the use of catchwords, such as "stone," or
phrases from Ps. 110, uncovers a whole complex of interwoven
Biblical passages and concepts.[21]

Another aspect of the problem to be considered is the extent to which whole blocks of Old Testament material are
placed within an interpretative framework, such as Paul's
treatment of the relation of promise to law (Gal., ch. 3).
Likewise the New Testament's reading of one Old Testament
passage through the perspective of another text, which is a
typical midrashic technique, results in an interpretative stamp
on the larger units. For example, the Old Testament "call
narratives," such as that of Moses or Jeremiah, tend to be

viewed in the New Testament from the perspective of II
Isaiah, and the "First Exodus" from Egypt is subordinated to
the promise of an eschatological "Second Exodus." Lastly,
many uses of the Old Testament, such as the controversies in
Matthew regarding legal questions of the tradition, are viewed
as illustrative of a wider stance that affects one's understanding of the Law and the Prophets. In summary, the scope of
the New Testament's use of the Old Testament is extensive
when the full ramifications of its method of reference are
understood.

The second objection to the theological use of citations is
the claim that they are often incidental and curious in application which would vitiate the importance for Biblical Theology.[22] Certainly the variety in the New Testament's use of the
Old must be recognized and properly evaluated. It remains
the exegete's responsibility to distinguish between the levels
of seriousness in the interpretation offered. For example, Heb.,
ch. 3, with a whole chapter devoted to an interpretation of
Ps. 95, must be evaluated differently from the passing reference in I Cor. 9:9 to "muzzling the ox."

Again, an important rubric for Biblical Theology often
emerges even when the New Testament's exegesis is considered "curious" when measured by the criteria of modern
critical scholarship. Usually it is at the points in which the
time-conditioned elements of the New Testament's handling
of the Old appear most evident that an important debate between the church and the synagogue is being carried on respecting Biblical interpretation. For example, Paul's interpretation of the "seed" in Gal., ch. 3, or the "fading splendor"
of II Cor., ch. 3, gives evidence of a midrashic approach that
is foreign to the present critical age. Nevertheless, the issues
at stake remain those fundamental ones which continue to
divide Christianity from Judaism.

The use of Old Testament quotations in the New Testament
is one important approach of Biblical Theology in seeking to

take seriously the context of the whole canon. That it is not
the only method will be illustrated in Part III, which attempts
to test the proposal for a new shape to Biblical Theology.

THE RELATION OF THE BIBLICAL WITNESS
TO THE EXTRA-BIBLICAL

Up to this point we have focused on the problem of the relation between the original function of a passage and its later
theological role within the canon. But what is the relation of
extra-Biblical perceptions of reality to the Biblical witnesses?
The Bible is not alone when it speaks of God, man, and the
world. How do these assertions, confessions, and reflections,
which are made from a context apart from that of Israel and
the church, relate to those made from within the community
of faith? Obviously the problem is too large to be treated thoroughly, but a few lines of direction are in order as it touches
on the shape of a Biblical Theology.

This perennial problem has taxed the intellectual powers of
Christian theologians from the beginning of the church's
history. It is no small wonder because the problem has already been clearly posed by the Bible itself. Throughout the
whole Bible its authors have made use of the language, vocabulary, thought patterns, and culture of the world in which they
lived to bear witness to God and his work. It has become
commonplace to recognize that the writers of Genesis employed mythopoeic language of the Ancient Near East in
describing the primeval history. The Biblical sages made use
of the common treasury of family and court wisdom to speak
of man in relation to God and his fellows. Again, the Fourth
Evangelist employed a vocabulary strikingly different from
that of the Synoptic traditions, but one in which a precise
religious terminology had already been developed outside of
the Christian community. In the light of this clear evidence,
the question of the relation of the Biblical witness to non-
Biblical witnesses cannot be avoided.

There are two classical reactions to the problem which can be readily dismissed. The first refuses to admit any real validity to a religious assertion outside the Bible. This position would argue that the Biblical writers did make use of common material, but they so transformed it as to sever any lines of continuity. The second classical response represents the other extreme. The Biblical witness can claim no special prerogatives to divine truth. The Bible represents one expression of human experience that must be related on the same level with all other human responses to the religious dimension of life. The first alternative protects the uniqueness of the Bible by making it irrelevant to all general areas of human experience. The second seeks for relevance by reducing the Biblical witness to the lowest common denominator. In our opinion, neither of these two solutions is helpful.

It is highly doubtful whether anyone will ever be able to solve this problem theoretically or by means of one overarching proposal. It remains a burning issue that must be continually faced by the interpreter, yet it is one that emerges in innumerable different forms. For this reason, an essential part of the exegetical activity is to wrestle with the Biblical witness in constant relation to the world outside of the community of faith. The interpreter must hear the Biblical word along with other words, and reflect on both in the light of the reality toward which they point. Involved in the reflective process of Biblical Theology is the movement from the witness—whether Biblical or not—to the subject matter of the witness.

In many ways this last dialectic movement is the most difficult of all. It requires a high level of theological sensitivity to avoid the obvious traps when moving from the general sphere of human experience to the area of divine activity. So, for example, the human spirit is not just a little spark of the divine, nor is God's love for the world just a bigger instance of a man's love for his family. Almost every page of the New Testament seeks to elucidate the Kingdom of God in terms of human experience. Yet it is done with consummate skill and an amazing sense of reticence before the mystery of the interaction of the divine with the human. "The kingdom of God is like unto . . ." "If you being evil know how to give good gifts, how much more will your heavenly Father give the Holy Spirit." "There are times when someone might even dare to die for a good man, but God shows his love for us in that while we were yet sinners Christ died for us."

We are able to understand the gospel's message of God's love for mankind, his forgiveness in Christ, and his offer of joy and reconciliation, in relation to our human emotions of love and forgiveness, of joy and reconciliation. Yet exactly how God's love and our emotions relate remains an unsolved problem. There is a delicate balance between cause and response, fundamental to the Christian faith, which dare not be destroyed by psychological bridges, hermeneutical leaps, or philosophical theories. Rather, it remains an ongoing task of the Biblical theologian, working from the context of the canon, to struggle with the witness of his faith in conjunction with other voices from other contexts.

Lest one gain the impression that the "other voices" are always those of outsiders, it is important to remember that the Biblical interpreter is himself a human being, with his own individual context, shaped by his own emotions, personality, and culture. The dialectic between the witness and other apprehensions of reality must take place within the mind and heart of each interpreter. Part of the greatness of Luther as a Biblical interpreter lies in the intensity with which he sought to use his humanity as a transparency for testifying to the Word of God.[23]

CHRISTIAN AND JEWISH SCRIPTURES

There is one final issue that remains an essential part of the understanding of the canon's relationship to other contexts. How does the Christian interpretation of Scripture relate to the Jewish? [24] Historically Judaism was the bearer of the Old Testament traditions and the instrument through which the traditions received their first canonical shape. But Judaism is also a living community of faith, which continues to find in its Bible the revelation of the divine will for the covenant people. It is a community of faith that has its own context from which to read the Old Testament. By interpreting the Bible through the oral tradition of the synagogue fathers, Judaism also makes use of a theological context. The tensions that have arisen between the two communities in the reading of the Bible cannot be judged as an accidental historical disagreement, for they reflect issues that are fundamental to both sides. The New Testament feels constrained to define much of its witness in conscious opposition to Jewish tradition, and most often by an appeal to the Old Testament. The centrality of Paul lies in large measure in his having formulated Christian theology in a polemical debate with the synagogue. If for this reason alone, one cannot speak adequately of the church's canonical context without a serious consideration of classical Jewish exegesis.

A comparison of Judaism and Christianity's use of the Bible is of great theological importance because neither of the two communities shares the original historical context of Israel. Both faiths set the Old Testament within another normative tradition, the oral tradition of Judaism, the New Testament tradition for Christianity. Conversely, the Biblical text serves as a determinative force in forming the normative traditions of both communities. Both arose as responses to the text and cannot be divorced from it. This means that both faiths relate themselves in a dialectical movement to the text on the basis of a context of faith. It involves coming to the Biblical text from tradition, and going to the tradition from the text. The confusion in the exegetical disputes of the second and third centuries between Christians and Jews rested to a large extent in the mutual failure to recognize this indirect relationship to the Bible. Neither side could prove or disprove its

basic religious structure from the Old Testament text alone,
nor could either side afford to abandon the exegetical task as
irrelevant to the theological issues at stake.

A comparison of the classical exegesis of Judaism and
Christianity is of importance within the discipline of Biblical
Theology for several reasons. By seeing how the Old Testament can be understood from another context of faith, the
exegete is made more conscious of the precise manner in
which the text has become a vehicle for Christian revelation.
He is made aware of the fact that the Old Testament does not
"naturally" unfold into the New Testament. It does not lean
toward the New Testament, but the Christian interpretation
within its new context is fully dependent on the radical new
element in Jesus Christ. Again, the Jewish interpretation high-
lights by its divergence those elements in the Old Testament
which are being emphasized, transformed, or rejected in the
larger context of the Christian canon. Finally, the dialogue with
Judaism in relation to a common text is a constant reminder
to the church of the mystery of Israel. Here is a community
that has not recognized the claims of Christ and yet at times
bears witness in her life to a reality that the church confesses
to be that of Jesus Christ. The church thus is reminded that
God has not abandoned his people, and that his purpose is
not accomplished "until all Israel is reconciled to God."

To summarize: The concern of this chapter has been to
propose a form of Biblical Theology that takes as its primary
task the disciplined theological reflection of the Bible in the
context of the canon. The crisis in the discipline has come
about by a failure to clarify the major task of Biblical Theology. As a result, Biblical scholars exert most of their energy
on historical, literary, and philological problems which, while
valid in themselves, have not provided the scholarly Biblical
research of the sort the church sorely needs.

7

BIBLICAL THEOLOGY'S ROLE
IN DECISION-MAKING

THE BIBLE AND ETHICAL NORMS

One of the characteristics of American theology, particularly in this decade, is the intense concern with the problem of making ethical decisions. This is not a new phenomenon of modern theology. It is as constitutive to Christianity, as it is to Judaism, to lay tremendous emphasis on responsible ethical behavior. Yet the form in which the problems have been posed, and the solutions that have been offered, have assumed a particular form that makes the modern period distinctive. Within the last decade the focus of Christian responsibility toward the problems of war, poverty, sex, and race has greatly intensified. Along with this has gone an unparalleled growth in complexity. The Christian church has been forced to come to some terms with the new role of the government and social agencies in the area of human welfare which has had no precedent in former periods.

The question is not one of abandoning the need for a life of personal faith and obedience. Rather, added to this traditional dimension of ethics has come a cluster of problems of a corporate and social nature that are related to the so-called "common good." There are few pastors who do not find a large proportion of their time taken up with concerns of general human welfare in which they are called upon to work with men of goodwill. The pastor may be deeply involved in open housing, school reform, civil rights, and ward politics, but often there seems to be little direct relation between these necessary activities and his Christian faith. Conversely, he seems to find little help from his faith—other than the most general principles—in coming to the difficult decisions that confront him on all these fronts.

Interest in this problem focuses on the role of the Bible for the Christian within the complex world of modern ethical decision. The Biblical Theology Movement failed in the end to provide an adequate theological approach to the Bible that could have been successfully used by pastors, theologians, and laity who stood on the firing line between the church and the world. Suddenly it appeared to many that the older emphases of revelation and history, exodus and covenant did not speak to the burning issues of the day. Whatever shape a new Biblical Theology will take, surely it must be one that will aid in the process of making the knotty ethical decisions that daily confront the Christian.

It has been characteristic of American theology, both for the period of the Social Gospel and during the height of the Biblical Theology Movement, that the relation of the Bible to questions of social ethics remained a nebulous one. Within most American divinity schools, in respect to both faculty and students, there was a rather sharp line dividing the "Biblical phalanx" from the "social ethics boys." Only infrequently did scholars such as Paul Minear and Amos Wilder attempt to bridge the gap between the fields. In spite of the great interest in ethics, to our knowledge, there is no outstanding modern work written in English that even attempts to deal adequately with the Biblical material as it relates to ethics.[1] Of course, into this vacuum there has come a host of ethical treatises that usually make some use of the Bible. For one group the Bible—usually the New Testament is meant—provides a sort of atmosphere of ethical concern but little more. Others use the Bible as a backdrop, and justify their recourse to tough-minded realistic ethics by contrasting the simple directives from the Biblical world with the complex intertangle of modern society. Occasionally, one finds moral theologians working with ethical principles, which are related to the Bible, but which require a system of casuistry in order to impinge on concrete problems of the day. Within the last five years among the activist wing of the church even this vague appeal to the Bible has often been dropped, and replaced by an appeal to intuition, human conscience, and the sense of the community's welfare. Although it remains easy to criticize the excessive subjectivity by which ethical decisions have been sought by modern Christians, no clear-cut answer in respect to the use of the Bible has emerged. Perhaps the chief blame falls on the Biblical scholars themselves who have provided little material which the ethicists could make use of within their field.

The concern of this chapter focuses on how the Bible functions in establishing ethical norms in the life of the church as it confronts the world. Obviously there remains the equally difficult, but separate, question of how Biblical norms, even when correctly understood by the church, relate to those outside the community of faith. On the one hand, to suggest that the Biblical imperatives are to be confined strictly to the church imposes an a priori restriction in scope that the Bible itself resists, and that renders them ultimately irrelevant to modern Christianity. On the other hand, to find an easy analogy that allows the imperatives of the Bible to be translated into ethical norms for society in general runs the acute danger of impairing the radical newness of the gospel which provides the sole grounds for an obedient life before God. The difficulty is one that has taxed the great theologians of the past and will certainly continue to require even greater attention in the future. The present essay does not deal with this issue directly, but addresses itself to a prior and more

modest question. How does the Bible function for the Christian when making ethical decisions? Of course, this question
has an important relation to the larger one, but it is an issue
that lends itself more properly to the reflection of the Biblical
theologian. It is our conviction that only when some clarity
has emerged regarding the Christian's use of the Bible will
important insights be forthcoming respecting the Bible and the
world.

What can one say about the Christian's use of the Bible in
relation to the problems of ethics, and particularly those of
decision-making? Usually at this juncture one launches into
the problems raised by historical criticism and the time-conditioned elements of many of the Biblical prescriptions.[2]
Although we do not wish to denigrate the importance of some
of these issues, these questions are not regarded as central for
the reasons that have been outlined in the preceding chapters.
Rather, the case is being argued that the central problem
for the study of Biblical ethics has already been posed within
the Scriptures themselves. The issue turns on the question to
what extent God's will has been made clear and unequivocal
for his people.

On Knowing the Will of God

On the one hand, there are numerous passages in both
Testaments that imply that God has made known his will to
his people with great clarity. In the Old Testament the giving
of the covenant brought with it a way of life that was constitutive to the relationship. Throughout the rest of the Old Testament there is constant reference made to the divine imperatives in the legal, prophetic, and wisdom literature. For
example, Deut. 30:11, 14: "This commandment which I
command you this day is not too hard for you, neither is it
far off. . . . But the word is very near you; it is in your mouth
and in your heart, so that you can do it." Again, Micah's

response to those who inquire what God requires of them is quite typical for the prophets: "He has showed you, O man, what is good; and what does the LORD require of you but to do justice, and to love kindness, and to walk humbly with your God?" In the New Testament the approach to the question of the will of God is basically the same. God has not left his people in the dark in respect to what is required for the obedient life. To the rich young ruler who inquired after eternal life in Mark, ch. 10 (cf. parallels), Jesus replied: "You know the commandments." Similarly, Paul offers a summary of the law as had Jesus: "The commandments . . . are summed up in this sentence, 'You shall love your neighbor as yourself.'"

Yet on the other hand, it is equally clear from a large number of passages that knowing the will of God, apart from the question of doing it, cannot be simply taken for granted. In the Old Testament, Israel has to "seek and inquire after" God. The will of God has not become a lifeless list of precepts; rather, the Israelite is constantly reminded to "listen to the voice of God." Particularly in the Wisdom Literature there is a large vocabulary of words denoting different aspects of testing, discerning, using insight and understanding in order to live the good life. Similarly, in the New Testament, Paul admonishes the Romans to be transformed "that you may prove what is the will of God, what is good and acceptable and perfect" (Rom. 12:2). The will of God must be "discerned" (cf. Phil. 1:10). Of course, in both Testaments the discerning of the will of God is never conceived of as a merely cognitive function, but learning and doing the will of God are tightly joined.

How does one understand this obvious tension between the different witnesses of the Bible regarding the will of God? It seems apparent that the tension cannot be resolved by contrasting the approach of the Old Testament with the New, nor is the heart of the problem touched by distinguishing the approach to revelation in prophetic and wisdom literature, however valid such a distinction may be for other subjects. Rather, the tension seems to be constitutive to the Bible's understanding of how God reveals his will to his people. Several important implications arise from the tension. First, the will of God can be formulated in clear, straightforward imperatives. The Decalogue is the classical expression of the divine law that remained fundamental to the covenant throughout the entire Old Testament and into the New. In spite of variations and function in the law the centrality of the one divine will remained unchanged. The point of emphasis is the continuity of content within the tradition regarding God's will for his people. He does not demand one thing at one period which is denied or reversed in another. Regardless of the fact that critical scholarship has concentrated its attention on changes and developments in ethical behavior and attitudes, the Biblical tradition stressed the one, unchanging will of God. Thus, Jesus argues against the practice of divorce on the grounds that God's intent was absolutely unequivocal from the beginning in spite of the accommodations to human sinfulness (cf. Mark 10:2 ff.). Nowhere is there a hint of criticism made by the New Testament writers of the Old Testament to suggest that God was unable to make known his clear will to Israel. Even the book of Hebrews, which stresses the frailty and incompleteness of the Old Covenant, does not suggest a break in the continuity of tradition regarding God's revealed will for Israel.

Secondly, the tension is constitutive to the Bible because God remained the living author of his law, who continued to confront his people throughout their history with his will. For Israel the law could never be abstracted into precepts that functioned independently of God himself. Particularly in Deuteronomy, the Prophets, and in the preaching of Christ, the law underwent a dramatic radicalization that cut through the layers of religious interpretation and confronted the hearers with God himself who could not be boxed into a religious system. The prophets recovered the terrifying dimensions of God's holiness when confronting human sinfulness. They spoke of the mystery and awe of the covenant God before whose presence the best of human aspirations were judged as pretension and folly.

Thirdly, the tension in the Biblical witness arose from the fact that the commandments of God were always addressed to particular persons in concrete situations. The word of the Lord came to a Jeremiah and a John the Baptist. He spoke "in the year that King Uzziah died" and "in the fifteenth year of the reign of Tiberius Caesar." The Biblical accounts are filled with elements of extreme particularity. The commission given to Jeremiah for the people of Judah during the reign of Josiah differed radically from the word spoken to II Isaiah in behalf of an exiled people. Paul was conscious of his unique commission and of his special assignment to the Gentiles. Along with this extreme regard for concrete persons and situations went an extreme amount of freedom in bearing witness to the eternal will of God. Ezekiel confronts the despondent exiles with the individual choice of life or death by a radical reinterpretation of the law. To the rich young ruler Jesus' challenge to sell all and follow him was an *ad hoc* commission that was designed to elicit an unequivocal response. Consistently the specific application of the divine imperative of obedience took on an unexpected and radical form that could never be deduced from an ethical principle.

It is of fundamental importance to recognize that at no point within the Bible is there ever spelled out a system or a technique by which one could move from the general imperatives of the law of God, such as found in the Decalogue, to the specific application within the concrete situation. The Bible reckons throughout with the unchanging divine will of God, and yet at the same time it describes in an inexhaustible variety of examples the unexpected and radical application of God's will to particular persons in definite situations. There is a continuity in God's will, a consistency of purpose that extends from the past to an anticipated future, an ongoing movement from promise to fulfillment. But the tension remains between this revealed will of God and the struggle for obedience in the concrete situation of specific moment before a living God. The effort both to know the will of God and to do it remained inseparably linked. In specific acts of obedience one learned to know the will of God, and the knowledge of his will carried with it the imperative for doing it.

To summarize: The Bible is consistent throughout in confessing that God had made known his will to his people. Yet at the same time the tradition continues to testify to the need for his people to seek and discern his will in the concrete situations of life. The obedient life, which is lived in the knowledge of God's election, functions as a struggle both to know and to do the works of God.

THE REFLECTIVE PROCESS IN SEEKING WARRANTS

We return to our original question: How does the Bible aid the Christian in the making of concrete ethical decisions? We have attempted to sketch in broad outlines one aspect of the Bible's approach to the problem of knowing God's will. But our context is a different one from that of either the prophets or the apostles. It is therefore incorrect to use the Bible with the assumption that the modern Christian functions like a prophet or an apostle in respect to the tradition. Rather, the thesis being defended is that the Christian's relation to the Biblical tradition is different and this difference is reflected in the formation of the canon. But within the context of the canon Scripture affords a warrant for seeking the will of God by virtue of its inner dynamic. God has revealed his will to his people, yet they must constantly strive to discern it. How does this process work within the Scripture of the church?

First, the Scriptures provide the normative tradition that the church confesses to contain the revealed will of God for his people. To the query: "What does God want of me/us?" the Christian replies: "Read the Scriptures." Yet the context of the canon serves to remind its users that the Bible does not function as Scriptures apart from the community of believers. Nor can the witness be separated from the subject matter of which it speaks. The Scriptures continue to point to a living God who spoke through his servants in the past, but who continues to confront the church and the world with his divine will. The Scriptures remain the vehicle through which he communicates afresh to his people by the activity of his Spirit. Finally, each new generation standing in its particular moment of history searches the Scriptures in order to discern the will of God, and strives to receive guidance toward the obedient life that must be pursued within concrete issues of the world.

Yet how does one discern the will of God within the Bible, and what has this to do with Biblical Theology? What we are suggesting is a process of disciplined theological reflection that takes its starting point from the ethical issue at stake along with all its ambiguities and social complexities and seeks to reflect on the issue in conjunction with the Bible which is seen in its canonical context. This manner of using the Bible in relation to decision-making can properly be called Biblical Theology because of its emphasis on a disciplined theological methodology. It opposes a Biblicistic use, common to theological Conservatives and Liberals alike, which seeks an immediate warrant for social action either from a verse of the Bible or from an action in the life of Jesus.

Normally the process of theological reflection will start from the modern question or issue that calls forth some response. Obviously there are many nontheological factors immediately at work in determining the nature of an issue and in describing its components. The lack of attention to those factors is not intended to denigrate their importance, but arises from the need to focus on the one issue of how to use the Bible in respect to decision-making. Once the issue has been established, the descriptive task of making use of the Bible consists in two major approaches to the Biblical tradition. First, the Biblical theologian attempts to sketch the *full range* of the Biblical witnesses within the canonical context that have bearing on the subject at issue. Secondly, he seeks to understand the *inner movement* of the various witnesses along their characteristic axes when approached from within the context of the canon.

The first step, that of sketching the full range, has as its purpose to determine the variety of approaches to a question. It attempts to hear the complete scale of notes that are played, first in terms of their original setting, and secondly in relation to the whole canon. To an issue such as sex ethics and the relation of a man to a woman obviously there is a variety of approaches to be found when comparing Gen., ch. 2, with the Song of Songs, Prov., ch. 7, with Lev., ch. 19, or I Cor., ch. 7, with I Peter, ch. 3. The descriptive task attempts to determine to what extent the witnesses are addressing similar elements of the same problems, and to what extent the subject matter is so diverse as to be only loosely related. Again, it is important to plot the outer limits of the area within which the Bible addresses itself. So, for example, the concept of conscience plays no role within the Old Testament, and has a very restricted function within the New. Again, it is significant to determine areas that relate to the field of ethics, but into which the Bible does not enter.

For example, it is of great importance for the subject of Christian ethics to realize that nowhere does the Bible deal with the problem of how the receiver of a "word of God" knows that it is from God. Indeed, in both Testaments the problem of the legitimacy of office causes a prophet or apostle to defend his commission before challengers, but never does a patriarch or prophet seem to be in doubt himself as to whether

God spoke to him or not. Nevertheless, modern Christians still regard it as important to know whether an imperative "comes from God" or simply reflects an inner compulsion. The recognition of such areas in which the Bible does not speak prevents the Biblical theologians from forcing the Bible to address every issue or of bending Biblical testimonies to accommodate utterly alien questions. The interpreter who paraphrases the opening of Gen., ch. 22, with the words, "Abraham *thought* God commanded him to sacrifice his son," has introduced a fundamental confusion into the story and into any subsequent theological use of it.

The second step of the descriptive task is concerned with understanding the inner structure of the area that has been marked out by the first. It attempts to chart the inner dynamic of Biblical thought regarding an issue, to determine whether there are characteristic patterns or familiar axes along which the witnesses can be grouped. For example, it is characteristic of the Bible to defend the need for impartial justice for the poor before the courts of justice by an appeal to the ultimate justice of God before whom all men will be judged. (Cf. Ex. 23:6 ff.; Isa. 1:21 ff.; Ps. 50:20 ff.; Matt. 7:1 ff.; I Cor. 6:1 ff.; James 4:11 ff.) Conversely, the Pauline emphasis on the law as a divine imperative that evokes a crisis within sinful man because of his inability to meet the divine demands is not a characteristic concept for the Old Testament legal material or for Israel's psalmody. Again, this second step seeks to establish inner relationships between the various witnesses and to examine the important inner action and tensions between subjects. Basic to this task is the need to understand the various historical contexts out of which the witnesses arose and to whom they were addressed when seeking to systematize the material. Thus, the relation of "faith and works" in Paul and James cannot be simply juxtaposed without an examination of the differing contexts in which they functioned.

The effect of such a study of both the scope and the inner

structure of the Biblical witness is to have uncovered a
dynamic grid within the normative tradition. Now the issue
turns on how this material functions within the context of the
canon in the making of moral decisions. The grid reflects as
clearly as possible the various warrants respecting different
subjects and situations in which a Christian is forced to decide
on an action. Biblical Theology in turn attempts to relate by
a process of disciplined theological reflection the issue at stake
with the Biblical warrant to which it is most closely related.
This warrant does not function as an infallible rule of thumb,
nor as an instance of an eternal principle, but as a time-conditioned testimony to God's will in which word the Christian
seeks to discern afresh his own obedient action in a new historical moment. The warrant may function as a direct imperative, or it can provide a set of guidelines, or offer a sequence of
priorities.

To give some examples. At times a warrant may provide a
clear and unequivocal imperative for a given situation. The
whole of Scripture is unified in demanding of the believer
that he love God with all his heart, soul, and strength. The
Old Testament commandment is never withdrawn or mitigated
throughout the Bible. The Bible provides many examples, as
does church history, in which men and women were called
upon to denounce their faith in God in order to save their
lives. The Bible provides an unequivocal warrant for prefer-
ring death to apostasy. Somewhat less dramatic, but no less
clear, is the Biblical imperative "to love one's neighbor as
oneself." This is not a suggestion but a commandment that
is unaffected by differing kinds of neighbors.

Again, at times the Biblical warrant appears in the form of a
tension between two conflicting responsibilities, both of which
exercise imperatives. Both Testaments demand obedience to
God rather than man when these issue in a conflict (Dan., ch.
1; Acts, ch. 5). Yet obedience to the civil authorities is also
required because these offices are representatives of God's

authority (Rom. 13:1 ff.). In the lives of the prophet Jeremiah and the apostle Paul the Bible offers examples of men who strove for obedience to God and to men within the tensions of conflicting claims. The warrant consists not only in recognition of both imperatives as valid but also in establishing the imperatives as polarities on an axis between which the responsible decision must be found.

Once again, a Biblical warrant can serve to establish a set of priorities in the order of which the wise decision is made. Most of the Wisdom Literature is concerned with questions of whether an action is wise or foolish, fitting or inappropriate, timely or premature, prudent or rash.

Many of Paul's comments on marriage are given in the spirit of sound advice, gained from experience, which charts the advantages of one set of action over against another (cf. I Cor. 7:32 ff.). Also, the parables of Jesus are filled with warrants that do not contain an imperative or even a warning, but offer directions and guidelines to wise decisions in matters of the world (cf. Luke 14:7 ff.).

Finally, there are Biblical warrants that offer a series of options depending on the situation and the person who is called upon to act. Paul gives his advice in a modified conditional form when he writes: "If possible, so far as it depends upon you, live peaceably with all." (Rom. 12:18.) And to Philemon: "If he has wronged you at all, or if he owes you anything, charge that to my account." (V. 18.) The writer of Proverbs also makes use of the conditional form, but often in order to attach a warning to his sound advice (cf. ch. 6:1 ff.).

The task of Biblical Theology is to reflect carefully on the issue that calls for a moral decision in the light of the various warrants that the Biblical tradition provides. It is obviously a mistake to approach every issue with only one Biblical model in mind. Many a pastor has decided on a question of social ethics in the spirit of Paul before Agrippa or Luther before the Emperor, when the issue was one which called for compromise after the manner of the sage in Proverbs. Although the best efforts of the Biblical theologian in providing the correct Biblical warrants may in the end prove to be misleading, this ever-present possibility does not take away the value of a rigorous and systematic study of Scripture with an eye toward using it in the area of ethical decision.

The question must be faced as to how the Christian moves from the Biblical warrant to the decision for action itself. We have stressed the point that there is no system that leads one infallibly from the Biblical warrant to the appropriate decision. The revelation of the will of God to the prophets and apostles did not function this way, nor does the Bible have this role. Rather the church, individually and corporately, studies the Bible in prayer and expectation, often in agony and confusion, awaiting God's guidance through his Word. The bridge from the past to the present is not irrational and arbitrary. It does not abrogate the continuity of the one covenant God's directing and leading his people according to his will. Nevertheless, the movement from past to present remains creative, new, and it is full of potential surprise and mystery because it issues from God.

At times a warrant from the Bible becomes an immediate transparency for a fresh imperative. "Who then is my neighbor? . . . Go thou and do likewise." The differences in setting and personnel between the past and the present become irrelevant. The old imperative takes on a new form as it speaks to a particular person in a concrete situation. Then the major question is not what does God want of me, but will I do it! Because of the complexity of many ethical issues, when the Christian is genuinely uncertain how to act, we tend to forget or ignore the fact that life is constantly filled with moral issues concerning which the Christian can have no doubt whatever. One cannot live a day in the company of people without being challenged to respond as a Christian "to one for whom Christ died." Most often the Christian knows all too well what he should do. It is, therefore, not accidental that much of the ethical emphasis in the Bible focuses on questions of the will. The Christian life is pictured as a struggle, not because its demands are uncertain and confusing, but because of the battle between the forces of good and evil that includes dimensions far more comprehensive than simply the cognitive.

At times the Biblical warrant serves simply to delimit the area in which the decision must be sought. A tension between conflicting responsibilities is established and the Christian may simply have to struggle and wait until he finds the obedient response. The Bible speaks of proceeding "from faith to faith" to suggest that one learns the good by the doing of it. The call to discipleship issued by Christ did not commence with a briefing session, but was simply an appeal to follow. This aspect of faith remains an essential part of the Christian life which cannot be dispelled by more information regarding theological ethics.

Then again there are situations in which the Biblical warrant offers a variety of alternatives for moral decision. The choice between alternatives may depend on the peculiarities of the historical situation, or on a variety of nontheological factors. The result is that Christians may disagree radically with one another on a particular course of action, and yet both positions may rightly appeal to some Biblical warrant. Many of the political and economic issues that divide churches fall within this category. It is hard to believe that there is one Christian answer to the problems of military conscription, population explosion, and the Middle East crisis. The implication from this is not that Christians should stay out of politics, but rather that Christians should be more discerning when claiming a Biblical warrant. Particularly in these cases in which a variety of alternative decisions rightly fall within the Biblical warrant, it is the primary task of the church to hold together the dissenting factions in Christian love. The real danger arises when the pastor identifies his position with the Christian answer and becomes the mouthpiece for one party line. At times the church's task would be to serve as a forum in which fresh empirical evidence is brought to bear on the issue in the hope of overcoming the conflict. But in the end there is no reason to expect Christians to agree on every issue. This is to confuse consensus with the gospel. Especially in the coming decade one would sincerely wish that the church would produce more "wisemen" and fewer "prophets" for the responsible guidance of the people of God.

Lastly, there will be instances of extreme crisis in which the church, both individually and corporately, will find itself in great straits without any clear directives in a given situation. One thinks in this regard of the Christian church in East Germany and Czechoslovakia in the years following the Second World War, and their agonizing struggle to maintain a responsible witness. Then the church is called upon to wait and to pray earnestly for some fresh alternative in which God's redemptive power can be realized. One searches the Scriptures because of the promise that the doors to heaven will not always remain closed.

These moments of crisis are important in reminding the church that the criteria for judging the rightness or wrongness of a moral decision lie ultimately in God's hands. Human criteria of successful outcome, exercise of power, and cultural impact are ancient traps to be shunned. Certainly in the end, Paul's formulation of justification by faith undergirds the whole Christian ethic. The confidence in God's forgiveness and justification offers a type of freedom that makes possible a bold and daring grappling with the hard decisions of moral judgment. It is in the light of this goal that the Bible functions, not as a pious book of religious aphorisms that knows nothing of the risk of faith, but as the arena linking heaven and earth, in which the faithful Christian continues to wage life's battle.

8
RECOVERING AN
EXEGETICAL TRADITION

The rise of the historicocritical approach to the Bible, which had completely won the field by the middle of the nineteenth century in Germany and by the end of the century in England, resulted in a sharp break with the church's exegetical traditions. The new critical approach seemed so strikingly new in contrast to the traditional interpretation as to effect a wholesale lumping together of pre-nineteenth-century exegesis under the caption of "precritical." All the earlier disputes regarding exegetical method, whether between the Alexandrians and the Antiochians, the Reformers and the church fathers, or the Calvinists and the Wesleyans, were suddenly reduced to virtual insignificance before a method that called into question the common ground on which they all stood. In the modern period it has become standard procedure to treat the history of Biblical scholarship as a slow growth of insight that finally culminated in the ushering in of the critical method. In fact, the significance of a man's contribution is measured by the extent to which he abetted or aided in reaching the critical goals. As a result Spinoza, Hobbes, Colenso, and Strauss are treated in every standard history, while one searches usually in vain for even a mention of the English Puritan expositors, the French Jansenists, or the influence of Matthew Henry and Adam Clarke. If it were not for our Eng-

lish departments, it would have been long since forgotten that
Donne and Milton were in fact Biblical expositors. In most
Protestant seminaries the curious impression is given that
serious interpretation of the Old Testament began with Wellhausen, who was unfortunately wrong in most of what he said!
The New Testament department has done a little better in
remembering the earlier works, but even here, except for the
antiquarian interest of scholars, little importance is attached
to the so-called "precritical" period except in those instances
in which the later approach was adumbrated.

In our opinion, this evaluation of the historicocritical scholarship, and its relation to the exegetical work that preceded
it, is highly one-sided to say the least. While we do not deny
but heartily endorse the tremendous contributions that have
been derived from the critical method *in certain areas,* the
danger has arisen in assuming that only the historical method
has a validity for Biblical studies. The point that needs reiter-
ating is that the correct exegetical method is determined in
large measure by the context in which the discipline is pursued. To draw an analogy: Biblical interpretation contains
elements that can be classified both as a science and as an art.
As a science there is a constant advance in knowledge that is
commensurate with a refinement of research method. Who
could deny the tremendous achievements of Biblical science
in the fields of textual criticism, of literary and historical
questions? Moreover, the study of the history of religions in
relation to both Testaments has likewise been profoundly
altered by the critical methods.

But Biblical interpretation as an art does not operate by a
precise accumulation of scientific data, nor is its method so
easily outlined. One rather tends to describe the product as
illuminating, profound, or brilliant. Auerbach's interpretation
of Gen., ch. 22, is a classic example of Biblical interpretation
as an art. It has a timeless quality about it whose validity lies
in its self-authenticating character. Or again, one recalls

Kierkegaard's reflections on Abraham's testing, Father Mapple's sermon on Jonah in *Moby Dick*, or even T. S. Eliot's "Journey of the Magi" in order to sense a totally different dimension of reflection on the Bible. The overemphasis on the critical approach has eclipsed this entire side of interpretation by claiming to be the only truly modern interpretation.

However, the analogy between art and science, while helpful in part, does not touch the heart of the problem, which is theological. The historicocritical method is an inadequate method for studying the Bible as the Scriptures of the church because it does not work from the needed context. This is not to say for a moment that the critical method is incompatible with Christian faith—we regard the Fundamentalist position as indefensible—but rather that the critical method, when operating from its own chosen context, is incapable of either raising or answering the full range of questions which the church is constrained to direct to its Scripture.

Surely some will object to this line of argument by asserting that the exegete's only task is to understand what the Biblical text meant, and that the critical methodology is alone capable of doing this correctly. The historical reading is exegesis; everything else is "eisegesis." Our response to this type of objection is by now familiar. First, what the text "meant" is determined in large measure by its relation to the one to whom it is directed. While it remains an essential part of Biblical exegesis to establish a text's function in its original context(s), the usual corollary that the original function is alone normative does not follow. Secondly, the question of what the text now means cannot be dismissed as a purely subjective enterprise suitable only to private devotion and homiletics. When seen from the context of the canon both the question of what the text meant and what it means are inseparably linked and both belong to the task of the interpretation of the Bible as Scripture. To the extent that the use of the critical method sets up an iron curtain between the past and the

present, it is an inadequate method for studying the Bible as
the church's Scripture.

The inadequacy of the historicocritical method for the theological task of exegesis of Scripture is painfully evident in the
modern concept of the Biblical commentary.[1] First of all, there
is the standard critical commentary, exemplified in English by
the International Critical Commentary series. The basic problem is not that the commentary is too technical, but its range
of interest is too narrow to cover a wide spectrum of issues
that are of primary importance for the Biblical theologian. The
material that is collected is indispensable for certain kinds of
research, but the scale of priorities used to determine which
material is included and which emphasis is given often taxes
the patience of Biblical theologians in the extreme. The commentary is filled with material that has only remote antiquarian
interest. On issues where help is genuinely needed often there
is a painful silence. Thus in the highly provocative story of
the two prophets in I Kings, ch. 13, which deals with how the
word of God functions through a prophet in the most paradox-
ical manner imaginable, a modern commentator provides detailed information on the different kinds of trees in Palestine,
the variety of lions, and the grave furniture of Early Bronze
family tombs.[2] Although it would not be fair to blame the critical method for the author's tone-deafness to theological issues,
the method is at fault in attributing such high priority to questions that are of such tangential importance to the story's own
perspective.

Of course, because of the pressure exerted by the working
clergy toward providing commentary aids for preaching, the
critical commentary has been often supplemented by a homiletical section. The well-known deficiencies of this compromise
hardly need to be rehearsed. The most serious objection is that
the real task of doing exegesis as a theological discipline has
been lost. In its place the reader is offered an exegesis that provides random critical information on the text, and homiletical

exposition that is only loosely connected with either the text or the exegesis. The Exegesis on Genesis in *The Interpreter's Bible* spends much of its allotted space when discussing Joseph's betrayal by his brothers in distinguishing between J^2, E, and R^{JE}. Then the Exposition comments: "Joseph is thrown by his brothers into a pit . . . but morally and spiritually, too, it may often seem that the soul of man is in a pit."[3] Granted that such a caricature of Biblical interpretation is extreme, the fact remains that the overemphasis on the historicocritical method has fragmented the concept of Biblical interpretation. In the end, such old Victorian commentaries as George Adam Smith on the Twelve Prophets or Godet on John remain far better guides to exegesis because the reader can at least get some impression of the reflective process at work that joins together the various elements of interpretation.

Significantly, the Biblical Theology Movement made little important contribution toward improving the situation. Although there was much talk about the need for the theological dimension to be attached to the historicocritical work, in practice these theologians found great difficulty in achieving this goal. Usually, the result was a popularization of the critical results along with a loosely related essay on Biblical Theology.

One of the major concerns of this monograph has been to sketch the shape of a new concept for doing Biblical Theology that should result in a different approach to writing a commentary. Its goal would be to take seriously the responsibility of interpreting the Bible as the Scripture of the church, and in developing rigorous exegetical skills that are commensurate to this task. However, instead of projecting an ideal form for such a commentary, which has been already adumbrated in the earlier chapters, it is of prime importance to regain an exegetical tradition that has always existed in the church and that has been largely misunderstood because of the rise of the historicocritical study of the Bible. Precritical interpretation of the Bible has much of great value to offer the modern Biblical theologian. It is either arrogance or ignorance to suggest that a completely new start is necessary. Much of what has been characterized as "precritical" is in fact highly sophisticated theological exposition that has been faulted by applying totally inappropriate historicocritical canons. Admittedly the older exegetes lacked precision and method when they came to many problems in history, literature, and theology. Notwithstanding, they did certain exegetical tasks exceedingly well and provided some highly significant models for the doing of theological exegesis.

First of all, many of the precritical commentators attempted to deal seriously with the Bible as the Scriptures of the church. This often meant that they worked consistently from the context of the whole canon. Much of the later criticism that was directed against an alleged "nonhistorical" interpretation failed to see that by working from the church's context a confessional context had been purposefully substituted for the historical. Calvin's commentaries are classic examples of an exegesis that works consistently from a theological context. Calvin can be justly criticized for failing to hear a whole range of Biblical witnesses—he understood Paul far better than John —but not for his hearing Old and New Testaments in concert. If these early interpreters often failed to distinguish adequately between the original context in its historical usage and its later function within the canon, they nevertheless provided an excellent antidote against modern historical one-sidedness.

Because the canon is taken seriously, one finds in the older commentaries a vital interest in relating the various parts of Scripture to one another. Of course, at times this meant that divergent witnesses were forcefully harmonized, but often this deficiency has been exaggerated. One only has to examine such "precritical" interpreters as Augustine Calmet and Adam Clarke to be astonished at the freedom and imagination at work. Many modern critical commentators on the Psalms avoid scrupulously any reference to the New Testament while providing every conceivable Babylonian parallel, whereas an

older commentator such as J. J. S. Perowne carefully provides
the usage of the Psalms in the New Testament, and recognizes
the transformation of the text as it passes through the Septuagint. Again, one learns from the great masters of the past the
art of genuine theological dialectic. Augustine, in spite of his
allegorical method, often was able to penetrate to the heart of
the theological problem and grapple with a profundity that
has seldom been matched. It is surely not by accident that he
provided the glasses through which generations of Christians
read the Psalms and were stimulated to ponder afresh on the
Sermon on the Mount. Again, Calvin's exposition of the
Psalms is without parallel in the precision with which he brings
the whole spectrum of Biblical teaching to bear on a particular
verse. And how impoverished is any study of Romans that
has not wrestled through Luther's magnificent exposition and
caught some glimpse of a theological struggle that confronted
the text in order to grapple with God himself.

Then, again, many of the older commentaries such as
M. Poole's *Synopsis Criticorum* or Cornelius à Lapide's *Commentarii* are invaluable aids to theological exegesis by providing a history of interpretation. Such a historical perspective
is important for several reasons. First, it often demonstrates
the variety of possibilities within a text, many of which are
complementary rather than exclusive. There is a sense in which
the text is in as much movement as the reader. Again, by studying how a passage has been interpreted in different ages and
by many persons, one learns to evaluate the range of questions
that have been addressed to the text and stimulated by it.
The result is often a clearer understanding of one's own perspective and a profounder appreciation of the personal context
that each individual brings to his interpretation. The joy of
reading Luther's exposition arises in part from seeing how the
Word of God was mediated through the personality and emotions of a man to be shaped in a form that spoke to the people
of Saxony.

There is another important side of Biblical interpretation,

often overlooked by modern exegesis, which is found in the
classic commentators. Because of the emphasis on the diachronistic dimensions of the text, little attention is given to a
passage in its final stage. Surely questions of historical development cannot be ignored, but the study of the text as a whole
remains the fundamental task. The older commentators took
the Bible seriously as a book, and as a result often have a
penetrating analysis of the themes and motifs of whole chapters. Matthew Henry is generally known for his piety, but
much of the real strength of his exposition lies in his lucid literary analysis of large blocks of material. Surprisingly enough,
one often gains a better impression of the Bible as great literature when reading the older, classically trained expositors than
from modern critical exegesis (Alford, Trench, Westcott, are
good examples of the English tradition). Von Rad once characterized exegesis as the retelling of the story. Few have ever
surpassed in this art the brilliance of Chrysostom or caused
their audiences to resonate to the Biblical characters, as did
Joseph Hall.

Lastly, one learns from the great classical expositors of the
church how Scripture becomes the "bread of life." Many of
the modern problems of building hermeneutical bridges from
the text to the sermon or from the past to the present arise from
first treating the Bible as ancient grafitti and still expecting it
to produce great spiritual truths. Augustine[4] approached Scripture as a man who had been invited to a banquet table, and
in sheer delight partook of its richness. Tyndale[5] pictured the
Scriptures as "comfort in adversity," "medicine which every
man applies to his own sores." And Bengel wrote: "The bible
is, indeed, the true fountain of wisdom, which they, who have
tasted, prefer to all mere compositions of men, however holy,
however experienced, however devout, or however wise." [6] Far
from being a collection of pious aphorisms, the Bible spoke
to the heart of these men of dreadful judgment and glorious
redemption. They could pass with complete ease from the detailed study of syntax to the anatomy of the soul because they

saw God at work in all levels of Scripture. They learned to
scrutinize its parts with utmost rigor, and yet to confess at the
same time that in that process they themselves were being
examined.[7] Perhaps of all the tasks for modern Biblical Theology the hardest will be to rediscover the Bible as devotional
literature. There are no easy techniques that will assure success, but in the great expositors of the church there are countless examples of men whose learning has led them to the
throne of God.

To sum up: The attempt to recover the church's exegetical
traditions does not imply for a moment an uncritical reading
of the great masters; in fact, just the opposite. Unless modern
scholars once again learn how to read critically the scholars
of the past, there is little hope or purpose in rediscovering their
works. Obviously there is much within the fathers of little
value. Admittedly the Reformers are time-conditioned in their
running battle with Rome, and the Victorians often confused
the gospel with good manners. The modern reader must have
the ability to read with discernment and to recognize treasure
when he sees it. A new approach to Biblical Theology has as
one of its important functions the perfecting of these theological skills. Up to now little direction has been given as to what
to look for in the earlier exegesis. Usually the ancients are
judged by modern critical criteria and found wanting. If a
new Biblical Theology can establish the right for doing its
exegesis within the context of the canon, it will provide at the
same time criteria, compatible to the church's discipline, by
which to judge what is excellent in theological interpretation,
whether ancient or modern. A major obstacle to this goal continues to be a type of critical training that has the effect of
closing the Biblical student to all but a few questions. When
our seminary-trained pastors find Augustine incomprehensible,
Luther verbose, and Calvin dull, then obviously the problem
lies with the reader and his theological education and not with
the old masters.

PART III

Testing a Method

Introduction

ANY CRITICISM of a theological position that does not offer
a positive alternative can be righty faulted. Any proposal for
a new shape to a theological discipline that does not offer
concrete examples in support of it can also be judged deficient.
The final part of this monograph is intended to illustrate different elements of the proposal for doing Biblical Theology according to a new model.

In the first two chapters an attempt is made to outline the
shape of an exegesis that is done within the context of the
canon. The emphasis in the study of Ps. 8 falls on seeing the
different functions that a text can have within the canon and
in showing the significance of this development for theological
reflection. The focus in the exegesis of Ex., ch. 2, is somewhat
broader in scope although the method is the same. It attempts
to show the theological necessity for understanding the original setting of a text. Moreover, it illustrates the use of the
history of interpretation as part of the exegetical discipline
and points out a variety of exegetical moves that are involved

in genuine theological reflection. The third chapter wrestles with the problem of taking seriously the context of the canon when there is no explicit reference to an Old Testament text within the New Testament by which to be guided. The final chapter is an attempt at constructive theology that reflects in a disciplined way on a Biblical topic from within the framework of the two Testaments.

9
PSALM 8 IN THE CONTEXT
OF THE CHRISTIAN CANON

---

1. O Lord, our Lord,
   how majestic is thy name in all the earth!
   Thou whose glory above the heavens is chanted
2. by the mouth of babes and infants,
   thou hast founded a bulwark because of thy foes,
   to still the enemy and the avenger.
3. When I look at thy heavens, the work of thy fingers,
   the moon and the stars which thou hast established;
4. what is man that thou art mindful of him,
   and the son of man that thou dost care for him?
5. Yet thou hast made him little less than God,
   and dost crown him with glory and honor.
6. Thou hast given him dominion over the works of thy hands;
   thou hast put all things under his feet,
7. all sheep and oxen and also the beasts of the field,
8. the birds of the air, and the fish of the sea,
   whatever passes along the paths of the sea.

> 9. O Lord, our Lord,
>   how majestic is thy name in all the earth!
>   (Ps. 8.)

I

The first task is to determine, as well as possible, how this psalm functioned within its Old Testament setting. What did it mean to the ancient Hebrew people? Regardless of whatever else we shall want to do with the psalm, the responsibility rests upon the interpreter for dealing accurately with the passage within its Old Testament context. Otherwise the witness of the whole canon is impaired.

The psalm is a good example of what Gunkel described as a hymn, and represents the basic form in which Israel expressed her worship of praise to God. Briefly stated, the hymn consists of three major parts. There is an introduction, followed by a brief transition that leads to the body of the hymn, and a conclusion. The psalmist moves from the initial address to God in the vocative to an exclamation of praise to God's majesty: "How excellent is thy name in all the earth!" The verses that follow are more difficult and we shall skip over vs. 1b-2 at first because their interpretation does not affect the major problem at hand. The actual body of the psalm begins in v. 3 and extends through v. 8. Looking at the heavens at night, the psalmist breaks forth into praise of God who has established man within his creation. The poem concludes with a return to the refrain of the introduction.

Much of the content of the psalm is familiar from earlier parts of the Bible. In spite of the specific reference to his nightly meditation, the psalmist did not create his material simply from the inspiration of the moment, but was dependent on the tradition of the Priestly writer, which is reflected in Gen., ch. 1. Because Ps. 8 is an obvious reference to this body of tradition, it is important to see how the psalmist made use of this material. There were various possibilities that the poet could have used to praise God's great power. He could have spoken of the effortless control by which God ruled his world. Again, he might have chosen to emphasize the magnitude of the accomplishment of creation or even to describe the harmony of the product. However, the poet focuses on only one aspect of this creation tradition, namely, the role of man in his relation to God the Creator. Although in Gen., ch. 1, the creation of man was not the culmination of the account, it is nevertheless apparent that the creation of man did form a special act of self-reflection on the part of God which distinguished it from the creation of the rest of the world. Man bears the image of God—admittedly a difficult verse—and with the image also the blessing and imperative of subduing the earth and exercising dominion over it.

Now the psalmist goes beyond the Genesis tradition in reflecting on the position that God has given man. When he observes the magnitude of God's creative power seen in the heavens, the moon and the stars in their overwhelming splendor, a spontaneous reaction grips him. How insignificant then is man! His confession that man is lord of the creation and his recognition of the vastness of the creation clash in his mind. Yet the exciting part of this reaction is the fact that the experience does not call forth a wave of skepticism. Rather, in the light of his experience and the apparent contradiction between that which he confesses and that which he sees, the psalmist breaks forth in praise and adoration. First, he affirms that man has indeed been given dominion over all things. In the words of the tradition, he has been made little less than the Elohim, those divine beings which make up God's court. This is clearly a reference to the image of God. Secondly, he testifies that his position within the creation rests on an act of divine grace. The psalm, therefore, is neither a eulogy on mankind after the pattern of Hamlet's soliloquy nor an expression of praise to the creation itself, but above all, a hymn to God the Creator who placed man lord over all. "How majestic is *thy* name in all the earth!" In his name God has disclosed to men what he is like. For this psalmist there is no rupture between the creation and the Creator. Man can know God in the works of his hand.

We have skipped over a discussion of the several lines that separate the initial introduction from the body of the psalm. Let us return briefly to see what we can make of them. "Thou whose glory above the heavens is chanted by the mouth of babes and infants, thou hast founded a bulwark because of thy foes, to still the enemy and the avenger." If one looks into a modern commentary, or even an ancient one for that matter, he will be immediately made aware of the long history of difficulty that these verses have caused. First of all, the text is in some disorder and many suggestions have been made to amend it, either by following the reading of the versions or by reading a different Hebrew text. Certain commentators suggest a translation that differs considerably from the RSV: "Thou hast a stronghold planted with thy foes in mind to make an end to the enemy and him who claims revenge." [1] Such a suggestion has much to commend it. However, the exegetical problem remains essentially the same. There is no clear evidence in the Old Testament to give us a lead on how to interpret these verses. Obviously one can easily read a theological meaning into them. For example, one can say that the minds of children have an openness to God that is not there later on. Or one can understand it as suggesting that the apparently weak vehicle, such as children, serves God as a stronghold against man's foolish pretension. This is not to imply that these are in error, but only that such familiar interpretations can claim little exegetical warrant from the Old Testament. Therefore, it is a sound principle to work from the clearer portions and later attempt to place these more difficult verses in the larger context that emerges.

To summarize: In this hymn the psalmist moves to affirm

man's place as lord of the creation because of the will of God. The psalm is a praise to God the Creator who in his infinite wisdom and power has placed man at the head of his creation.

II

We turn now to the use of this psalm in the New Testament, where it is quoted explicitly a number of times. It appears in Matt. 21:16 with its parallels, again in I Cor. 15:27 and possibly Eph. 1:22, and finally in an extended reference in Heb. 2:6 ff. An examination of these passages will indicate that there is a wide variety in the use of the psalm which is characteristic of the New Testament. Our attention will focus on the one occurrence in Hebrews because it offers an extended and detailed interpretation. Even more important, the function of the psalm in its New Testament setting is totally different from that in its original one.

The first thing to notice is that the book of Hebrews is no longer making reference to the Hebrew psalm, but is dependent on the Septuagint. A closer look at the Greek translation of the psalm indicates that some important changes have taken place. The issue is not that the Greek writer has misunderstood the psalm or that he has mistranslated it by introducing tendentious elements. Rather, the very nature of translation from one language into another has effected a change. This alteration results more from the fact that words that had a wide semantic range in Hebrew are often rendered in Greek with words of a more limited range. Or the reverse—words that in Hebrew have a narrow scope are rendered in Greek with words that are more inclusive in meaning. The Greek translates vs. 5-6 as follows: "What is man that thou art mindful of him, or the son of man that thou carest for him? Thou didst make him for a little lower than the angels and hast crowned him with glory and honor." There are two changes from the Hebrew that strike one immediately. First, whereas

the Hebrew has: "Thou hast made him little less than God,"
the Septuagint has rendered it: "a little lower than the angels."
In the Hebrew the word for God (*ĕlōhīm*) is somewhat ambiguous. Elohim is the general Semitic name for God, but it
is also the name for that class of heavenly beings which serves
God, especially in his court. The Greek translator has offered
an interpretation, but one that does not in itself do an injustice
to the Hebrew. Second, the Hebrew word "a little" has been
translated by a literal Greek correspondent. However, the
Greek appears to have a more specific connotation than does
the Hebrew. The Greek word more frequently designates a
temporal distinction of "for a little time" (cf. Acts 5:34). However, the Septuagint still remains unclear whether the designation in v. 5 is one of time or of degree.

The important exegetical move is evident when one sees
what the writer of the Hebrews has done with the Septuagint
translation of Ps. 8. The translation made possible a new direction of interpretation that had not been available to the reader
of the Hebrew text. The Hebrew had stated that man in his
exalted position lacked only a little from being a god himself.
The Greek now opened the possibility of understanding this
lack as a temporal distinction, "to lack for a little time." The
writer of Hebrews seizes upon this new avenue as a means of
elaborating his understanding of the incarnation of Jesus
Christ. In the Hebrew text the juxtaposition of "man" and "son
of man" in v. 4 illustrates a common technique of Hebrew parallelism with no distinction being suggested. But for the New
Testament writer the term takes on a new meaning when read
in the light of Jesus, the Son of Man. Taking this as his lead,
the writer proceeds to read into the psalm a full Christology.
In his humiliation the Son of Man was made a little lower than
the angels for a while, but then he was crowned with honor in
his exaltation. Thus for Hebrews, the problem of understanding Ps. 8 is an entirely different one. The tension does not arise
between man as ruler of the creation and man in his insignifi-

cance, but rather from the obvious fact that man does not have control of the world. It is not now in subjection to him. "As it is, we do not yet see everything in subjection to him." (Heb. 2:8.) The writer of Hebrews makes the point that man in his actual state has not fulfilled the promise of the psalmist. Taking this then as his clue, he moves into his Christological confession: We see rather "Jesus, who for a little while was made lower than the angels, crowned with glory and honor . . . , so that . . . he might taste death for every one." As the Exalted One, Jesus has already assumed Lordship over the new age, "the world to come" (v. 5). For this Christian writer the ancient psalm is a testimony to the life and death of the Incarnate One whom God acknowledged as the representative for mankind.

Again to summarize: The New Testament writer, working on the basis of the Greek Old Testament text, has been able to move his interpretation into an entirely different direction from that of the Hebrew Old Testament. The psalm becomes a Christological proof text for the Son of Man who for a short time was humiliated, but who was then exalted by God to become the representative for every man.

III

The point to be stressed is that the psalm clearly functions in two distinct ways. We have oversimplified a number of issues in order to allow this one problem to emerge in all its clarity. What is now our exegetical move? The fact that the New Testament has read such a different and—in the minds of many—strange interpretation into an Old Testament psalm has convinced many that one should not attempt to relate these two entirely different points of view. In all honesty the Biblical interpreter should stick with the Old Testament and its original meaning. Most Old Testament commentators do just that! One should have no objection to this position within a clearly defined context. If the interpreter is content with simply describing what the psalmist believed, then it is sufficient to remain within the world of the Old Testament. However, if one wants to use the psalm in some broader fashion, if one is concerned to speak *theologically* about the content of the psalmist's faith, the simple descriptive task is not adequate. Certainly not for Christian theology! We are no longer in the community of Israel. We no longer have the temple in which to bring our praises to God. There is a break that separates, not only a Christian, but also any modern man from the world of the Old Testament. It is usually at this point that those who insist most vigorously on working from only the Old Testament context make a transition. They introduce some other framework by which to move from the world of the Old Testament to the world of modern man. For systematic theologians the overarching categories are frequently philosophical. The same is often the case for Biblical scholars even when cloaked under the guise of a theory of history. From the point of view of Christian theology it seems highly dubious that one can speak meaningfully of man and his relationship to God and the creation without speaking Christologically. This position is not a simplistic "Christomonism," but a theological conviction held in common by Christian theologians from Augustine to Calvin, and beyond.

The history of interpretation illustrates how consistently interpreters have tried to use the New Testament's interpretation, particularly that of Hebrews, as the key to the Old Testament psalm. For example, in Luther, one sees an attempt to find in the psalm only Christian teaching. Summarizing his exegesis, he says: "Thus the Holy Spirit through the prophet David instructs us . . . about the following topics: Christ; the two natures in Christ, His divine and human nature . . . Christ's dominion and kingdom . . . and of Christ's resurrection, exaltation, and glorification." [2] Now the objection to this type of traditional interpretation is that in its endeavor to deal seriously with the New Testament as Christian Scriptures, it has obliterated the Old Testament. No longer is one able to hear the original witness of the psalm; he hears only the content of the New Testament revelation. Surely something is wrong with an interpretation that is no longer concerned to hear the Old Testament on its own terms.

Calvin has a more interesting interpretation of the psalm. Characteristically he is concerned that the witness of the Old Testament is not lost in a Christianization of the old covenant. Therefore, he attempts to join together the two witnesses while at the same time recognizing the peculiarities of each. According to Calvin, both Old and New Testaments are speaking of the same *doctrine*. The task of the Biblical interpreter is to harmonize and fit them into a larger whole. Calvin reads into the psalm the doctrine of the fall of mankind and suggests as the context for the Hebrew psalm the ideal state of man before his disobedience in the Garden of Eden. The difficulties of this position are entirely obvious. A dogmatic context has been constructed from material outside both texts which fits the various parts into a whole foreign to both.

Our own hermeneutical suggestion is that the Christian interpreter, first of all, commit himself only to hearing both witnesses as clearly as possible, but then in relation to one another. To seek a relation between Old and New Testaments is to take seriously the church's confession of a canon of Scripture, and to reject an appeal to a "canon within the canon." The acknowledgment of the role of the canon in interpretation serves in staking out the area of theological reflection. It establishes a context that differs from both that of the Old Testament and that of the New Testament when seen in isolation from one another. To change the metaphor, the recognition of the canon influences which instruments are playing in the orchestra, but it does not determine the composition. This decision cannot be predetermined. One simply must listen. Secondly, the challenge to the Christian theologian is to penetrate these texts of Scripture and grapple with the reality that called both of them forth. Can we use both of these sets of testimony to guide us to God himself and to speak of his creation? In our opinion, this is the goal of interpretation as a discipline of the Christian church. Let us then move from the descriptive task to the constructive, reflective task of interpreting Ps. 8.

IV

The Old Testament witnesses to the apparent insignificance of man in the creation and yet the place of honor that has been given him. The New Testament writer of Hebrews testifies that man has not possession of the world; everything is not in subjection to him. Rather, the author finds in the psalm a witness to the humiliation and exaltation of Jesus through whose suffering man's salvation was won. How is it possible to make any meaningful bridges between these divergent witnesses? Are they even talking about the same issue? Many interpreters are convinced that the New Testament is not really interpreting the Old Testament, but merely using or even abusing it. The charge is that this is an arbitary reading in of Christology that is fundamentally alien to the intent of the psalm. Is this really so? Do the two witnesses have nothing in common?

In approaching this set of problems one needs to establish a somewhat larger basis from which to reflect. How does the Old Testament as a whole see the problem between man as a creation of God and man living life as it actually is? What is the relationship between man as the lord of creation and man as a human being, limited in time and space, formed in communities, striving to maintain his life? The Old Testament is filled with reflections on this problem. The issue is not so much that man is constantly seeking to wrench himself free from God and to become divine himself, but rather that Hebrew man finds himself so overwhelmed by the powers of the world as to threaten any sense of his special role in God's creation.

The psalms are filled with human struggle to maintain a life of faith among the dangers of everyday existence. The complaint psalms particularly oscillate between the confession that all things are in God's control and a protest against the actual state of affairs in which the psalmist is slowly being ground to pieces. Specifically in The Book of Job one has articulated in the most terrifying fashion the threat that a man experiences in relation to his basic existence. Job acknowledges man as a creation of God, even using Israel's traditional vocabulary. In ch. 7 he addresses God: "I loathe my life; I would not live for ever. Let me alone, for my days are a breath. What is man, that thou dost make so much of him, and that thou dost set thy mind upon him, dost visit him every morning, and test him every moment?"

It is interesting to hear in this Job complaint the same vocabulary of Ps. 8. "What is man, that thou makest so much of him?" (Cf. Ps. 144:3b.) But the amazing thing is the change in its function. For Job, God's visitation is no longer a sign of God's grace. It has become part of his affliction. Life in its grim actuality is only a "vale of tears." The presence of God serves only to remind him of his insignificance. Israel's confession of a special place in the creation has become a burden. Job reflects on the tension between life as it actually is lived and the religious tradition of man's special place in the creation. The issue is not that he is driven into the position of thinking that God does not exist, or that God is dead, but that man is dead and lacks utterly any value. "Let me alone that I may swallow my spittle."

A similar threat is seen in the book of Ecclesiastes (ch. 3:11) in which again the writer is caught in the hard realities of human life as he experiences it. He writes: "He [God] has put eternity into man's mind, yet so that he cannot find out what God has done from the beginning to the end." Therefore, the writer questions the advantage that man has over the beasts. "For the fate of the sons of men and the fate of beasts is the same; as one dies, so dies the other. They all have the same breath, and man has no advantage over all the beasts. . . . All go to one place."

Now it is only when one hears the confession of Ps. 8 in this light that one can begin to make sense of what the New Testament writer is doing. He affirms with the psalmist in the face of the threats of life that man's role in the creation is not simply an idea or wishful thinking on his part. The writer of Hebrews is not divorced from human suffering. He knows man who is threatened with the agony of everyday existence. But he comes face-to-face with the problem of man's promised role and man as he really is by testifying to God's work in Jesus, the Son of Man. Only when one understands man in the light of the man, Jesus Christ, can he see what God intended humanity to be—not a man who was freed from the threats of daily life, but one who himself entered for a while into the full sufferings of humanity in order to bring life to all men. This is to say, the New Testament now sees the basic problem that lies behind the Old Testament witness in the light of Jesus Christ, and gives its own clear witness. First, the psalmist was right in confessing that man has a special role in God's creation. It was because God so loved this world that he sent his Son. Secondly, the way by which man attains his position of honor is through suffering and death. There is a chasm that separates him from his intended role in the creation. He has floundered and lost himself, and has succumbed to the threats of the world. Finally, the New Testament writer points to the way of hope. Because of what Jesus as the "pioneer of salvation" (Heb. 2:10) has done in bringing into fulfillment the new world to come, the invitation is extended for man to enter into the full honor of his rightful estate as son of God. If we read the Old Testament from the light of the New Testament in the context of Christian faith, we confess that in Jesus Christ true manhood has already appeared.

However, it is equally important to read this New Testament confession in the light of the Old Testament. The reverse movement of the dialectic belongs to theological reflection in the context of the canon. If we subject the witness of Hebrews to the testimony of the Hebrew psalm, we are reminded that the redemption in the man Jesus is not an escape from the world of human affairs. The "world to come" of Heb. 2:5 must retain its essential continuity with the created world of Ps. 8. The psalmist's confession, "How majestic is God's name in all the world," is an essential part of the redemption in Christ. The Old Testament witness prevents the New Testament's testimony from moving toward the Gnostic heresy. What Christ achieved was not an escape for the pious, but a redemption of the world—not a gathering together of the saints, but a salvation for all men. Whatever redemption means in the full context of Christian faith, both Old and New Testaments, it has universal implications. It is cosmic in its dimensions. Because of the man Jesus Christ, all the creation will confess: "How majestic is thy name in all the world."

The challenge of the Christian interpreter in our day is to hear the full range of notes within all of Scripture, to wrestle with the theological implication of this Biblical witness, and above all, to come to grips with the agony of our age before a living God who still speaks through the prophets and apostles.

10
MOSES' SLAYING IN THE THEOLOGY OF THE TWO TESTAMENTS

11. One day, when Moses had grown up, he went out to his people and looked on their burdens; and he saw an Egyptian beating a Hebrew, one of his people. 12. He looked this way and that, and seeing no one he killed the Egyptian and hid him in the sand. 13. When he went out the next day, behold, two Hebrews were struggling together; and he said to the man that did the wrong, "Why do you strike your fellow?" 14. He answered, "Who made you a prince and a judge over us? Do you mean to kill me as you killed the Egyptian?" Then Moses was afraid, and thought, "Surely the thing is known." 15. When Pharaoh heard of it, he sought to kill Moses.

But Moses fled from Pharaoh, and stayed in the land of Midian; and he sat down by a well. 16. Now the priest of Midian had seven daughters; and they came and drew water, and filled the troughs to water their father's flock. 17. The shepherds came and drove them away; but Moses stood up and helped them, and watered their flock. 18. When they came to their father Reuel, he said, "How is it that you have come so soon today?" They said, "An Egyptian delivered us out of the hand of the shepherds, and even drew water for us and watered the flock." 20. He said to his daughters, "And where is he? Why have you left the man? Call him, that he may eat bread." 21. And Moses was content to dwell with the man, and he gave Moses his daughter Zipporah. 22. She bore a son, and he called his name Gershom; for he said, "I have been a sojourner in a foreign land." (Ex. 2:11-22.)

The Old Testament Context

The passage is connected with the birth story that precedes although somewhat loosely. The writer moves immediately to his first major theme: Moses goes out to look with sympathy on the toil of his kinsmen. No words in the story are wasted on describing where Moses lived or how he knew that he was a Hebrew. Rather, the concern focuses on Moses' purposeful seeking out his kinsmen and his regard for their toil. The repetition of the phrase "from his kin" (v. 11) connects the slaying of the Egyptian in a causal relation with Moses' identification with his Hebrew brother. Then the second major theme of the first story is introduced. Moses is anxious that his act be done in secrecy. The sequence indicates that the slaying was not initiated in a burst of passion or following a vain attempt to dissuade the oppressor (so Benno Jacob). Verse 12 emphasizes the note of secrecy and stealth in the piling up of clauses: he looked both ways; he observed no one; he struck him (there was no struggle as in v. 13); he buried him quickly because the ground was sandy.

In v. 13 the narrative returns to the first motif: again he goes out to his brothers, and to his surprise (wehinneh) two Hebrews are fighting. Moses attempts to mediate. The use of the technical legal term for the offending party (larasha̒) expresses succinctly Moses' concern above all with the issue of justice. His is not a sentimental identification with the Hebrews. The reference to "his fellow" (re̒eka) is a neutral one and does not express explicitly the incongruity of kinsmen fighting together (cf. Acts 7:26). Now the tension of the story mounts as the two chief themes clash. The offending Hebrew rudely rejects

the mediation of Moses, and challenges his authority to play
this role. The second question referring to the killing of the
Egyptian does not arise out of a genuine self-fear, but is a
cynical means of warding off the reproach and turning it into
a threat. The knowledge of the act is no longer a secret but
shared by one who has already started to use it as an insidious
weapon. The reaction of Moses confirms the point. Moses is
afraid because his secret is out, and with good reason. When
Pharaoh hears, he seeks to kill him.

The point of the first story emerges in the conflict between
the motifs of active sympathy and required secrecy. The latter
motif leads to the heart of the issue: Moses must act in secrecy
because he has no authority. The impudent Hebrew saw this
correctly. The story ends on two related notes. First, Moses
does not succeed in his attempted deliverance. He must flee
for his life like every other political fugitive.[1] Secondly, his
failure was initiated by the betrayal of his own kin who rejects,
not only his authority, but his demand for justice as well.

The reader is led immediately to the second episode. Some
commentators have tried to speculate on how much time
lapsed between stories, but the text lends no support whatever
to the question. The story is recounted in extremely simple
Hebrew prose—note the recurrence of the verb "to go"—
which alternates between description of action and conversation. Moses is seated at the well. In v. 16 the writer brings the
bare minimum of background information that is needed for
understanding the event that ensues. The setting at the well is
paralleled in several patriarchal stories and is the natural loca-
tion for human encounter in the semidesert areas of the Near
East. Since water was the source of all life, it is obvious that
strife regarding its control was common. With a few strokes
the writer pictures the deliberate ruthlessness of the shepherds. They wait until the women have finished the tedious
work of drawing water and filling the troughs before driving
them away with force.

Then Moses arises and comes to their aid. The writer is extremely restrained in his description of this intervention. He is not interested in portraying Moses as a folk hero. (Contrast this with the description of Sampson or Jonathan.) A more elaborate description issues from the women's conversation which is skillfully evoked by the use of Jethro's questions, and the daughters' answers. The emphasis falls on the unusual circumstance that an Egyptian rescued them, and the added surprise that he both drew water and watered their flock. Jethro's three remarks, each of which reflects a slightly different emotion, not only serve to express the reaction of a Bedouin whose deep-seated sense of responsibility for hospitality has been aroused, but they also work as a literary device to enhance the contrast in response between an earlier example of aid that had been rejected and one of true gratitude. Once the main point has been made the story hastens toward completion. The return of the daughters to Moses, the invitation of a meal, the meeting with Jethro, are passed over as unessential. Only the bare outline of essential history is sketched. Moses agrees to stay with Jethro; he is given a wife; he has a son; and the child is named. Although the formula for the naming is traditional, it serves as an essential conclusion to the episode. The name indicates that Moses still remembers that he is a sojourner in a foreign land. He belongs to another people, in another land.

The two stories that now form one unit have been linked together in an interesting manner. There is the initial continuity of fleeing to the land of Midian (v. 15) and the priest of Midian (v. 16). But more significant are the contrasts drawn between the two episodes. In the first, the Egyptian is the enemy who oppresses; in the second, Moses is called an Egyptian but offers aid against the oppressor. In the first, the strife is between an Egyptian and a Hebrew; in the second, between two non-Hebrew peoples. In the first, Moses flees from his home; in the second, he finds a home.

However, these contrasts serve to highlight the larger similarities that tie together the stories into a unit. First, the emphasis falls in both on Moses' active concern for justice for the
weak that transcends the narrow bounds of nation and peoples.[2] Secondly, Moses is an exile who is forced to live apart
from his people whom he has not succeeded in delivering.

THE NEW TESTAMENT CONTEXT

The Old Testament text receives two extended interpretations within the New Testament.

Acts 7:23-29, 35

23. "When he was forty years old, it came into his
heart to visit his brethren, the sons of Israel. 24. And
seeing one of them being wronged, he defended the oppressed man and avenged him by striking the Egyptian.
25. He supposed that his brethren understood that God
was giving them deliverance by his hand, but they did
not understand. 26. And on the following day he appeared to them as they were quarreling and would have
reconciled them, saying, 'Men, you are brethren, why do
you wrong each other?' 27. But the man who was wrong-
ing his neighbor thrust him aside, saying, 'Who made you
a ruler and a judge over us? 28. Do you want to kill me
as you killed the Egyptian yesterday?' 29. At this retort
Moses fled, and became an exile in the land of Midian,
where he became the father of two sons. . . .
35. "This Moses whom they refused, saying, 'Who
made you a ruler and a judge?' God sent as both ruler
and deliverer by the hand of the angel that appeared to
him in the bush."

In the Stephen speech[3] the recounting of Israel's history
continues with the story of Moses' slaying the Egyptian and
his flight to Midian. As one would expect from the author of

Luke-Acts these verses reflect several features of the Hellenistic Jewish midrash. In general, the parallels to Philo's treatment (*De Vita Mosis*) are closer to Acts than the early Rabbinic exegetical traditions, although the differences with both remain striking. Along with Philo, Acts, ch. 7, understands the slaying of the Egyptian as an abortive attempt to carry out a deliverance that became the mission of ch. 3. However, the Acts account connects the passages in terms of prophecy and fulfillment within a redemptive history of God (cf. v. 17), whereas Philo has Moses exhorting the people to patience in the light of the changing fortunes of nature (II, VIII, 40 ff.). The style of the two interpretations also has common features. Both offer a subjective motivation for the slaying: "Moses considered that his action . . . was a righteous one" (line 44); "he supposed that his brethren would understand" (Acts 7:25). In both cases the description goes considerably beyond the Old Testament text. It also differs from the style of the Rabbinic midrash which is also vitally interested in providing a motivation, but provides it after a different fashion.

There are several elements in Philo's treatment that stem from an inherited midrashic tradition that is common to the Rabbinic traditions, such as Moses' initial attempt to assist the Hebrews, the particular cruelty of the overseer, and the concern to justify the killing as an ethical act.[4] The account in Acts does share some of these common features such as the chronological datum (v. 23), and the toning down of the fear element in the flight. However, more characteristic of Acts is the restrained use of the midrashic tradition. The strong theological interest of the author forces the interpretation to move along quite different lines.

The category of prophecy and fulfillment by which the Old Testament traditions are read leads to the New Testament writer's attributing a purpose to Moses' act that is not given in the Old Testament account. He thought that his brethren would understand the true significance of his intervention as the instrument of God's deliverance. The lack of understanding, which is certainly an important Old Testament theme in the passage, is then employed apologetically by the New Testament writer as an example of a larger pattern of disobedience that extends throughout Israel's history (vs. 35 ff.). The pattern of disobedience culminates in the rejection of Jesus, the Righteous One (v. 52), which unleashed the implied threat of Deut., ch. 18.

Again, it is significant to note how the New Testament writer has interpreted the theme of deliverance in terms of reconciliation from his new perspective. Of course, the Old Testament text provided the starting point for his interpretation. The Exodus account stressed the incongruity of two Hebrews fighting which called forth Moses' intervention. But Acts 7:26 is explicit in describing his act as an attempt at reconciliation (*sunēllassein*). His appeal in v. 26 goes far beyond the Masoretic text and the Septuagint. The neutral "fellow" (*rea*) becomes "brother"; the interrogative is replaced by the indicative, and both men rather than just the offending party are addressed. "Men, you are brothers!" The closest parallel is in Gen. 13:8 (LXX). The callousness of the rejection is emphasized by the addition of the phrase "he thrust him aside." The second episode in Ex., ch. 2, of Moses in Midian is reduced to a bare minimum in Acts since the interest falls on the revelation at the bush which confirms Moses' authority by divine sanction. The mention of the two sons born in Midian perhaps reflects the common midrashic harmonization of Ex. 4:20 and ch. 18:4. Of more importance is the interpretation of Moses as an "exile" (Acts 7:29).[5] The word has already occurred in Acts 7:6. In the Old Testament the term *gēr* designated originally a social class of the landless sojourner who lived without the protection of a clan. But the term had already been greatly expanded theologically when the people of Israel were described as a *gēr* in Egypt (Deut. 23:7). A further spiritualization of the terms is evident in Chronicles and in the Psalms (cf. I Chron. 29:15; Ps. 39:12; 119:19). Philo quotes Ex. 2:22 (*De Confusione Linguarum* XVII, 82) to prove that man only sojourns in the body, but his real home lies in the realm of the spirit.[6] In the book of Hebrews the term reflects to some degree this Hellenistic polarity between earth and heaven, but within an eschatological framework.

In the light of these different alternatives, it is significant to see that Acts 7:29 holds to the original concrete meaning of the term. The fact that Moses was forced to become an exile serves to emphasize his rejection by his own people and perhaps even his persecution (v. 52). This interpretation illustrates very clearly the striking difference in setting between Acts, ch. 7, and Heb., ch. 11. In the former, the Old Testament is used for an apologetical purpose against the synagogue in order to establish the grounds of Israel's history of disobedience, while in the latter the Old Testament message functions as an encouragement to a Christian audience.

Heb 11:23-28

23. By faith Moses, when he was born, was hid for three months by his parents, because they saw that the child was beautiful; and they were not afraid of the king's edict. 24. By faith Moses, when he was grown up, refused to be called the son of Pharaoh's daughter, 25. choosing rather to share ill-treatment with the people of God than to enjoy the fleeting pleasures of sin. 26. He considered abuse suffered for the Christ greater wealth than the treasures of Egypt, for he looked to the reward. 27. By faith he left Egypt, not being afraid of the anger of the king; for he endured as seeing him who is invisible. 28. By faith he kept the Passover and sprinkled the blood, so that the Destroyer of the first-born might not touch them.

Exodus 2:11 ff. receives another surprisingly full interpretation in Heb., ch. 11. In the light of the compression of the exodus events into a few verses, this interest in the one story is even more remarkable. The literary form of the chapter is striking, and sets the interpretation immediately into a different context from Acts.[7] Under the theme of faith is presented a whole series of Old Testament figures who serve as witnesses of faith for the New Testament writer in his attempt to evoke a similar response in his readers (Heb. 12:1 ff.). Even Jesus is placed in the series, but then set apart as the "pioneer and perfecter of faith." The style has a strong rhetorical flavor, and has its closest parallels in the martyr literature of Hellenistic Judaism (cf. IV Macc., ch. 16). The dominant Hellenistic flavor is also evident in the vocabulary and religious perspective (cf. Josephus, *Antiquities* II, 51 ff.).

The writer uses the Moses story in a series to illustrate his understanding of faith. Windisch notes that the element of faith is not an explicit motif in the Old Testament stories chosen, and that the one explicit reference to Abraham's faith in Gen., ch. 15, is omitted.[8] It is evident that the New Testament writer is coming to the Old Testament with interests that are less dependent on the exact wording of the text. He uses a set of categories to transform the tradition for his own theological purposes in a way far more radical than Acts, ch. 7. In using the Moses story as an illustration of faith, the writer often goes beyond the limits of the original text.

First of all, the writer of Hebrews stresses the active choice of faith. Moses "refused to be called the son of Pharaoh, choosing rather to share ill-treatment with the people of God." The element of choice is emphasized by setting up the alternatives: "ill-treatment with the people of God" instead of "the fleeting pleasures of sin"; "abuse suffered for Christ" rather than "treasures of Egypt." The fact that Moses did make a choice appears, of course, implicitly in the Old Testament story, but the New Testament greatly expands on it. Especially in the description of Israel as the "people of God," the enjoyment of "the fleeting pleasures of sin," and "suffering the abuses for

Christ," the writer has introduced a vocabulary that is far removed from that of the Old Testament's.

The element of a real choice made in faith serves the writer's central concern of illustrating the power of faith that has been unleashed in Israel's history. A certain heroic element of those involved is present, but it is closely tied to the great events that faith evoked. The strong selective tendency is revealed in Heb. 11:27 which omits the Midian episode, and fuses the first leaving with the exodus.[9] The explicit reference to Moses' lack of fear of the king in the light of Ex. 2:14 shows the writer's freedom in respect to the actual wording of the text. However, that this freedom is not completely arbitrary can be defended in the light of the larger narrative context that portrays a consistent picture of Moses' bold confrontation with Pharaoh. In other words, the writer is interpreting the content of the exodus story and does not feel bound to the text of Exodus.

The boldest innovation of the writer, however, turns about his understanding of the event as "abuse suffered for Christ." This Christological interpretation is important in giving the writer's intention to the contrast between the "visible" and the "invisible," the "transient" and the "enduring" which pervades the chapter. In spite of the long history of scholarly debate on the meaning of the "abuse suffered for Christ" several things seem clear. The use of the term "abuse" stems from the Septuagint as is evident from Paul's explicit reference to Ps. 68:10 in Rom. 15:3. Moreover, in Ps. 89:50 f. the term appears in reference to the despised Anointed One, who suffers persecution for the sake of God. These verses seem to provide the specific background for the allusion in Hebrews.

What then is meant by Moses' suffering abuse for Christ? The attempt to interpret it merely typologically—Christ suffered once; so must also any who represent him (Westcott)— avoids the difficulty rather than explaining it. Nor can the phrase simply mean "suffering for Christ's sake" which would

call for a different Greek construction (cf. II Cor. 4:5, 11;
I Peter 3:14; Phil. 1:29). Rather, the phrase indicates an actual
participation by Moses in Christ's shame in the same way as
the saints who follow Christ later also share in it (cf. Heb.
10:33; 13:13). The statement does not appear to be dependent
on a theory of preexistence, but rather the whole emphasis
falls on the unmediated identification. The union that binds
the faith of Israel to the Christ is not merely a formal pattern
of hope in the invisible world, but actually shares in the selfsame content.

The striking feature in the thought of the New Testament
writer is his creative use of several separate theological alternatives. He speaks of a "timeless" identification of almost ontological homogeneity; he uses a polarity between the visible
and the invisible with its strong affinities to popular Hellenistic
thought; he retains the strong Old Testament flavor of prophetic expectation by placing all the stories within the framework of awaiting the promise (Heb. 11:39). Usually, modern
interpreters have isolated one element and used it to the detri-
ment of the others. However, this tends to destroy the sensitive
balance. The Christological reference provides the content to
the invisible: Christ was always present among God's people.
Nevertheless, the divine reality appears in a real polarity—
he does not speak of a not-yet-visible—which is not merely a
vehicle for eschatology. Still all the Old Testament history
must be read as a witness to God's promise, made to a wandering people, yet to be fulfilled.

Rabbinic Interpretation

Finally, the characteristic features of the New Testament's
hearing of the Old Testament can be illuminated when contrasted with the typical moves found in the Rabbinic midrashim. The aim of such an analysis is not to raise truth claims
for the Christian interpretation. Rather, the purpose is to
sharpen the lines in describing the New Testament's understanding by setting it over against an alternative hearing of a

common text. The plotting of both the common and the disparate elements will be useful for determining the way in which the Old Testament functioned in a later context.

In the first place, the Rabbinic midrashim, Philo, and the New Testament, all heard v. 11 of ch. 2 as a major theme of the Exodus passage: Moses' voluntary participation in the sufferings of his people. All these interpretations went beyond the Old Testament text in attributing to Moses' act a positive value judgment. Again, there was a common tendency to play down the explicit Old Testament reference to the secrecy of the act, and to Moses' subsequent fear at being discovered.

However, more striking are the different directions in which the later exegetical traditions moved. In the Rabbinic midrashim Moses' deed is used as the legitimation of his special status in Israel: "He delivered his whole soul to them." [10] Moreover, Moses' deed now functions analogically in providing a model for God's action toward Israel. "Thou hast put aside thy work and hast gone to share the sorrow of Israel. . . . I will also leave those on high." [11] This characteristic Rabbinic analogy operates under the rubric of "sufficient reward," or "measure for measure." The righteous deed of a man—usually a patriarch—provides the grounds for God's corresponding act of mercy.

The New Testament use of analogy is characteristically different from the Rabbinical, although the typology functions in distinct ways in Acts and Hebrews. In both, the Old Testament story provides a Christological pattern. In Acts the rejection of Moses foreshadows Christ's; in Hebrews the sufferings of Moses are anticipations of his. In the New Testament the analogy functions as an incomplete adumbration or a proleptic identification rather than as the grounds for the divine action. Particularly in Acts, the analogy is a negative one illustrating a pattern of unbelief, a point that would be unthinkable for the midrash. Moses functions as the bearer of the word of promise (Acts 7:37).

There are several other characteristic differences in approach to the Old Testament story. The Rabbinic midrashim see the major issue in both the episodes in Egypt and Midian to be Moses' attempt to execute justice for the oppressed. It is obvious that the midrashim found clear Scriptural warrant for this move in the Biblical text itself, but there is an expansion beyond the Old Testament text when the "beating of a Hebrew" is assumed to be an unjust beating with intent to kill.[12] However, the major issue is the question of justice. The midrash focuses its main attention on explaining and justifying Moses' act of slaying the Egyptian. A variety of reasons are given: he was the cruelest of all Egyptians; there was no one else to help; Moses saw that no proselytes would ever arise; the law demanded his death, etc.[13]

In the New Testament the issue of justice is subordinated to that of deliverance. Acts, ch. 7, does touch on the question of justice (cf. vs. 24, 26), but the writer understands Moses' intervention as the beginning of the fulfillment of the promised deliverance. For this reason the issue of justifying the killing by Moses does not emerge. In Hebrews the author is even farther removed from this issue in his focusing on the promise (cf. the western text of ch. 11:23). He omits both the killing and the betrayal.

Again, the issue of Moses' authority is treated by both traditions, but in different ways. The midrashim interpret his controversy with the Hebrew in Ex. 2:13 ff. as referring specifically to Dathan and Abiram.[14] In this respect, the movement of the interpretation leads to a narrowing of the problem of authority. The strife was caused by Dathan's characteristic wickedness, or it was evoked by recognizing that there was an unsolved halachic question regarding Moses' age and lineage. However, at one point the midrashic interpretation moves in another direction when it designates the sin of slander, which is illustrated in Moses' betrayal, as the cause for Israel's suffering. The New Testament's use in Acts is more akin to this second line of interpretation which generalizes from the one to the many. However, the New Testament position offers a far more radical turn by seeing here an example of a negative pattern, adumbrated throughout the whole history of Israel, which involves ontological dimensions of disobedience.

In summary: The midrash understands Moses' action to be the model of obedience to Torah even though it precedes in time the covenant at Sinai. The interpretation seeks to explore and develop the full implications of this central fact to the life of the community. Whereas, the fundamental eschatological interest of the New Testament controls the essential function of the text and establishes the new Christological setting for the new role of the ancient story.

History of Interpretation

In the history of the interpretation of this passage during the period that followed the fixing of the normative traditions, the commentators can be initially divided into two groups. One group gives Moses' slaying of the Egyptian a positive evaluation. Another group judges it in an unfavorable light.

The first group, which includes several of the church fathers (Gregory of Nazianzus, *Epistola* LXXVI; Tertullian, *Contra Marc.* IV, 28; Ambrosius, *De Officiis,* lib. I, 36), Luther, Calvin, and the bulk of orthodox Protestant exegetes of the seventeenth and eighteenth centuries (Henry, Patrick, Scott), generally takes its lead from the New Testament and sees the act as divinely inspired. Although the appeal to a nonrevelatory warrant is not absent (cf. Ambrose), Calvin's interpretation is typical, especially of the classic Protestant position. He writes: "He was armed by God's command, and, conscious of his legitimate vocation, rightly and judiciously assumed that character which God assigned to him." (Exodus, *loc. cit.*)

Although these interpreters have attempted to share the New Testament's perspective, the context in which they write has tended to alter the focus of the interpretation. The question of justice—the rightness or wrongness of the act—is very much in the foreground of the discussion. Luther addresses himself to the specific issue, and supports his affirmative answer by using reasons provided partly by the New Testament, but also partly from rational arguments which were borrowed from the Jewish midrashim. The tradition of combining reasons based on revelation and reason continues as a dominant one in both Catholic and Protestant orthodoxy[15] (cf. the summary of opinions in Cornelius à Lapide, *Commentarii in Sacram Scripturam*, and M. Poole, *Synopsis Criticorum*). Several commentators find themselves in the position of defending the rightness of the act while at the same time arguing that its special divine warrant removes it from the area of moral judgment (Henry). Moreover, the commentators who stress the revelatory character of Moses' act often feel constrained to explain the absence of an explicit reference to such in Scripture, and seek to supply the link through conjecture or deduction.

The other major alternative in the history of interpretation finds its authoritative representative in Augustine (*Contra Faustum* 22, 70) who contests Moses' authority to kill the Egyptian in spite of the injustice, and compares him with Peter who also sinned in his untrained impulsiveness (cf. later modification in *Quaest. in Hept.* II, 2). Frequently, the act is judged premature because it preceded the call in ch. 3 (Keil). However, the most characteristic element in this group of interpreters is the strong psychological interest. Very early, the "turning this way and that" in v. 12 was attributed to Moses' bad conscience. Driver is typical of the late nineteenth-century Liberal Protestant view, which appreciates Moses' sympathy for the oppressed, but in the end cannot but condemn it as ill-advised. H. Frey[16] speaks of "his all too human failing" in which Moses moved from a stance of faith to disobedience. Another typical position, which is closely akin, focuses to such an extent on the psychological traits of Moses as to subordinate almost entirely the ethical question (already Gregory of Nyssa). The interest falls on the traits of the hero, his courage, burning patriotism, and feelings for justice (cf. especially Dillmann, Baentsch, Beer). At times there is a tacit approval of his deed because of its passionate quality.

The classical Jewish commentators fit into the first group of interpretation. Taking their lead from the midrashim, they naturally evaluate Moses' act in a positive light. Rashi faithfully follows the midrashic tradition with little addition. Maimonides attributes to Moses the first degree of prophecy which spirit moved him to slay the Egyptian (*Guide for the Perplexed*, II, 45). Abravanel, after attacking the idiosyncrasies of Ibn Ezra, elaborates on the qualities of Moses that are revealed in this act of courage which would not tolerate insult to his brothers, even though he had to risk his life to avenge the sons of Israel. All these commentators are agreed in regarding Moses' action as just.

THEOLOGICAL REFLECTIONS

Finally, we consider the Exodus passage within the context of the Christian canon, keeping in mind the history of interpretation. First, if we take our lead from the book of Hebrews and attempt to understand the Old Testament in the light of the New, we see that Moses' act of identification with his brothers is judged to be a model of Christian faith. Indeed, the specific ingredients of this faith are spelled out in the terms of this story. He suffered the abuse of Christ; he shared ill-treatment with the people of God; he looked for his reward. Moses' decision is a pattern of Christian faith because he responded to God in obedience and endured by faith in his promise.

However, if we now turn to the Old Testament, the picture of Moses' decision is a wholly different one. Nowhere are Moses' motives discussed. He did make a conscious decision

in identifying with the plight of his kinsmen. This is emphasized in the Old Testament passage, but the emphasis is fully
on the act, and not on the decision itself. However, the events
that subsequently are described point in no way to a single-
hearted commitment to a divine purpose. Rather, an occurrence is described that touches off a series of incidents, most
of which are only accidentally connected with one another.
He kills an Egyptian thinking that his act was secret. But he
is seen, rebuffed by his fellow Hebrew, and betrayed. In terror
for his life he flees as a fugitive from his country to seek
shelter in Midian. There he remains shepherding sheep for
a livelihood, and raising a family. One finds little of the hero
of faith who decides for God.

Nevertheless, the relationship of these two portrayals is not
wholly arbitrary and poses by their juxtaposition an important
theological problem. In both the Old Testament and New
Testament passages there are elements of faith such as sharing
another's suffering, and faith as hope. But the perspective is a
totally different one. Hebrews describes Moses' whole behavior as eschatologically oriented; Exodus speaks of the here
and now, and only in the naming of the child is there a
momentary glimpse into a hope and a future. Hebrews brack-
ets all the story under the rubric of faith; Exodus has no one
such rubric but describes a series of actions. In a real sense,
the issue at stake, theologically speaking, is the understanding
of the nature of man's decision for God. Seen from one perspective the issue is unequivocal in its character, the clear
call to discipleship. In another sense, it is a living and decid-
ing among the variety of relationships in which we live, in
the complexity of mixed emotions and historical accidents,
seeking to live an obedient life. The selfless act is soon beclouded by violence, and nothing of lasting effect is accomplished for Israel's plight. To interpret from the context of
the canon would seem to mean that the Biblical witness to
the nature of Moses' faith is viewed from a double perspec-

tive: faith as eschatological hope and faith as response in the present. Faith as a clear-cut decision of commitment, and faith as confused action toward obedience in the complexity of several alternatives and mixed motivations.

Secondly, to reflect on the Exodus passage from the witness of Acts raises another set of issues. The sequence of Moses' identifying with his brothers' suffering, risking his life for his people, and then being misunderstood and rebuffed is interpreted as a recurring pattern of Israel's disobedience. This history of unbelief is brought in line with the Old Testament prophets and climaxes in the rejection of the Messiah. Is this not a completely arbitrary and tendentious reading of the facts? The Jews did not ever reject the authority of the Messiah. The issue at stake was that Jesus' claim to be the Messiah was not acknowledged. But this is exactly the theological issue that emerges when Old and New Testaments are seen together. The claim to authority was not accepted because the right to the office of God's deliverer was not acknowledged: "Who made you judge over us?"

Neither Moses nor Jesus was recognized, at least not by their own people. Still Moses was "recognized" by the Midianites—in spite of his looking like an Egyptian. And Jesus found a response among the poor and outcast. The basic point being made is that lack of recognition is disobedience because the nature of the act itself discloses the bearer to be from God. "Believe me for my work's sake." The quality of the deed was self-authenticating. This appears to be the answer of Jesus to John the Baptist's query (Matt. 11:1 ff.). The same issue is at stake with Moses. The fact that God's deliverer is not recognized reflects a condition of blindness on the part of his people. To the objection: "If you are the Christ, tell us plainly," the whole Bible answers: "The works that I do in my Father's name, they bear witness to me."

Finally, there is another way of using this text that tries to make use of the Bible in relation to specific problems that the

interpreter brings with him to his exegesis. Rather than begin
with the Bible and then seek its contemporary relevance, it
appears equally legitimate from a theological perspective to
start with the modern problem. The decisive theological move
does not depend on the starting point but on the interaction
between the Bible and the issue. As a modern Christian who
participates in an American culture I am concerned with the
issue of using physical violence as a means for social change.
I would like to know if it is ever justified, and if so, under
what conditions. What about the so-called "theology of revolution"? I approach the Exodus text with this problem, seeking
some guidance. What can I learn?

We have already noticed that the Old Testament does not
moralize on Moses' act of violence. Nowhere is there an explicit evaluation that either praises or condemns it. Rather, a
situation is painted with great realism and sensitivity, and the
reader is left to ponder on the anomalies of the deed. Moses
acts in order to make right an injustice, not for his own sake,
but for another. He is motivated to react with violence out of
love for his people which even jeopardizes his own life. But
the ambiguity of the situation is that the act does not carry
only one meaning. It is open to misunderstanding and a variety of possible interpretations. Moses supposed that his
motivation was obvious, but the Hebrew who was abusing his
fellow attributed a totally different intention from that which
Moses has envisioned. "Who made you a ruler over us?" Implied in both of Moses' acts, the killing of the Egyptian and
the attempt to reconcile the Hebrew, was a claim to authority
and a definition of justice. From the perspective of the offending Hebrew this man posed a threat because his own behavior
was being called into question. He was not willing to accept
Moses' help when it was offered under these conditions.
Therefore, he rebuffed Moses and sought to destroy him by
imputing an interpretation to his deed that impugned his
honesty. To his chagrin Moses discovered that his altruism

had made for him an enemy, and not an ally.

Again, the story points to Moses' attempt to act in secret. He killed the Egyptian thinking that he was not being observed, and even cautiously disposed of the incriminating evidence. Obviously, his being in hostile Egypt dictated this prudence. Yet one wonders whether an act of justice can really be done under these circumstances. Once Moses is discovered, he is unusually vulnerable. In terror he flees for his own life, leaving behind the repercussions of his act. He has become indistinguishable from every other political fugitive. Moreover, what did he really solve? The Biblical text, without drawing explicit conclusions regarding the ethics of the matter, does make it fully clear that no deliverance occurred. Moses had to be sent back to Egypt with a different authority and with a new mission.

Finally, the interpretation in Acts points to another aspect of the problem. The New Testament writer is concerned with the intervention as an attempt at reconciliation. Moses is cast into the role of Abraham and uses the patriarch's words in addressing the fighting Hebrews: "Men, you are brethren." But the incongruity of Moses' arguing for genuine reconciliation is pointed out by the impudent Hebrew. His act of killing had put him in a different position from Abraham. He was now unable to act as a reconciliator. The prior action had robbed all his later words of significance. Like a good many pastors who also tried to help, Moses was ready for another parish!

To sum up: Our text does not provide one clear answer to the complex problem of using violence for the sake of justice. But it does raise a whole set of issues that are inherent in such action. By uncovering the ambiguities in the act of violence, the reader is forced to confront rather than evade those basic factors which constitute the moral decision.

11
PROVERBS, CHAPTER 7, AND
A BIBLICAL APPROACH TO SEX

1. My son, keep my words
   And store up my commandments with you;
2. Keep my commandments and live,
   And my teachings like the apple of your eye;
3. Bind them on your fingers,
   Write them on the tablet of your heart.
4. Say to wisdom, "You are my sister,"
   And call discernment "Friend";
5. To guard you from the loose woman,
   From the adultress with her seductive words.
6. For at the window of my house
   I looked out through my lattice,
7. And I saw among the simple,
   I discerned among the youths a young man
      without sense,
8. Passing along the street near her corner,
   Strolling along the road to her house,
9. In the dusk, in the evening,
   At the time of night and darkness.
10. And then a woman comes to meet him,
    Dressed as a prostitute, wily of heart,[1]
11. Boisterous and aggressive,
    Never does she stay at home;
12. Now in the street, now in the market,
    And at every corner she lies in wait.

13. Then she catches hold of him and kisses him,
    And with shameless face says to him:

14. "I have sacrificial meat on hand
    For today I have discharged my religious
        duties;

15. That is why I have come out to meet you,
    To seek you eagerly and I have found you.

16. I have spread my couch and coverlets,
    Colored spreads of Egyptian linen;

17. I have sprinkled my bed
    With myrrh, aloes, and cinnamon.

18. Come let us take our fill of love until
        morning,
    Let us delight ourselves with love-making.

19. For the good man is not at home;
    He is gone on a long journey;

20. He has taken the money bag with him,
    He will not come home until the full moon."

21. She persuades him with much seductive talk;
    With smooth words she urges him.

22. All at once[2] he is accompanying her,
    Like an ox being led to the slaughter
    Or as a stag is caught fast,[3]

23. Until an arrow pierces its entrails;
    As a bird hastens into the net,
    Not knowing that it will cost him his life.

24. And now, my sons, listen to me,
    And pay attention to the words of my mouth.

25. Let not your heart incline to her ways,
    Do not stray into her paths,

26. For many a victim she has laid low;
    And numerous are her slain,

27. Her house is the way to Sheol,
    Descending into the chambers of death.

(Prov., ch. 7.)

IN THE CONTEXT OF THE BOOK OF PROVERBS

The chapter gives an immediate impression of a literary unity in spite of the fact that, form critically speaking, the central section (vs. 6-23) falls outside the normal pattern of the discourses in chs. 1 to 9 of Proverbs.[4] There is the familiar introduction that commends wisdom by means of a string of imperatives and then in v. 5 moves to the specific threat to life in the form of the "loose woman." The concluding section (vs. 24-27) is clearly marked by the initial adverb "and now," and the repetition of an explicit addressee. The familiar warnings (ch. 5:1-6, etc.) are again issued in the imperative style. However, the main interest of the chapter focuses on the extended description of the harlot at work in seducing her victim, which is related by an unobserved narrator.

The description is a literary masterpiece. An old sage watches the city street from the privacy of his window as dusk begins to fall. A young man catches his attention from among the others who move along the street. He is not pictured as an evil, corrupt, or stupid fellow; rather, a young, naïve, inexperienced youth, without discernment, and thoughtless. The Hebrew calls him "simple"; he "lacks sense." He walks along aimlessly with no fixed intention, but unwittingly he passes near "her corner," strolling along "her street." The unmodified pronoun anticipates the introduction of the loose woman which is to follow, but serves to heighten the suspense by its veiled allusion. The narrator knows more at this moment than the simple youth who remains unsuspecting at the cool of the evening, when the heat of the day has subsided.

Then the narrative tempo shifts. Suddenly a woman moves swiftly out to meet him. Both her dress and her behavior portray her profession. Without appreciably slowing down the story's pace the narrator pauses momentarily to picture the harlot. With a quick stroke he produces a vignette of calculated, restless activity. Wily and cunning, garrulous and brazen, she is much too impatient to wait for her customers. She must be out, stalking her game, flitting from one street to another, into the market and back to her corner. The contrast between the aimless, unwitting simpleton and the designing adventuress is complete.

She sights the slow-moving figure and hastens to meet him. In the darkness of the night she accosts him, seizing him. Had he perhaps sought to retreat? In an instant she smothers any inhibitions with caresses, throwing herself at him. She has just come back from the temple—she is one of those harlots with a sense of religious duty—and her table is already prepared with the meat for a luxurious banquet. Of course, not prepared for just anyone, but "for you." "I have come out to meet you, to seek you eagerly, and I have found you." But the feast is only the beginning. The couch is ready, decked with the finest of Egyptian linen, dripping myrrh and aloes. The air is thick with heavy perfume. The sensuous appeal to taste, smell, sight, and touch fuses together in one voluptuous revelry of delight. "Come, let us saturate ourselves in love until the morning."

Still he hesitates. The simpleton does not speak, but his reaction is mirrored in her running conversation. She anticipates the resistance and deftly overcomes it. He need have no fear of discovery. "The good man is on a trip"—she does not mention her husband by name. "Surely he will not return for days."

She beckons, "with much seductive speech she persuades." Then all of a sudden he finds himself accompanying her:

"Like an ox being led to the slaughter . . .
Not knowing that it will cost him his life."

The sage has finished. He concludes with a word of advice. "Now, my sons, listen: do not stray into her path. . . . Her house is the way to Sheol, going down to the chambers of death." He does not mount a theological argument, nor appeal to sacred tradition, but from the world of experience he relates what he knows of the world. This is simply the way it is. Such action always leads to death. So, my son, do not be a fool!

The passage, in spite of its unusual literary style, presents a theme that is typical of Wisdom Literature, both within and without the Christian canon.[5] The contrast between the way of wisdom leading to life and that of folly leading to death is illustrated, above all, in the repeated warning against the loose woman. The teaching of the sage is designated as "commandments." It possesses an authority that goes beyond simple advice. Yet it does not rest on prophetic inspiration nor cultic sanction, but rather reflects the tested observations of wise men on the ways of the world. Nevertheless the imperative of these teachings has already been equated with the sacred tradition that bears the claim of direct, divine revelation. Like the Decalogue of Deut. 6:4, these instructions are also to be "bound on the fingers" and "written on the tablets of the heart." Like obedience to the word of God (Ezek. 3:16; 18:32; 33:10 ff.) the observance of these teachings leads to life. Again, these words function as the law in keeping a young man from going astray (Ps. 119:9 ff.).

Besides the major theme of the passage, which warns of the dangers of folly and points to life on the path of wisdom, several other features reflect elements of theological interest. The passage describes in detail the psychology of temptation, portraying with great sensitivity the delicate mechanism of influencing the will toward evil. Again, the understanding of the fool as one inexperienced, lacking in discernment, and without inner resolution is repeatedly pictured as exposed and helpless before evil which is described as cunning, alert, and aggressive. Lastly, the inevitable connection of the deed with its effect is assumed by the writer as part of the order of the world.

If one now attempts to place the passage within the context of the book of Proverbs, several important observations can be made. First of all, the theme of wisdom contrasted with folly continues with great consistency throughout the other discourses in chs. 1 to 9, and, in slightly varying form, in chs. 10 to 31. Repeatedly the theme of the loose woman personifies the life of folly. She is one with "smooth words," who has forsaken "the companion of her youth," who has forgotten "the covenant of her God," and whose "house sinks down to death" (ch. 2:16 ff.). She is noisy, takes her place in a public place where she can tempt all passers-by (ch. 9:13 ff.). The sage warns against infatuation, of being captured by her beauty, and spells out the risks involved (ch. 6:25 ff.). Yet, surprisingly enough, the same vocabulary of the harlot is used throughout Proverbs to describe the activity of "Lady Wisdom." [6] She also cries in the streets (ch. 1:20), stations herself in a public place where she can accost all (ch. 8:3). She allures, calls, beckons with outstretched hand (ch. 1:24). Her way is pleasant (ch. 3:17). She also has slaughtered her beasts and set the banquet table (ch. 9:2). She seeks to be loved (ch. 4:6) and embraced (v. 8).

The effect of using the one set of imagery serves to intensify the struggle between the way of wisdom and the way of folly. Wisdom like folly is active, aggressive, and persistent. Both offer the rewards of happiness and pleasure. Yet one leads to life and one to death. The decision lies in the hands of man. The stakes are high; his life is laid on the line.

There is a second movement that one discerns by placing ch. 7 within the larger context of the book. In ch. 5:15 ff. the sage admonishes his son:

> Drink water from your own cistern,
> Flowing water from your own well. . . .
> Rejoice in the wife of your youth,
> A lovely hind, a graceful doe.
> Let her affection fill you at all times with delight,
> Be always infatuated with her love.

In contrast to the false infatuation with the loose woman, the sage commends love for one's own wife with enthusiasm. The ideal of monogamy is already fully explicit. He is to be "infatuated with her," "filled with delight," and to rejoice in her beauty. Once again, a similar vocabulary is used to describe the sexual attraction for one's wife and the infatuation aroused by the adventuress. The issue is obviously not between sex and celibacy, which is a polarity totally foreign to the Old Testament, but between misused sex that leads to destruction and sex that belongs to the fullness of life and blessing. Nowhere in the discourses of chs. 1 to 9 is this latter thought developed, but it is assumed as essential to the good life and commended as a delightful antidote to the temptations of folly.

BROADENING THE CONTEXT

Now the task is to move beyond the confines of Proverbs and view the passage within even a larger context, if possible, within the context of the whole canon. How is this move made when there are no explicit quotations in the other witnesses that would indicate how the text was heard and used? As has been suggested in an earlier chapter the method that is being suggested for Biblical Theology is not confined to the use of explicit quotations. The occurrence of citations serves only as one useful aid when broadening the context by which to establish the perimeter of the Biblical witnesses and by which to determine with considerable precision the specific axes along which the reflections of Scripture moved. Above all, this method allows the interpreter a means of measuring how the same text functioned in a different context which is far more difficult to ascertain when one moves directly to the study of motifs or themes. However, a variety of other means are available by which to achieve a similar goal when broadening the context within the canon. The present objective is to explore one of these other alternatives.

An exegetical move that is akin to the use of citations is one that seeks to discover in other Biblical material the use of a cluster of similar vocabulary that functions in a coherent manner. By concentrating on similar vocabulary the interpreter assures himself of a linguistic control in determining that the subject matter being investigated is closely related. The study of vocabulary, as in the use of citations, brings far more precision to bear in delineating a common subject matter than does simple conceptual analogy. Again, by seeking a cluster of similar vocabulary one avoids the inherent danger of individual word studies, which arises when the word is treated apart from its role within the sentence.[7] Moreover, the stress on coherent function assures that the peculiar shape the material has assumed will be recognized. This control guards against the tendency of word studies to isolate words from their genuine context. Yet it affords a check to larger conceptual constructs that are not congruent with the Bible's own inner movement. Lastly, the use of function instead of concentrating on meaning affords the interpreter a more reliable guide in tracing the change that occurs within the same material when serving in different settings.

Having delineated a methodology, we return to the problem of broadening the context of Prov., ch. 7. An analysis of the chapter revealed that the call to wisdom was contrasted with the way of folly. The latter was most clearly illustrated by the enticement of the loose woman. However, already within the book of Proverbs a positive role of sex was set over against the negative, although this side of the issue remained undeveloped.

Now the question arises as to whether there is another use of the language of Prov., ch. 7, one in which a cluster of similar vocabulary functions in a coherent manner. It should come as no surprise to find the greatest concentration of erotic language in the Song of Songs. Whatever may have been the original setting for this material—and no scholarly consensus has emerged—the book now consists of a series of love poems in which the speaker is at times the woman addressing her lover, and at times the situation is reversed with the man courting the woman. The remarkable feature is the way in which the same erotic language used in Prov., ch. 7, by the harlot to entice the simpleton on the road to death is now employed by the lovers without the slightest negative overtones. Indeed just the opposite! Throughout the whole book their words reverberate with the sheer joy of unrestrained delight in their mutual sexuality. "Love is strong as death" and the greatest treasure of human life (Song of Songs 8:6 f.). Like the brazen harlot who goes forth to "seek and find" her victim (Prov. 7:15), "now in the street, now in the market" (v. 12), the lover of the Song of Songs pursues him in "the streets and square" (Song of Songs 3:1), calls after him (v. 1), and seeks to lead him back to her house (v. 4). When she finds him (v. 4), she holds him fast (v. 1), and would kiss him outside (ch. 8:1). Like the harlot who entices her victim with the invitation of love upon perfumed couches until the morning breaks (Prov. 7:18), so the lover in the Song invites her lover to her couch at night (Song of Songs 3:1) to remain until the morning comes (ch. 4:6). Her hands drip with myrrh (Songs of Songs 5:5; Prov. 7:17); she is compared to a garden filled with aloes and cinnamon (Song of Songs 4:14; Prov. 7:17). Her lips "distil nectar"; "honey and milk are under the tongue" (Song of Songs 4:11), which parallels the harlot in Proverbs whose "lips drip honey" and whose "palate is smoother than oil" (ch. 5:3). Whereas the sage warns the youth of the dangers of the harlot's beauty who captures a man "with her eyelashes" (ch. 6:25), the lover of the Song of Songs confesses that his heart has been ravished with "a glance of your eyes" (ch. 4:9). Continually physical beauty is exalted and human passion ignited by sexual attraction (chs. 4:1 ff.; 5:2 ff., etc.).

Moreover, there is an additional use of the erotic language in the Song of Songs which goes beyond the perimeter of the Proverbs, but which constitutes an essential part of the poem's function. In Proverbs the misuse of sex is described with the harlot's aggressively seeking the man. In contrast, the man in Proverbs exercises the active force in the relation of properly used sex, and his needs are placed at the center (ch. 5:15 ff.). How strikingly different is the Song of Songs at this point. Not only is human, physical love praised and exalted, but the relation of the man to the woman is completely mutual. At times the initiative is assumed by the man when courting the woman, but even more frequently, the passionate yearning for her lover is the woman's. Far from being a delightful antidote to the temptations of the flesh, love is inextinguishable, a "vehement flame," "strong as death," the most valued of all human prizes.

Moreover, the Song of Songs is even more radical in its approach to erotic love, in fact so radical that the average Christian hesitates to recognize it as Scripture. The book of Proverbs had commended in one place love for one's own wife. Within this framework it was able to find a positive role for erotic love. In the Song of Songs there is no mention of marriage or the institution of the family. The love that is exalted in the Song is not between husband and wife, but simply between lovers. This greatest of human joys, this cruel and vehement fire, is described on its own terms. What is binding is love itself without any sociological or religious function. In itself, and for itself, it is prized and feared.

To summarize up to this point: By placing Prov., ch. 7, within the context of the whole book an important theological movement emerged as dominant and typical for the Wisdom Literature. Man is called to seek wisdom and eschew folly. Particularly is the loose woman to be avoided who exemplifies par excellence, the latter path. How much wiser to be satisfied with one's own wife. We then turned to the Song of Songs and traced another use of the same erotic language. That which appeared as a minor note in Proverbs, namely, the positive role of sexual love, became the major theme of the Song which portrayed the full dimensions of human love completely apart from any utilitarian function that it might serve.

What is the effect of reading Proverbs in the light of the Song of Songs, and the Song of Songs in the light of Proverbs? Does the juxtaposition of these two books within the canon exercise any influence on their interpretation? First, by reading Proverbs in the light of the Song of Songs the polarity emerges with even greater sharpness between misused sex as foolish self-destruction and rightly used sex as a joyous possession of the wise. The witness of the Song of Songs corrects and opposes the tendency within Proverbs to view the positive value of sex chiefly in its function as an antidote to sexual incontinence. Rather, human love is recognized and acclaimed for itself. The physical and spiritual sides of love form an inseparable unity. Love unleashes the deepest of all human feelings. It can be cruel and deadly in terrifying bursts of jealousy. It is strong as death itself and most to be valued among all human achievements.

Conversely, the reading of the Song of Songs in the light of Proverbs exercises an important canonical control in another direction. Proverbs testifies that wisdom is a divine order and true human knowledge of the world leads unswervingly back to God. Because God's order provides the framework for all human activity, the "fear of God" affords a guide to the wise man for leading him to the fullness of life. Proverbs places human love within the established order of the world, and relativizes its function by confining its scope. Love is a human attribute; it does not provide the bridge to the divine. Nor does it remove the major ethical imperatives constitutive to the good life because the call to wisdom is also the path of righteousness (Prov. 4:10-27).

Again it is necessary to pause and reflect on the next exegetical move. What does one do when he has exhausted the study of those passages which allow for linguistic control such as is provided by a citation or by a cluster of similar vocabulary? Clearly if one is to do Biblical Theology within the context of the whole canon, there is a necessity for broadening the subject matter beyond the confines of material which is suitable to such linguistic tools. Once the area has been outlined in which a Biblical approach to a subject moves, and once the inner motion along its characteristic axes has been traced, then it is necessary to enlarge the context by means of conceptual analogies and affinities of subject matter. However, right at this point great care is needed lest the precision of the earlier steps in remaining close to the text be sacrificed in the broadening process.

There are some negative controls that aid in moving correctly from the area of linguistic parallels to similarity of subject matter. First, the similarity of subject matter must be one that is integrally related to both the inner and the outer movement of the original Biblical passage. This test is not to serve as a rigid structure into which all subsequent material is forced; rather, its function is to assure a genuine relationship instead of an incidental parallel. To illustrate the point: The loose woman in Prov., ch. 7, speaks of having just performed her cultic duties. One might wish to see a relation between this text and Isaiah's condemnation of sacrifice and immorality (Isa. 1:13 ff.). But the fact that the relation of sacrifice to immorality is not integral to Prov., ch. 7, but tangential to its purpose, would speak against developing this connection.

Secondly, the similarity in subject matter must be one that shares more than one point in common. There must be at least two points of contact in order to establish its relation to the movement of the original passage. Often a Biblical word, image, or concept is used in a variety of ways to address distinct issues. If the Biblical theologian follows every movement that an image allows within the whole Bible, the sharp

lines of the distinct Biblical movements are lost. For example, Prov., ch. 7, portrays a harlot tempting an Israelite to sin.
Now the imagery of the harlot is used elsewhere to depict
Israel's disobedience to God, particularly in the prophets
(Hos. 2:1 ff.; Jer. 3:1 ff.; Ezek. 16:1 ff.). However, the similarity lies chiefly in the word "harlot." The prophetic use of
the term belongs to another Biblical theme and is not to be
related to the use in Prov., ch. 7.

Thirdly, there must be a functional as well as conceptual
similarity to establish a genuine parallel between passages.
Even though two passages might reveal similarity of content
at several points, a radically different function in nonrelated
contexts would afford a major obstacle in establishing an
integral relationship. For example, I Tim., ch. 5, in the context of outlining family responsibility of children for parents,
warns of the danger of young widows gadding about the
city. There is a certain parallel here to the description in
Prov., ch. 7, of the loose woman prowling about the city
while her husband is on a trip. But clearly the New Testament
setting in which the warning is given is so different that one
would be ill-advised to draw any lesson that could bridge
the diverse contexts of the passages.

Keeping these strictures in mind, we now attempt to broaden
the context in which one reads Prov., ch. 7, to include material that is only conceptually related. The story of Potiphar's
wife in Gen., ch. 39, affords an immediate parallel of subject
matter but without a close linguistic connection. An unfaith-
ful wife attempts to entice the young Hebrew into committing
adultery. The setting is not far removed from that of Prov.,
ch. 7. The woman is portrayed as aggressive and deceitful
while Joseph, up to this point in the narrative, is described as
a naïve, sheltered youth who has carried his father's special
favor. The nature of the temptation is carefully portrayed in
the story. Potiphar is completely detached from the affairs
of his household. Indeed, he may well have been a eunuch.[8]

Joseph has charge of the entire household. There is no chance of discovery (Gen. 39:11), and the temptation is constantly repeated.

However, the Genesis story adds several new elements to the pattern that goes much beyond Prov., ch. 7. First, the focus in the story now falls on Joseph's response. Not only does he refuse to be tempted, but voices his reasons in a theological confession. He expresses his loyalty to his master, Potiphar, who has entrusted him with his possessions. Next he reminds the woman of her position: she is his wife and as such has a position unique in the household. Lastly, and above all, Joseph refuses to yield because of his commitment to God in whose sight adultery is a great wickedness. His reference is not to Yahweh, God of the covenant, nor does he draw a warrant from a divine commandment of the law. Rather, his appeal to God is fully congruent with the wisdom schools in Proverbs that relate God to the moral order as the world's creator. Nevertheless, the confession of personal commitment by Joseph to God reflects the influence of covenant theology and points to a close union in Israel between the two originally diverse theological approaches. The additional motif of the story that Joseph was willing to suffer an unjust punishment adds the note of the suffering righteous servant of God which lay close to the heart of Israel's piety. While von Rad [9] is probably correct in seeing the strong influence of wisdom on the Joseph stories, it must also be said that it is a form of wisdom that has been joined to the center of Israel's faith in Yahweh.

There is another closely allied point that should also be made. The wisdom teacher and the lawgiver brought a different set of sanctions to bear in condemning sexual vagrancies. The Decalogue forbade adultery in an apodictic prohibitive that arose from the covenant demands laid upon Israel as the people of God. Leviticus, ch. 18, grounded its prohibitions of sexual abuse in the community on God's at-

tribute of holiness which was contained in the formula of
self-introduction: "I am Yahweh your God." However, in spite
of the differing vantage points in approaching the subject,
the end result in terms of ethical response issued in a unified
imperative. The whole Bible remains unswervingly consistent
in condemning adultery as a threat to the individual and corporate life of Israel. The story of David and Bathsheba with
its detailed commentary by Nathan (II Sam., chs. 11 and 12)
makes it absolutely clear that even kings are not exempt from
God's order.

THE NEW TESTAMENT CONTEXT

When one turns to the New Testament, there is no direct
use made, either of the text of Prov., ch. 7, or of its peculiar
idiom. Nevertheless, there are several passages in which similar subject matter is treated in a way that reveals that the
writer moves along the familiar lines of the Old Testament.
Indeed, the case can be made that the New Testament makes
such little explicit reference to the subject because the Old
Testament's understanding of the role of sex has been simply
assumed as normative. In I Thess. 4:1 ff. Paul instructs the
congregation in the "will of God." A Christian has been called
to a life of holiness that abstains from immorality. Each man
is to have his own wife and live in holiness, not according to
the "passions of lust like heathen." The apostle concludes by
alluding to the judgment of God against immorality by means
of a catchword from Ps. 94:1.

Paul reflects his inherited Jewish revulsion against the
sexual abuses that he identifies with the heathen. When instructing Gentile converts in the manner of the Christian
life, Paul does not need to develop a new Christian approach
to sex and marriage. Rather, he assumes the Old Testament
teaching to be normative. The will of God has already been
made clear in demanding a life of holiness commensurate with

God's holiness. Nevertheless, the context in which Paul spoke has effected several changes in the tradition that he inherited. He characterizes the relationship to one's wife as demanding "holiness and honor" in contrast to the heathen whose relationship he describes as dominated by "passions of lust." One notices increasingly the tendency of certain New Testament writers to identify sin with concupiscence (I Tim. 6:9; II Peter 1:4, etc.; cf. Heb. 11:25). In the Old Testament the contrast was between proper and misused sex. The New Testament does not contest this distinction, but the passage in I Thess. does shift the emphasis by sharply denigrating misused sex as lust in contrast to the proper relationship that appears in a form completely devoid of erotic overtones. The wife is to be treated with "holiness and honor," whereas the term "love" (*agape*) is reserved for the Christian community (I Thess. 4:9 f.). Of course, the New Testament does contain explicit imperatives instructing husbands to love their wives (Eph. 5:5; Col. 3:19), but still this does not offset the general tendency of the New Testament to assign sexual passion to the category of heathen immorality, or at least to regard it as a danger to be extinguished (I Cor. 7:9).

In the Pauline discussion of the problems of marriage in I Cor., ch. 7, the general tone of Paul's advice is roughly akin to the stance of Proverbs in emphasizing marriage as an antidote to the misuse of sex. Nevertheless, the negative side has been pushed considerably beyond anything in the Old Testament. The seeds of asceticism are certainly present with abstinence seen as a higher way of life. Once Paul's remarks were cut loose from their Old Testament setting in the process of Christianizing the Greco-Roman empire, a new stance to sex and marriage emerged that was completely alien to the Old Testament.

The Pauline discussion of the role of sex and marriage is a good illustration of the need of the theologian to understand the New Testament in the light of the Old. Two obvious, but

200 BIBLICAL THEOLOGY IN CRISIS

faulty, hermeneutical moves are thereby avoided. Either one seeks to absolutize the Pauline teaching for Christian ethics in every age or one dismisses the Pauline teaching as a distorted and time-conditioned human judgment. By insisting on its place within the normative tradition, and yet subjecting it to the criticism and balance of the other witnesses, another theological alternative is opened up for the serious handling of Scripture in the life of the church.

12
THE GOD OF ISRAEL
AND THE CHURCH

THE PROBLEM OF METHOD

A common way of treating the subject of God in Biblical Theology—a method inherited from the pre-nineteenth century—is to assemble passages from the Old Testament into a doctrine of God and to assemble passages from the New Testament into a doctrine and then to compare them.[1] The method suffers from several deficiencies that have often been pointed out in recent years, particularly by those in the Biblical Theology Movement. First, it is very dubious whether one can correctly talk of doctrines when dealing with the Biblical material. Secondly, the process of systematization overlooks how statements about God and his work function in specific contexts. For these reasons, besides others, this older approach has been generally abandoned when doing Biblical Theology.

Several alternative proposals have been attempted in dealing with the subject of God. The "History of Redemption" approach usually begins with Old Testament theology and organizes the various statements about God around institutions (covenant) and events that are connected by means of a concept of revelation in history. The New Testament witnesses are then lined up as testimonies to the climactic event of the one history. The problem with this approach is that it suggests a framework that, while appearing in the New Testament, is not at all the only one used. Moreover, many of the important elements in both Testaments are not dealt with adequately within the system of *Heilsgeschichte*.

Another attempt has been to deal with the subject from an eclectic perspective that combines historical development with a topical approach. Thus Manson[2] treats "God as Father" and "God as King" by tracing the development of these concepts, first in the Old Testament and then in the New. But Manson has difficulty moving from his discussion of the Old Testament development to the New Testament. Because the method makes little use of form criticism, the material is given no setting within Biblical traditions. The bridge between the Old and New often becomes a matter of historical conjecture. Because a concept of God was current in the religious thought of the people with whom Jesus lived, "it could hardly have been unknown to him." [3] As a result the method does not satisfy either the historian or the theologian.

In more recent years most Biblical scholars have given up the attempt to combine the two Testaments,[4] which simply reflects the crisis of envisioning Biblical Theology as one discipline. While not wishing to minimize the problems involved, we would like to suggest a method that takes more seriously the canonical form of the church's Scripture. The concern would be to determine how the Old Testament's witnesses to the covenant God of Israel functioned within the New Testament. An examination of Old Testament citations with the New which relate to this subject would seem to be the place to begin. If the Old Testament verses function in an entirely different way in their new Christian context from their original role, one would have a means of measuring the changing concept of God as well.

THE OLD TESTAMENT IN THE NEW

First of all, one finds a series of Old Testament texts that appear to function within the New Testament in unbroken continuity with their role within the Old Testament. Christians assume a common front with Judaism against all forms of paganism by making use of the Old Testament witness to monotheism. Mark 12:29 has Jesus using the Shema (Deut. 6:4) in his disputation with the scribes: "Hear, O Israel: The Lord our God, the Lord is one." Again in Matt. 4:10 Jesus, as a faithful Jew, repels Satan's demand for worship with a quotation from Deut. 6:13: "You shall worship the Lord your God and him only shall you serve." He rejects the title "Good Teacher" with the retort: "No one is good but God alone" (Mark 10:18). Likewise Paul makes use of the Shema in a somewhat paraphrased form, when he argues against the existence of idols that "there is no God but one" (I Cor. 8:4; cf. I Thess. 1:9). The monotheism of the Old Testament is everywhere assumed in the New Testament and at no point repudiated. There are no gods beside the one God, neither mammon (Matt. 6:24), nor cosmic powers (Gal. 4:8 f.), nor Caesar (Matt. 22:21).

The identity of the Christian God with the God of the Old Testament was so taken for granted that it became the grounds for exhortation and disputation. James argues against the separation of faith and works by noting that even the demons believe that God is one—to their agitation (James 2:19). Paul's somewhat obscure line of reasoning regarding the inferiority of the law because of its agencies is deduced from the axiom that God is one (Gal. 3:20). The writer of Hebrews cautions his hearers against disobedience by reminding them that God who judged Israel formerly in his wrath is the completely all-knowing one "with whom we have to do" (Heb. 4:13). The Christian God is the "God of the Fathers" (Acts 22:14), "God of Israel" (Matt. 15:31), and "Abba! Father!" (Rom. 8:15).

At times the formulas used of God show a later stage of development beyond the Old Testament, which had received its stamp in Jewish Hellenistic circles,[5] but the continuity with Jewish monotheism is again confirmed (cf. Rom. 1:20, "God's

invisible nature and eternal power"; I Cor. 8:6, "from whom
are all things and for whom we exist"; James 1:17, "Father of
lights with whom there is no variation or shadow due to
change," Heb. 2:10, "he, for whom and by whom all things
exist"; ch. 11:27, "the invisible one"; etc.).

The Old Testament's witness to God functioned in the
church as part of the Christian proclamation of divine promise
and divine judgment. Paul invokes the classic covenant formula, "I will be their God, and they shall be my people" (Isa.
52:11; Lev. 26:12; etc.), when admonishing the Corinthians
to lead a holy life separate from unbelievers (II Cor. 6:16).
He draws the ethical implications for eating meat sold in the
common market with good conscience from Ps. 24: "The earth
is the Lord's, and everything in it" (I Cor. 10:26). He warns
the Romans of the Final Judgment in the words of Isa. 45:23
(Rom. 14:11).

Moreover, Old Testament affirmations about God serve as
a basis for Christian exhortation to moral action. Particularly
Paul makes use of this form. The Christian is not to avenge
himself because God said "vengeance is mine" (Rom. 12:19
quoting Lev. 19:18; Deut. 32:35). Be generous in sharing one's
possessions because God supplies generously the needs of
those who are obedient (II Cor. 9:6 ff. quoting Ps. 112:9).
Do not act according to the wisdom of the world because
God "catches the wise in their craftiness" [1] (I Cor. 3:8 ff. quoting Job 5:13 and Ps. 94:11). "Owe no one anything, except to
love one another" because the commandment is: "You shall
love your neighbor as yourself" (Rom. 13:8 ff. quoting Lev.
19:18; Deut. 5:17 f.). Moreover, I Peter 3:9 finds a warrant
in Ps. 34:12 f. for not returning evil for evil, and the writer
of Hebrews in ch. 13:5 f. cautions against the love of money
by reference to Deut. 31:6, 8; Josh. 1:5.

Finally, there are a few texts that show that Old Testament
passages were used liturgically by Christians to praise God
in a manner that continued in unbroken continuity Israel's

worship. In Luke, ch. 1, Mary and Zechariah praise God with hymns which, both in form and content, are in direct continuation with the synagogue worship when rendering thanks for the birth of Jesus and John. Again, in the book of Revelation the worship of God is carried on in the same divine liturgy that Isaiah saw in his vision (Rev. 4:8 quoting Isa. 6:2 f.), or in a liturgy that combines passages from Daniel and the Psalms (Rev. 11:15 ff.).

To summarize: The use of Old Testament quotations referring to God by the New Testament writers shows an unbroken sense of continuity between the God of Israel and the God worshiped by Christians.

Secondly, one finds a series of Old Testament texts that function within the New Testament to maintain continuity with the Old Covenant while at the same time serving to develop a Christology. Old Testament faith in God is cited explicitly to establish faith in Jesus Christ. Because God is a fearful God—did he not say: "Vengeance is mine, I will repay"—do not incur his wrath by rejecting the Son of God (Heb. 10:26 ff. quoting Deut. 32:35 f.). A similar argument occurs in Heb. 12:29, "God is a consuming fire" (Deut. 4:24); therefore see that you do not refuse him, but offer to him an "acceptable worship." Particularly Paul has frequent recourse to an Old Testament proof text that relates to the hidden purpose of God to explain the gospel as both redemption and judgment. In Rom. 11:7 ff. he argues that Israel as a nation failed to obtain salvation. Only the elect obtained it; the rest were hardened. He cites Isa. 29:10 to indicate God's purpose: "God gave them a spirit of stupor," and concludes his whole discussion of Israel's final redemption with a doxology taken from Isa. 40:13 f. and part of Job: "For who has known the mind of the Lord or been his counselor?" Again in I Cor. 2:9 he argues that Christ is the secret wisdom of God, and if men had only understood, they would not have crucified him. Then he cites from Isaiah (chs. 64:4; 65:17). Finally the cross seems folly to those who are perishing, but it really reveals the power of God, as Isaiah said: "I will destroy the wisdom of the wise" (I Cor. 1:19 citing Isa. 29:14).

Moreover, the Old Testament is repeatedly used in the New Testament to interpret God's relation to Jesus Christ. "It is the God who said: 'Let light shine out of darkness,' who has shone in our hearts to give the light of the knowledge of the glory of God in the face of Christ." (II Cor. 4:6 quoting Gen. 1:3.) In II Cor. 5:17, Paul again relates the work of Christ to creation, but this time to the new creation by paraphrasing Isa. 65:17; 66:22. God's promise of a new heaven and earth is realized in the man who lives "in Christ." In Heb. 1:5 ff. God addresses Jesus in the words of Ps. 2 to designate him as his Son: "Thou art my Son, today I have begotten thee" (v. 7). In the same way the baptismal texts (Matt. 3:17 and parallels) have the heavenly voice announce the Sonship of Jesus in the words of Ps. 2:7 and Isa. 42:1 (cf. Mark 9:7). Conversely, Jesus' relation to God is consistently formulated in terms of Old Testament texts. Jesus is the "Messiah of God" promised by David in Ps. 110:1 (Mark 12:36); the "Son of God" in Matt. 22:41 ff. quoting Ps. 110:1 (cf. II Sam. 7:14); the "image of God" in II Cor. 4:4 quoting Gen. 1:27; the "Word" of God in John 1:1 referring to Gen., ch. 1, and Prov., ch. 8, etc.[6]

Again, Jesus assumes the titles of God by explicit reference to the Old Testament. In Heb. 1:8 he is identified with the "God" (theos) of Ps. 45:7. He is "Lord" (kurios) in Rom. 10:8 f. with reference to Deut. 30:14. He is the "first and last" of Isa. 44:6 in Rev. 1:17, the "I am he" of II Isaiah in John 8:58, and the one who is and "who was and who is to come" of Rev. 1:8 with an allusion to Ex. 3:14.

Moreover, Jesus shares or fully assumes the functions of the God of the Old Testament for the church. He is the giver of the new law in Matt., ch. 5. He is the one before whose judgment seat all must stand (II Cor. 5:10 with reference to Eccl. 12:14). Jesus is now the one at whose name "every knee should bow . . . and every tongue confess," whereas God was the object of this adoration in Isa. 45:23 (cf. Rom. 14:11). The Old Testament "day of the Lord" is now identified with the coming of Jesus (I Thess. 5:2). Finally God's table of Mal. 1:7 has become the "table of the Lord" who graciously feeds his people (I Cor. 10:21). Accordingly, the liturgical forms of Old Testament worship of God have been transferred to Christ. Christians now "call upon the name" of Christ (Acts 19:13; Rom. 10:14; I Cor. 1:2), and baptize "in his name." Angels worship him (Heb. 1:6; cf. Deut. 32:43, LXX; Ps. 97:7), and give praise to God and "the Lamb" (Rev. 5:13).

To summarize: The New Testament writers, even during the process of developing their Christologies, see no tension between the Old Testament understanding of God and their own understanding of Jesus Christ, but explicitly make use of the Old Testament to formulate their Christian confessions.

Finally, there are a variety of New Testament passages that attempt to defend the continuity between Christ and the God of the Old Testament, but without the explicit use of quotations. The threat to the Christological unity with the Old Testament came from two sides: first, from the synagogue that rejected the claim as incompatible with monotheism; secondly, from "enthusiasts" and proto-Gnostics who would reject the connection with the old covenant as impairing the new. The New Testament's defense against both fronts strove to show that the person and work of Jesus Christ was not something simply added to the Old Testament faith in God, but issued in an inner expansion because there was an integral relationship between the two.

A number of New Testament writers attempt to relate the work of Christ to what God had been doing in the history of Israel. Particularly in the speeches in Acts, Luke sets Jesus' coming in direct line with God's great deeds of the past. Similarly, the writer of Hebrews witnesses to the same God who once spoke to the fathers by prophets, but now has spoken through his Son (Heb. 1:1 f.). He recalls the Old Testament history of men's faith in the God of Israel which, however, already had Christ as its object (ch. 11:26). Again, Paul's speech in Athens (Acts, ch. 17) begins with God as creator of heaven and earth before speaking of the resurrection of the dead. In I Thess. 1:9 f. the work of Jesus is set within the context of turning from idols and serving the "living and true God" who comes as judge.

Again, there are numerous passages that attempt to point out both the unity and diversity between God and Christ by means of the double formula. Particularly, John works out the relation of the "Father and the Son." Jesus is the "only begotten Son," who was "sent" by the Father, and who makes him known. One honors the Father by honoring the Son (John 5:23). Likewise, Paul emphasizes that the confession of Jesus as Lord is done for the honor of God because it is God who acts in Jesus Christ (Phil. 2:11). In I Cor. 8:6 the uniqueness of both God and Christ is guarded by the repetition of the adjective "one": "There is one God, the Father, . . . and one Lord, Jesus Christ." First Timothy stresses the difference of function when he speaks of "one God, and one mediator between God and men, the man Christ Jesus" (ch. 2:5). First Corinthians 15:27 ff. makes use of Ps. 8 when interpreting the final subjection of the world to God as the work of Christ. Throughout these passages, in spite of a variety of approaches, the common note struck is on the unity of creation and salvation. The "God of our Lord Jesus Christ" (Eph. 1:17) has revealed his power in him in order to bring to completion his one divine purpose for all ages and men.

Lastly, the relation of God to Christ has been expressed in a series of triadic formulas. The benediction of II Cor. 13:14 speaks of "the grace of the Lord Jesus Christ and the love of God and the fellowship of the Holy Spirit." Matthew's baptismal form uses the "name of the Father and of the Son and of the Holy Spirit." One of the clearest statements of the diversity of divine function within complete unity is found in I Cor.

12:4 ff. (italics added): "There are varieties of gifts (*charisma*), but the *same Spirit;* and there are varieties of service (*diakonia*), but the *same Lord;* and there are varieties of working (*energyma*), but it is the *same God* who inspires them all in every one." As is well known, these are not trinitarian formulas because the inner unity among the parts has not been worked out at this early stage of the Christological development. However, the foundation on which the later creeds built has already begun to emerge within the New Testament.

To summarize: The New Testament confronts the various attacks, which seek to sever the Christian witness to Jesus Christ from the Old Testament understanding of God by confessing a dynamic unity, both in terms of person and work, between God and Christ, which admits of no dissolution.

TESTING THE SCOPE OF THE METHOD

An objection comes to mind. Is this conclusion regarding the unity of the New Testament's understanding of God with the Old really only dictated by the method of using Old Testament quotations and related formulas? Is it possible that a wholly different side of God's character and action is witnessed to in the New Testament apart from the Old Testament? Ever since Harnack's famous article[7] that pointed out the lack of explicit quotations in sections of the New Testament, certain scholars[8] have questioned whether the use of the Old Testament is basically an accommodation to an audience rather than being a formulation of an essential relationship. Did in fact a new understanding of God emerge through the person and work of Jesus which stood in striking discontinuity with the Old Testament? While a comprehensive treatment of this subject lies beyond the scope of this chapter, the question is serious enough to require at least a test respecting its validity.

An obvious place at which to probe the issue would be in

terms of the New Testament's understanding of God as a God
of love. Traditionally many Christians have felt that the
greatest strain between the Testaments lay at this point.
First, we turn to Paul to see his approach to the problem in
Rom. 8:28-39.[9] Paul works out his understanding of the love
of God within the framework of justification which, however,
does not mean that Paul has replaced love with faith. Following Old Testament and Rabbinic tradition, Paul sees God's
love revealed in terms of his election. Love to God stems from
being loved by God. It is the fruit of the Spirit (cf. Gal. 5:22)
and not a particular quality or virtue. Because God is "for you"
there can be no force or power to separate God's elect from
the love of God in Jesus Christ. And because of what Christ
has done, there can be no accuser, not even God himself. God
is the helper in terms of Isa. 50:9. This foreknowledge of God
working for the Christian's good calls forth man's love for
God. Then Paul quotes Ps. 44 to demonstrate that the Christians, as the Old Testament saints, confess in dire straits that
God is for them and they are, therefore, "more than con-
querors through him who loved us." Even in terms of the "love
of God" Paul finds complete continuity in God's nature which
was working out the one divine will in love from the beginning.

When we turn to John, ch. 5, we find a typical Johannine argument with strong parallels in ch. 9. Jesus answers the criticism of his healing on the Sabbath in v. 17: "My father is
working still [up to now], and I am working." The logic of the
response is that only God's work takes away sin and death.
Jesus manifests God's work in the act of healing. By healing
on the Sabbath, he claims to be continuing the life-creating
work of God. Indeed, he fills the Sabbath with the power of
God. He is not detracting from God's work. It is just the opposite: This is God at work. Then there follows a commentary
on the Son's relation to the Father. The Son does nothing of
his own accord, but comes in the name of the Father. His work
bears witness to his unity with the Father. In ch. 14 the love

of God to Christ and of Christ to God, and of the disciples to Christ, is worked out. At no point is there a rupture with the Old Testament's understanding of God's love, in spite of the fact that the Johannine idiom has moved far beyond the confines of the Old Testament. John simply is not talking about some new idea of God. The same divine reality that manifests itself as love is at work in the God who revealed himself in the Old Testament and in Jesus Christ.

We conclude that there is no reason to suggest that the New Testament insistence on continuity between the Old and New Testaments is one of accommodation, but lies at the heart of the gospel itself.

TESTING THE CLAIM OF CONTINUITY

Our study confirms that the New Testament consistently makes a claim to be in continuity with the Old Testament's understanding of God. Yet is this claim, in point of fact, true? Or is it the case that the Old Testament's witness to God simply cannot be treated as the New Testament attempts to do, and that the alleged continuity is a contrived one that does injustice to the Old Testament? One way of approaching the issue would be to determine how the Old Testament's understandings of God functioned in their original, historical contexts, and then to compare them with the New Testament's usage. The method does not consist in matching doctrines or ideas of God. Rather, the goal would be to see if one can determine the particular role of a witness within its setting, then sketch its inner movement within the whole range of Old Testament usage. Finally, one would seek to relate the inner movement and the outer structure of the Old Testament witness to its function within the New Testament. An additional control is applied when one begins with a specific Old Testament passage that is quoted in the New. This assures a common subject matter, at least at the outset.

1. Deut. 6:4, the "Shema Israel" is frequently quoted or

alluded to in the New Testament (Mark 12:29; Rom. 3:29; etc.). This formulation, which was to become the classical expression of monotheism for Judaism, comes as a summary statement in the book of Deuteronomy of the covenant relation between Yahweh and Israel. The unity in the person of God demands an absolute allegiance to the one covenant God. As is well known, the Deuteronomic statement is not a theoretical proposition that addresses the question of the existence or nonexistence of other gods, but arises out of the context of the covenant, and is directed toward maintaining that relationship. The Deuteronomic formulation reflects the concern of the whole book for the unity and holiness in the worship of the people of God, which was in danger of fragmentation because of pagan inroads. However, the tradition is ancient and already formulated in the Decalogue: "You shall have no other gods before me." In the later prophets the confession of Yahweh's claim over Israel was extended to become a claim for absolute uniqueness. Other gods are a delusion. There is no god beside Yahweh (Isa. 45:14). Yahweh alone is God (ch. 37:16). "I am the first and I am the last; besides me there is no god. Who is like me?" (Ch. 44:6 f.)

Nevertheless, this radical claim of the Old Testament for monotheism, which excludes idolatry in all forms, is not a form of monism. It is not a theory of God's unity that excludes the tensions between his immanence and his transcendence. The Old Testament can still speak of theophanies, of the "messenger of Yahweh" (*malak YHWH*), of his "glory" (*kabod*), "name," and "face." Nor is the tension between his eternality and temporality eliminated. He is "from everlasting to everlasting" and yet he participates in a history of revelation with new disclosures of his will for mankind (Ex. 6:2 ff.; Isa. 43:19). He is a God who reveals himself and yet who is also hidden (Job 13:24)—one in whom the tensions between his righteousness and mercy are not theoretically related.

The New Testament use of the Shema indicates that the

church saw itself in absolute agreement with the Old Testament and Judaism regarding God's uniqueness. Yet at the same time it sought to relate Christ to God within the framework of Old Testament witnesses to God. The church did so by utilizing the polarities within the Old Testament itself. Jesus was the "word" who was with God at the creation; he was the divine "wisdom" (Prov., ch. 8), and the "image of God." The New Testament, like the Old Testament, did not begin to formulate its theology as an exercise in philosophical reflection. Rather, within a covenant that the people of the early church had inherited and a discipleship to which they were committed they sought to understand what God was doing in Jesus Christ.

2. The Genesis testimony to God as creator of the heavens and the earth is solved continually in the New Testament, and is reflected in Christian liturgy and theology from the beginning (II Cor. 4:6; Col. 1:15; Heb. 4:4; etc.). However, the New Testament lays even greater importance upon the concept of redemption as a new creation and the expectation of a new heaven and earth. Obviously this polarity between the old and new creation is not peculiar to the New Testament, but was an inheritance from the Old. The prophets and apocalyptic writers testified to the final act of God—sometimes conceived of as a restoration of the old, sometimes as a totally new creation—which would bring to completion the plan of God for the world in spite of the enormity of human sin and cosmic evil. In parts of the Old Testament the writers witness to a new creation without attempting to relate it to the first creation. But particularly in II Isaiah, creation and eschatological redemption are fused into the one great act of God, in whose will creation and redemption are one (Isa. 51:9).

The problem of relating the church's eschatological hope to the faith of the Old Testament did not arise at the point of an eschatological hope of redemption as a new creation, but rather from the side of those within the church who sought to dissolve the Old Testament tension between the new and the old by rejecting the first creation. If this movement had been successful, then indeed a wedge would have been driven between God the Creator of the Old Testament and Christ the Redeemer of the church. As it happened, the struggle with Marcion in the second century resulted in a developing creedal formulation that affirmed the New Testament's solidarity with the Old in confessing God as creator and redeemer. Both Testaments are one in testifying to God's redemption, not as a dissolution of his creation, but its completion.

3. God's covenant relation to Israel is confirmed in the New Testament. At times the New Testament writers simply assume themselves to be part of Israel to whom the covenant was given (Acts 5:30). At other times the covenant is used as an illustration of God's goodness and Israel's disobedience (John 1:49). But most often the New Testament speaks in terms of a new covenant by which the church understood primarily its relationship to God in Christ. Obviously the New Testament found the warrant for its theology of the new covenant in the prophets, especially in Jer. 31:31. The controversy between the church and the synagogue arose in regard to whether the Mosaic covenant was inviolable or conditional, and whether the new covenant was a ratification of the old or its abrogation.

We turn to the Old Testament to examine the original function of the covenant to Israel to trace its inner movement. First of all, the tradition in Exodus and Deuteronomy is unified in seeing the covenant as a gracious act that stemmed from the initiative of God. Israel did not achieve the covenant status, nor was it granted in a form that was conditioned on her fulfilling certain stipulations. Nevertheless, once Israel became the covenant people, the imperative for obedience followed, and the covenant blessings were conditional upon a faithful response. Israel was set apart from all the nations as God's "own possession . . . a holy nation" (Ex. 19:5 f.).

Secondly, although the prophets seldom use the term "covenant," they do address themselves continually to the subject. They assume Israel's special prerogative before God, but conclude that special favor has incurred special judgment (Amos 3:2). The prophets speak of an impending divine judgment on God's disobedient people that shatters utterly and irreconcilably the past relationship. Isaiah addresses Israel as the "people of Gomorrah" (Isa. 1:10) and is commissioned to harden their hearts until the full judgment is executed (ch. 6:9 ff.). Hosea reverses the covenant formula: "Call his name Not my people, for you are not my people and I am not your God" (Hos. 1:9); Ezekiel portrays the entire redemptive history as one of perversity and disobedience, which went from bad to worse (Ezek. 16:1 ff.).

Thirdly, in spite of the unmitigated judgment Israel remains the people of God, and the dialectic between God's judgment and his redemption is never completely broken. Hosea envisions a day when God "will say to Not my people, 'You are my people'" (Hos. 2:23). Second Isaiah writes: "Fear not, . . . for your Maker is your husband. . . . For a brief moment I forsook you, . . . but with everlasting love I will have compassion on you." (Isa. 54:4 ff.) Finally, Jeremiah announces in an oracle from God: "Is Ephraim my dear son? Is he my darling child? As often as I speak against him, I do remember him still. . . . I will surely have mercy on him." (Jer. 31:20.)

How does the New Testament's understanding of God's covenant with Israel relate to the Old Testament's range of witness? Paul is the key witness on whom to run a test. Interestingly enough, Paul approaches the problem of God's relation to Israel in a dialectical fashion.[10] On the one hand, he stresses in Galatians the radical discontinuity between "Israel according to the Spirit" and "Israel according to the flesh." The church consists of people who are different in quality from those of the "old age." They are God's "new creation"

(Gal. 6:15). Because the new has come, the church lives in the present eschatological moment and neither circumcision (the covenant sign) nor uncircumcision counts for anything. Rather, a new people, called out of darkness, walk by the Spirit to whom the things of the law are past. The rupture with the past is so radical that Paul can even address the church as the "Israel of God" (v. 16).

On the other hand, Paul speaks in terms of the complete continuity with Israel in Rom., chs. 9 to 11, and insists that there is only one people of God, namely, Israel. Non-Israelites are only engrafted into the one trunk. Paul denies categorically that God has rejected his people. The judgment of Israel was used in God's purpose as a blessing to the nations and as the unbelief of Israel served the Gentiles, so, in turn, their faith will benefit Israel. In the end "all Israel will be saved" (Rom. 11:25 ff.).

In conclusion, although Paul's message regarding the covenant is radically different from the Old Testament, nevertheless his witness has caught the inner movement of the Old Testament's testimony to the elements of judgment and salvation, of discontinuity and continuity within God's covenant with his people.

THEOLOGICAL REFLECTIONS
ON THE CANONICAL WITNESS

We should now like to attempt some theological reflections that go beyond the descriptive task of Biblical Theology, and use as the context the witness of the whole Christian canon. It is interesting to recall the other recent theological attempts to develop an understanding of God from a different context.[11] One thinks especially of Tillich's ontological approach from "the ground of being," of Bultmann's existential stance that cannot talk of God except through the medium of anthropology, of Altizer and the "death of God" theologians who speak of the God of the Old Testament dying with Jesus to signal a freeing of man from superstition, and of the "new left" who identify God with service toward one's fellows and the humanizing of the structures of society. Perhaps the only things held in common among these various contemporary alternatives is their failure to take the Biblical canon seriously.

What does it mean to interpret the New Testament in the light of the Old? First, the Old Testament witness to the God of Israel provides the matrix in which the Christological statements of the New Testament are made. We cannot understand Jesus Christ apart from what God was doing as creator of the world, convenanting with Israel, guiding and directing the nations in judgment and mercy. The faith of the Christian church is not built upon Jesus of Nazareth who had a Jewish background, but its faith is directed to God, the God of Israel, Creator of the world, the Father of our Lord Jesus Christ. The Old Testament testimony to God serves the church, not as interesting background to the New Testament, nor as historical preparation for Christ's arrival, but as the living vehicle of the Spirit through which it continues to confront God.

Secondly, the Old Testament witness to God as the context from which to understand the New Testament guards the Christian against any truncated interpretation of God's work in Christ that would separate the physical world from the spiritual, the objective action from the internal motivation, the people of God from the individual believer, and commitment to a covenant from authentic existence. Most of the heresies of the Christian church stem from a distorted emphasis of the New Testament that has been cut adrift from its Old Testament moorings.

Thirdly, the Old Testament witness to God continues to provide the primary witness to dimensions of God's nature and purpose which, far from being corrected, are sustained and reiterated in the New. The righteousness of God is not bypassed but fulfilled in the cross. The holiness of God is not reduced by the incarnation but radicalized. The unity of God is not endangered by the Son but confirmed. The mystery of God is not made obvious but projected to new dimensions of wonder and praise.

Conversely, what does it mean to interpret the Old Testament in the light of the New? First, the New Testament testifies to the failure of Israel in its response to the covenant will of God. The Old Testament does not present a history of growing obedience or increasing illumination, but ends in dissidence and uncertainty. The easy continuity expressed in the phrase "the Judeo-Christian heritage" is opposed by the New Testament's witness to Jesus Christ, which testifies to his suffering, rejection, and death at the hands of the chosen people. The New Testament remains an offense because it lays claim to the Scriptures of Israel and hears in them the testimony to the rejected Messiah of God.

Secondly, the New Testament's witness to Christ as the context for understanding the Old Testament points to the fact that there is no aspect of the old covenant's testimony which is unaffected by the Lord of the church. The New Testament confesses Christ as Creator, Eternal Wisdom, Redeemer of Israel, and Judge. There is no body of Old Testament teaching that stands by itself and is untouched by the revelation of the Son. This means that frequent appeal to the term "Christomonism" raises a false issue, which has failed to understand the dynamics of Trinitarian theology.

Thirdly, the New Testament's witness to Christ provides the context from which to understand the tensions within the Old Testament's witness to God. His justice and his mercy find a unity in the death of Jesus, his transcendence and immanence in the incarnation, and his Kingship over heaven and earth in the reign of his Christ. The claim for a unity within the Old Testament is a theological confession that views the promise from the perspective of its fulfillment.

Fourthly, the New Testament's witness to Christ guards

the Old Testament from distortions to which it is vulnerable
when isolated from its whole context. The God of the Old Testament is not the God of Israel alone, but of all the nations.
The physical blessings of this world—life, land, the people—
are an inheritance that points to the ultimate reward which is
God himself. Man's worship, his deeds of charity, and search
for God are vain and worthless strivings without the Spirit
of God who breathes life into dead forms.

Lastly, what does it mean to interpret the Biblical witnesses
to God in the light of God's reality, and his reality in the light
of the witnesses? First, the Scriptures are pointers to God
himself. To know about God is not the same as knowing God.
"Let him who glories glory in this, that he understands and
knows me." (Jer. 9:24.) The God of the Bible is not a theological system, but a living and acting Lord, the one with
whom we have to do—now. We are confronted, not just with
ancient witnesses, but with our God who is the Eternal Present. Prayer is an integral part in the study of Scripture because
it anticipates the Spirit's carrying its reader through the written page to God himself. Again, obedience is the source of the
right knowledge of God. Peter said to Jesus: "Lord, what
about this man?" Jesus said: "What's that to you? Follow me."
The Christian is led from faith to faith, but in the context of
faithful response to God and his people. Finally, the Christian
interpreter strives to learn to use the language of faith that he
reads in the Bible. The ancient medium becomes a living vehicle into the presence of God only insofar as it becomes the
witness of each new generation. He cannot ape the past, but
he can be instructed by the prophets and apostles toward the
end that he learns himself to speak the language of faith for
his age.

NOTES AND INDEXES

Notes

Chapter 1. *The Beginning of a Movement*

1. Cf. Otto Piper's high praise in *Interpretation*, I (1947), p. 83: "In the field of biblical theology this is the first creative reaction America produces to the theological renaissance of the continent." A different response was voiced by Robert M. Grant in the *Journal of Religion*, XXVII (1947), pp. 213-214.

2. James D. Smart, "The Death and Rebirth of Old Testament Theology," *Journal of Religion*, XXIII (1943), pp. 1-11, 125-136. Reprinted with significant alterations in a later form in his book *The Interpretation of Scripture* (The Westminster Press, 1961).

3. Paul S. Minear: "There are signs of spring" (*Theology Today*, I [1944–1945], p. 49); Bruce Metzger: "A fresh wind is blowing in many quarters of the field of New Testament scholarship. . . . As in Ezekiel's vision . . . so we are witnessing today a veritable resurrection of a living and vital understanding of the New Testament" (*ibid.*, p. 563); J. M. Gettys: "A new day is dawning in the interpretation of the Old Testament" (*Interpretation*, II [1948], p. 356).

4. Cf. especially the editorials in *Theology Today*, I (1944–1945), and *Interpretation*, I (1947).

5. *RGG*,³ II, pp. 168 ff.; Thomas F. Torrance, *Karl Barth: An Introduction to His Early Theology, 1910–1931* (London: SCM Press, Ltd., 1962); James M. Robinson (ed.), *The Beginnings of Dialectic Theology* (John Knox Press, 1968).

6. Some indication of Brunner's importance is seen in his frequent citation in articles and books during the late forties and early fifties. Cf. as typical examples: Theodore O. Wedel, *Theology Today*, II (1945–1946), p. 35; Robert J. McCracken, *ibid.*, p. 81; J. N. Thomas, *Theology Today*, III (1946–1947), p. 162; James I. McCord, *Interpretation*, III (1949), p. 144; S. Paul Schilling, *Journal of Bible and Religion*, XVI (1948), pp. 13 f.; Paul S. Minear, *Eyes of Faith: A Study in the Biblical Point of View* (The Westminster Press, 1946), pp. 11, 13, 24, etc.; G. Ernest Wright, *God Who Acts: Biblical Theology as Recital* (London: SCM Press, Ltd., 1952), p. 90.

7. Robert C. Dentan, *Preface to Old Testament Theology*, rev. ed. (The Seabury Press, Inc., 1963); C. T. Craig, "Biblical Theology and the Rise of Historicism," *JBL*, LXII (1943), pp. 281 ff.; and the classic article by Martin Kaehler, "Biblical Theology," *The New Schaff-Herzog Encyclopedia of Religious Knowledge*, Vol. II (Baker Book House, reprinted, 1952), pp. 183 ff.

8. Krister Stendahl, "Biblical Theology, Contemporary," *The Interpreter's Dictionary of the Bible*, Vol. 1 (Abingdon Press, 1962), p. 419.

9. Lefferts A. Loetscher, *The Broadening Church* (University of Pennsylvania Press, 1954).

10. J. Gresham Machen, *Christianity and Liberalism* (The Macmillan Company, 1923).

11. Louis Berkhof, *Systematic Theology* (Wm. B. Eerdmans Publishing Company, 1938).

12. John A. Mackay, editorial, *Theology Today*, I (1944–1945), p. 13.

13. G. Ernest Wright, "The Christian Interpreter as Biblical Critic," *Interpretation*, I (1947), pp. 138 ff. In his later reflections on the state of Biblical studies in America, Wright played down the significance of the American theological impasse in the thirties in favor of a theory regarding the place of history in American education. Cf. *Harvard Divinity Bulletin*, XXVII (1962), pp. 1-16; XXVIII (1964), pp. 85-96.

14. G. Ernest Wright, *The Challenge of Israel's Faith* (The University of Chicago Press, 1944), p. vii.

15. Editorial, "Criticism, and Beyond," *Interpretation*, I (1947), pp. 219 ff.

16. Alan Richardson: "Most British readers find Barth somewhat indigestible" (*Theology Today*, II [1945–1946], p. 371). John Lowe: "In this country the uncongenial 'theology of crisis' has played only a minor role" (in Clifford W. Dugmore [ed.], *The Interpretation of the Bible* [London: S.P.C.K., 1944], p. 118). A. Michael Ramsey: "Is it possible to learn from the shaking that Barth has given to us, and yet to return to use what Westcott had taught us?" (*The Resurrection of Christ* [The Westminster Press, 1946], p. 121).

17. Amos Wilder suggests in his article, "Biblical Hermeneutic and American Scholarship," in *Neutestamentliche Studien für Rudolf Bultmann* (Berlin: Töpelmann, 1954), pp. 24 ff., that there was a continuity in America between the early liberals who were "constructive, antipositivistic, and even evangelical" and the modern study of hermeneutics. American Liberalism could "deepen" without the need of a real break with the past because it had never been undermined by eighteenth-century rationalism. Certainly Wilder is correct in observing that there has been an unbroken continuity of theological liberalism in America. But Wilder fails to understand in this article why the members of the Biblical Theology Movement found themselves fundamentally at odds with the type of liberal scholarship represented by his list of the "best known biblical scholars in this country." However, in another article Wilder gives evidence of having a real appreciation for Paul S. Minear's position (*Journal of Religion*, XXVIII [1948], p. 183).

18. In a sympathetic review article, Bruce M. Metzger and Otto Piper conclude: "One is inclined to think that conservative biblical scholarship has grown somewhat complacent and has lost contact with the world in which Christians have to live" (*Interpretation*, II (1948), p. 229).

19. Cf. the dedication in H. H. Rowley, *The Re-Discovery of the Old Testament* (The Westminster Press, 1946).

20. Alan Richardson, "The Nature of the Biblical Theology," *Theology*, XXXIX (1939), pp. 166-176.

21. William Irwin, in *Journal of Bible and Religion*, XII (1944), p. 160. Cf. a similar complaint in I. G. Matthews' review of G. Ernest Wright's *The Challenge of Israel's Faith*, in *Journal of Religion*, XXIV (1944), p. 221.

22. Morton Enslin, in *The Christian Century*, LXIII (1946), p. 460. Cf. the readers' responses on pp. 529 f.

23. Norman Pittenger, in *Journal of Bible and Religion*, XIII (1945), p. 181.

24. Robert Pfeiffer, "Facts and Faith in Biblical History," *JBL* (1951), pp. 1-14.

25. Henry J. Cadbury, in *Interpretation*, III (1949), p. 333.

26. Cf. Henry J. Cadbury's criticism of Floyd V. Filson's essay in *Journal of Religion*, XXVIII (1948), p. 210: "We are on the edge of a highly controversial issue which American scholarship scarcely has grappled with, though it is reminiscent of the technique of Machen."

27. Cf. the careful evaluation of John Lowe in Dugmore (ed.), *op. cit.*, pp. 108 ff.

28. Stendahl, *loc. cit.*

29. A good example of an American book that grew out of ecumenical discussions and yet was itself influential in charting the direction of the ongoing debate was Paul S. Minear's *Images of the Church in the New Testament* (The Westminster Press, 1960).

30. Cf. William B. Kennedy, "The Genesis and Development of the *Christian Faith and Life* Series," unpublished Ph.D. dissertation, Yale University, 1957; James D. Smart, *The Teaching Ministry of the Church* (The Westminster Press, 1954); Kendig B. Cully, *The Search for a Christian Education —Since 1940* (The Westminster Press, 1965).

31. H. Richard Niebuhr, Daniel Day Williams, and James M. Gustafson (eds.), *The Advancement of Theological Education* (Harper & Brothers, 1957), p. 97.

32. Cf. the typical emphasis on preaching in such articles and books as: Robert J. McCracken, "Let the Preacher Preach the Word," *Theology Today*, II (1945–1946), pp. 77 ff.; P. C. Warren, "By What Authority?" *Interpretation*, I (1947), pp. 201 ff.; Samuel Terrien, "The Old Testament and the Christian

Preacher Today," *Religion in Life,* XV (1946), pp. 262 ff.; Editorial, "Biblical Theology and the Pulpit," *Interpretation,* V (1951), pp. 432 ff.; H. H. Farmer, *The Servant of the Word* (Charles Scribner's Sons, 1942); Donald G. Miller, *Fire in Thy Mouth* (Abingdon Press, 1954). For a different stance, cf. Edmund P. Clowney, *Preaching and Biblical Theology* (Wm. B. Eerdmans Publishing Company, 1961).

33. *From the Bible to the Modern World* (Study Department of the World Council of Churches, Geneva, 1948).

34. Alan Richardson and Wolfgang Schweitzer (eds.), *Biblical Authority for Today* (The Westminster Press, 1951).

35. Oliver S. Tomkins, *The Church in the Purpose of God* (London: SCM Press, Ltd., 1950), p. 43.

36. Harold R. Willoughby (ed.), *The Study of the Bible Today and Tomorrow* (The University of Chicago Press, 1947).

37. James H. Cobb, "Current Trends in Catholic Biblical Research," in Willoughby (ed.), *op. cit.,* pp. 116-117.

38. Cf. representative articles in John L. McKenzie (ed.), *The Bible in Current Catholic Thought* (Herder & Herder, Inc., 1963).

39. Albert Gelin, *The Key Concepts of the Old Testament,* tr. by George Lamb (Sheed & Ward, Inc., 1955); Louis Bouyer, *The Meaning of Sacred Scripture,* tr. by Mary P. Ryan (University of Notre Dame Press, 1958); Célestin Charlier, *The Christian Approach to the Bible,* tr. by Hubert J. Richards and Brendan Peters (The Newman Press, 1958); Claude Tresmontant, *A Study of Hebrew Thought,* tr. by Michael F. Gibson (Desclee Publications, 1960).

40. Bruce Vawter, *The Four Gospels: An Introduction* (Doubleday & Company, Inc., 1967).

Chapter 2. *Major Elements of the Consensus*

1. Smart, *The Interpretation of Scripture,* p. 27.

2. Donald G. Miller, in *Interpretation,* I (1947), p. 263.

3. Bernhard W. Anderson, *Rediscovering the Bible* (Association Press, 1951), p. 4.

4. H. H. Rowley, *The Relevance of the Bible* (The Macmillan Company, 1943), p. 15.

5. Joseph Haroutunian, "Recent Theology and the Biblical Mind," *Journal of Bible and Religion*, VIII (1940), p. 20.

6. *The Westminster Study Edition of The Holy Bible* (The Westminster Press, 1948), p. xx.

7. Editorial, *Interpretation*, I (1947), p. 224.

8. John A. Mackay, in *Theology Today*, I (1944–1945), pp. 7-8. Cf. a similar statement by Elmer G. Homrighausen, in *Journal of Bible and Religion*, XI (1943), pp. 16 ff.

9. G. Ernest Wright, "The Present State of Biblical Archaeology," in Willoughby (ed.), *op. cit.*, p. 87 and elsewhere.

10. H. H. Rowley, "The Relevance of Biblical Interpretation," *Interpretation*, I (1947), p. 11.

11. Wright, *God Who Acts*, p. 112.

12. C. H. Dodd, *The Present Task of New Testament Studies* (London: Cambridge University Press, 1936).

13. Wright, "The Christian Interpreter as Biblical Critic," *Interpretation*, I (1947), pp. 139 f.

14. *The Expository Times*, LVIII (1946–1947), had five articles on the unity of the New Testament. *Interpretation*, V (1951), had a symposium on the unity of the Bible. *The Christian Scholar*, XXXIX (1956), offered several classic articles on the subject.

15. H. H. Rowley, *The Unity of the Bible* (The Westminster Press, 1955), p. 98.

16. Wilhelm Vischer, *The Witness of the Old Testament to Christ*, tr. from the 3d German ed. by A. B. Crabtree (London: Lutterworth Press, 1949).

17. A. G. Hebert, *The Throne of David* (London: Faber & Faber, Ltd., 1941).

18. H. Richard Niebuhr used the term "christo-morphic" in *The Responsible Self* (Harper & Row, Publishers, Inc., 1963), p. 158. Cf. G. Ernest Wright, in *Interpretation*, V (1951), p. 311.

19. Rowley, *The Unity of the Bible*, p. 2.

20. *Ibid.*; Paul E. Davies, "Unity and Variety in the New Testament," *Interpretation*, V (1951), pp. 174 ff.

21. Rowley, *The Unity of the Bible*, p. 17.

22. James Muilenburg, "The Interpretation of the Bible," in Richardson and Schweitzer (eds.), *Biblical Authority for Today*, pp. 200 ff.

23. Robert C. Dentan, in *Interpretation*, V (1951), p. 173.

24. Floyd V. Filson, "The Focus of History," *Interpretation*, II (1948), p. 25. Cf. also Donald M. Baillie, *God Was in Christ* (Charles Scribner's Sons, 1948), p. 22, and Otto Piper, "How I Study My Bible," *The Christian Century*, LXIII (1946), p. 299.

25. J. Stanley Glenn, "Jesus Christ and the Unity of the Bible," *Interpretation*, V (1951), p. 265.

26. H. Richard Niebuhr, *The Meaning of Revelation* (The Macmillan Company, 1960), pp. 135 f. Cf. also the very popular book of Bernhard W. Anderson, *The Unfolding Drama of the Bible* (Association Press, 1957).

27. William Temple, *Nature, Man, and God* (London: Macmillan & Co., Ltd., 1934), p. 448.

28. Millar Burrows, *An Outline of Biblical Theology* (The Westminster Press, 1946), p. 36.

29. C. R. North, *The Old Testament Interpretation of History* (London: The Epworth Press, Publishers, 1946), pp. 147 ff.

30. H. Wheeler Robinson, *Inspiration and Revelation in the Old Testament* (Oxford: Clarendon Press, 1946).

31. Rowley, "The Relevance of Biblical Interpretation," *Interpretation*, I (1947), p. 8.

32. Rowley, *The Re-Discovery of the Old Testament*, p. 11.

33. Rowley, *The Unity of the Bible*, p. 15.

34. Rowley, *The Relevance of the Bible*, p. 17.

35. G. Ernest Wright, "Progressive Revelation," *The Christian Scholar*, XXXIX (1956), pp. 61 ff.

36. Wright, *God Who Acts*, p. 55.

37. G. Ernest Wright, *Biblical Archaeology* (The Westminster Press, 1957), p. 55: "Biblical theology and biblical archaeology go hand in hand, if we are to comprehend the Bible's meaning." Cf. also Wright's response to the attack of J. J. Finkelstein against the new "Historicity School," in *Biblical*

Archaeologist, XXII (1959), pp. 101-108, reprinted in the *Biblical Archaeologist Reader,* I, pp. 14 ff.

38. Wright, *Biblical Archaeology,* p. 127. This conservative American orientation to Old Testament history found Eichrodt's position most compatible among the European scholars. Cf. Walther Eichrodt, "Offenbarung und Geschichte im Alten Testament," *Theologische Zeitschrift,* IV (1948), pp. 321 ff.

39. Anderson, *Rediscovering the Bible,* p. 35.

40. Bernhard W. Anderson, *Understanding the Old Testament* (Prentice-Hall, Inc., 1957), p. 37.

41. *Ibid.,* p. 41.

42. Cf. Floyd V. Filson, *The New Testament Against Its Environment* (London: SCM Press, Ltd., 1950), p. 50. A somewhat mediating position in G. Ernest Wright and Reginald H. Fuller, *The Book of the Acts of God* (Doubleday & Company, Inc., 1957), pp. 236 f., and Alan Richardson, *The Miracle-Stories of the Gospels* (London: SCM Press, Ltd., 1941), p. 3.

43. Otto Piper, "The Bible as 'Holy History,'" *The Christian Century,* LXIII (1946), pp. 362 ff.

44. Oscar Cullmann, *Christ and Time,* tr. by Floyd V. Filson (London: SCM Press, Ltd., 1951), p. 99. Ethelbert Stauffer's influence remained only indirect because his *New Testament Theology* had not been translated.

45. H. Richard Niebuhr, *The Meaning of Revelation,* p. 17.

46. *Ibid.,* p. 66.

47. Paul S. Minear, "The Conception of History in the Prophets and Jesus," *Journal of Bible and Religion,* XI (1943), p. 156.

48. Paul S. Minear, "Christian Eschatology and Historical Methodology," *Neutestamentliche Studien für Rudolf Bultmann* (Berlin: Töpelmann, 1954), pp. 15 ff.

49. Minear, *Eyes of Faith,* p. 276.

50. Will Herberg, "Biblical Faith as *Heilsgeschichte,*" *The Christian Scholar,* XXXIX (1956), p. 25.

51. *Ibid.,* p. 31.

52. Minear, "The Conception of History in the Prophets and Jesus," *Journal of Bible and Religion,* XI (1943), p. 156. Cf.

Minear, *Eyes of Faith*, pp. 11 ff. Howard T. Kuist, *These Words Upon Thy Heart* (John Knox Press, 1947), had a similar thesis, but worked it out along different lines.

53. Anderson, *Rediscovering the Bible*, p. 22.

54. Muilenburg, "The Interpretation of the Bible," in Richardson and Schweitzer (eds.), *Biblical Authority for Today*, p. 200.

55. Cf. Piper's formulation in "The Bible as 'Holy History,'" *The Christian Century*, LXIII (1946), p. 362.

56. G. Ernest Wright, "History and Reality: The Importance of Israel's 'Historical' Symbols for the Christian Faith," in Bernhard W. Anderson (ed.), *The Old Testament and Christian Faith* (Harper & Row, Publishers, Inc., 1963), p. 195.

57. John Wick Bowman used the term "prophetic realism," but he seemed to have had a similar problem in mind in his *Prophetic Realism and the Gospel* (The Westminster Press, 1955).

58. Emil Brunner, *The Divine-Human Encounter*, tr. by Amandus W. Loos (The Westminster Press, 1943), p. 47.

59. James Barr's *The Semantics of Biblical Langauge* (London: Oxford University Press, 1961) is, of course, fundamental although his concern in this book was not to trace the history of the development of the method which he criticized.

60. Matthew Arnold, *Culture and Anarchy: An Essay in Political and Social Criticism* (1869), cited from the Macmillan Company edition (1883), pp. 110 ff. Cf. the recurrence of Arnold's vocabulary in O. C. Quick, *The Gospel of Divine Action* (London: James Nisbet & Co., Ltd., 1933), pp. 33 ff.

61. George Adam Smith, *The Legacy of Israel*, ed. by E. R. Bevan and C. Singer (Oxford: Clarendon Press, 1927), pp. 10 ff.

62. H. Wheeler Robinson, "Corporate Personality in Ancient Israel," *Werden und Wesen des Alten Testaments*, ed. by P. Volz (Berlin: Töpelmann, 1936), pp. 49-62. The article was adumbrated in several of his earlier books.

63. J. Aubrey Johnson, *The One and the Many in the Israelite Conception of God* (Cardiff: University of Wales, 1942); *The Vitality of the Individual in the Thought of Ancient Israel* (Cardiff: University of Wales, 1949).

64. Johannes Pedersen, *Israel: Its Life and Culture* (London: Geoffrey Cumberlege, 1926).

65. Thorleif Boman, *Hebrew Thought Compared with Greek*, tr. by Jules L. Moreau (The Westminster Press, 1961). Cf. his Catholic counterpart, Tresmontant, *A Study of Hebrew Thought*. The closest Jewish parallel is represented in the writings of M. Kadushin: *Organic Thinking* (Jewish Theological Seminary, 1938) and *The Rabbinic Mind* (Jewish Theological Seminary, 1952).

66. Cullmann, *op. cit.*

67. The mood of the times is clearly reflected in the report of H. Richard Niebuhr, Daniel Day Williams, and James M. Gustafson (eds.), *The Advancement of Theological Education*, pp. 92 ff.

68. Alan Richardson, *A Preface to Bible Study* (The Westminster Press, 1944), pp. 86 ff.

69. Cf. Balmer H. Kelly's review of Norman H. Snaith's *The Distinctive Ideas of the Old Testament* (The Westminster Press, 1946), in *Interpretation*, I (1947), p. 88.

70. Alan Richardson (ed.), *A Theological Word Book of the Bible* (London: SCM Press, Ltd., 1950). Cf. the classic Biblical Theology approach in John Marsh on "Time"; Alan Richardson on "Miracle"; etc., in contrast to Matthew Black on "Isaac"; J. Y. Campbell on "Son of Man"; W. A. Whitehouse on "Commandment"; etc.

71. William F. Albright, *The Biblical Period* (Biblical Colloquium, reprinted 1950), p. 29.

72. G. Ernest Wright, "How Did Early Israel Differ from Her Neighbors?" *The Biblical Archaeologist*, VI (1943), p. 6. Cf. a similar statement in Rowley, *The Re-Discovery of the Old Testament*, p. 58: "The most enduring things that Israel attained were not the things she had in common with others, but the differentiae."

73. Cf. the similar lists in William F. Albright, *From the Stone Age to Christianity*, 2d ed. (The Johns Hopkins Press, 1957), pp. 257 ff.; Wright, "How Did Early Israel Differ from Her Neighbors?" *The Biblical Archaeologist*, VI (1943), pp. 6 ff.; Anderson, *Understanding the Old Testament*, pp. 57 ff.

74. Filson, *The New Testament Against Its Environment*,

p. 9: "Therefore we can grasp the distinctive character of the New Testament message concerning God only by a clear discernment of the originality of its teachings about Jesus Christ."

75. Albright, *The Biblical Period*, p. 9.

76. Henri Frankfort and others (eds.), *The Intellectual Adventure of Ancient Man* (The University of Chicago Press, 1946), pp. 363 ff.

77. Walther Eichrodt, *Theology of the Old Testament*, Vols. I and II, tr. by J. A. Baker, from the German 6th ed. (The Westminster Press, 1961 and 1967). Cf. Eichrodt's critical review of Harry Emerson Fosdick's *A Guide to the Understanding of the Bible* (Harper & Brothers, 1938), in *JBL*, LXV (1946), pp. 205 ff.

78. Frankfort and others (eds.), *op. cit.*, p. 358.

79. Nelson Glueck, *Rivers in the Desert*, Evergreen Encyclopedia, Vol. 5 (Grove Press, Inc., 1960), pp. 65 ff.

80. Harry M. Orlinsky, *Ancient Israel* (Cornell University Press, 1954), p. 142.

81. Hezekiel Kaufmann, "The Biblical Age," in Leo W. Schwarz (ed.), *Great Ages and Ideas of the Jewish People* (Random House, Inc., 1956); Hezekiel Kaufmann, *The Religion of Israel*, adapted and tr. by Moshe Greenberg (The University of Chicago Press, 1960).

82. Roland de Vaux, *Ancient Israel: Its Life and Institutions*, tr. by John McHugh (McGraw-Hill Book Company, Inc., 1961), pp. 271 ff.

83. John L. McKenzie, "God and Nature in the Old Testament," *Catholic Biblical Quarterly*, XIV (1952), reprinted in his book *Myths and Realities: Studies in Biblical Theology* (London: Geoffrey Chapman, 1963), pp. 85 ff.

84. J. J. Finkelstein, "Bible and Babel: A Comparative Study of the Hebrew and Babylonian Religious Spirit," *Commentary*, XXVI (1958), pp. 431 ff. Finkelstein's second essay (which was directed chiefly against Nelson Glueck), "The Bible, Archaeology, and History," *Commentary*, XXVII (1959), pp. 341 ff., called forth a reply from Wright in *The Biblical Archaeologist*, XXII (1959), pp. 101 ff.

85. Ivan Engnell was best known in the English-speaking

world for his dissertation, *Studies in Divine Kingship in the Ancient Near East* (Uppsala: Almqvist, 1943). A selection of his articles has only recently been translated: *A Rigid Scrutiny,* tr. by John T. Willis (Vanderbilt University Press, 1969).

86. The school was originally defined by a volume of essays entitled *Myth and Ritual* (London: Oxford University Press, 1933), ed. by S. H. Hooke.

87. Floyd V. Filson, "The Central Problem Concerning Christian Origins," in Willoughby (ed.), *The Study of the Bible Today and Tomorrow,* pp. 343 f.

88. William F. Albright, *Archaeology of Palestine* (London: Penguin Books, Ltd., 1949), p. 255.

89. Sir Edwyn C. Hoskyns and Francis N. Davey, *The Riddle of the New Testament,* 3d ed. (London: Faber & Faber, Ltd., 1947).

Chapter 3. *Unresolved Problems*

1. Smart, *The Interpretation of Scripture,* p. 290.

2. Wright, *The Challenge of Israel's Faith,* p. 16.

3. Editorial, "The Foundations of the Apostles and Prophets," *Interpretation,* II (1948), p. 183.

4. Richardson, *The Miracle-Stories of the Gospels,* pp. 127 f. Cf. Anderson, *Understanding the Old Testament,* p. 44; Robert C. Dentan, in *Interpretation,* V (1951), p. 165.

5. Rowley, *The Relevance of the Bible,* p. 50.

6. C. H. Dodd, H. Cunliffe-Jones, A. G. Hebert, R. Abba, J. K. S. Reid, John Bright, R. H. Bryant, etc.

7. Richardson and Schweitzer (eds.), *Biblical Authority for Today,* pp. 240 ff.

8. Cf. James Barr, "Old Testament Theology and the History of Religion," *Canadian Journal of Theology,* III (1957), pp. 147 f. R. B. Y. Scott's review of B. Davie Napier's *From Faith to Faith* (Harper & Brothers, 1955), in *The Christian Scholar,* XXXIX, pp. 82 f.

9. H. Richard Niebuhr, with Daniel Day Williams and James M. Gustafson, *The Purpose of the Church and Its Ministry* (Harper & Brothers, 1956), p. 103.

10. Randolph C. Miller, *Biblical Theology and Christian Education* (Charles Scribner's Sons, 1956).

11. Wayne E. Oates, *The Bible in Pastoral Care* (The Westminster Press, 1953).

12. Edward C. Gardner, *Biblical Faith and Social Ethics* (Harper & Brothers, 1960).

13. Cf. Schubert M. Ogden, *Christ Without Myth* (Harper & Row, Publishers, Inc., 1961).

14. Karl Barth, *Church Dogmatics*, Vol. III, Part 2, p. ix, cited by James Barr in his *Old and New in Interpretation* (Harper & Row, Publishers, Inc., 1966), p. 96.

15. James M. Robinson, "Basic Shifts in German Theology," *Interpretation*, XVI (1962), pp. 76 ff.; "The New Hermeneutic at Work," *Interpretation*, XVIII (1964), pp. 347 ff.

16. Allen O. Miller, *Invitation to Theology: Resources for Christian Nurture and Discipline* (Christian Education Press, 1958).

17. Paul Ramsey, *Basic Christian Ethics* (Charles Scribner's Sons, 1950).

Chapter 4. *The Cracking of the Walls*

1. G. Ernest Wright could write unequivocally in 1949: "The best and most balanced biblical department is undoubtedly that of the University of Basel with Baumgartner, Eichrodt, and Stamm in the Old Testament department, and Schmidt and Cullmann in the New." (*Interpretation*, III [1949], p. 53.)

2. Rudolf Bultmann's *Theology of the New Testament* was first translated in 1951 (Vol. I) and 1955 (Vol. II) (Charles Scribner's Sons); "New Testament and Mythology," in *Kerygma and Myth*, ed. by Hans Werner Bartsch (Harper & Brothers, 1953); *Essays: Philosophical and Theological* (The Macmillan Company, 1955); *Primitive Christianity in Its Contemporary Setting* (Meridian Books, Inc., 1956); *Jesus and the Word* (Charles Scribner's Sons, 1934, reissued 1958); *History of the Synoptic Tradition* (Harper & Row, Publishers, Inc., 1963). Günther Bornkamm, *Jesus of Nazareth*, tr. by

Irene and Fraser McLuskey with James M. Robinson (London: Hodder & Stoughton, Ltd., 1960); Günther Bornkamm and others, *Tradition and Interpretation in Matthew* (The Westminster Press, 1963); Ernst Käsemann, *Essays on New Testament Themes*, tr. by W. J. Montague (London: SCM Press, Ltd., 1964).

3. Cf. Rudolf Bultmann's review of Cullmann's *Christ and Time* in *Theologische Literaturzeitung*, LXXII (1948), pp. 659 ff., translated in *Existence and Faith*, ed. by Schubert M. Ogden (Meridian Books, Inc., 1960), pp. 226 ff.

4. Pfeiffer, *JBL*, LXX (1951), pp. 1 ff.

5. Eichrodt, "Offenbarung und Geschichte im Alten Testament," *Theologische Zeitschrift*, IV (1948), pp. 321 ff.

6. James M. Robinson, *A New Quest of the Historical Jesus* (London: SCM Press, Ltd., 1959).

7. James Branton, "Our Present Situation in Biblical Theology," *Religion in Life*, XXVI (1956–1957), pp. 5 ff.

8. Winston L. King, "Some Ambiguities in Biblical Theology," *Religion in Life*, XXVII (1957–1958), pp. 95 ff.

9. Langdon Gilkey, "Cosmology, Ontology, and the Travail of Biblical Language," *Journal of Religion*, XLI (1961), pp. 194 ff.

10. *Ibid.*, p. 199.

11. James Barr, "Revelation Through History in the Old Testament and in Modern Theology," *Princeton Seminary Bulletin*, LVI (1963), pp. 4-14, and in *Interpretation*, XVII (1963), pp. 193-205. Cf. Barr, *Old and New in Interpretation*.

12. Barr, *Old and New in Interpretation*, p. 18.

13. Branton, *loc. cit.*, p. 12.

14. Cf. H. B. Huffmon, "The Covenant Lawsuit in the Prophets," *JBL*, LXXVIII (1959), pp. 286–295; James Muilenburg, "The Form and Structure of the Covenantal Formulations," *VT*, IX (1959), pp. 347-365; D. R. Hillers, *Covenant: The History of a Biblical Idea* (The Johns Hopkins Press, 1969).

15. Gerhard von Rad, "Typologische Auslegung des Alten Testaments," *Evangelische Theologie*, XII (1952), pp. 17 ff.

16. Gerhard von Rad, *Old Testament Theology*, Vol. II, tr.

by D. M. G. Stalker (Harper & Row, Publishers, Inc., 1965), pp. 319 ff.

17. Cf. Hans Conzelmann, "Fragen an G. von Rad," *Evangelische Theologie*, XXIV (1964), pp. 113 ff., and von Rad's response in *Evangelische Theologie*, XXIV (1964), pp. 388 ff.

18. Hans Conzelmann, *The Theology of Saint Luke*, tr. by Geoffrey Buswell (Harper & Row, Publishers, Inc., 1960).

19. Cf. the critical review of the major redactional studies by Joachim Rohde, *Rediscovering the Teaching of the Evangelists* (The New Testament Library) (The Westminster Press, 1969).

20. Käsemann, *op. cit.*

21. Millar Burrows, "Thy Kingdom Come," *JBL*, LXXIV (1955), pp. 1 ff.

22. One of the most incisive criticisms, prior to Barr, was L. Knothe, "Zur Frage des hebräischen Denkens," *ZAW*, LXX (1958), pp. 175 ff., but cf. the reviews of Rudolf Bultmann in *Gnomen*, XXVII (1955), pp. 551 ff.; J. Hempel, *ZDMG*, CIV (1954), pp. 194 ff.; R. Marcus, *JBL*, LXXIII (1954), p. 111.

23. Henry J. Cadbury, "The Peril of Archaizing Ourselves," in *Interpretation*, III (1949), pp. 331 ff.

24. Cf. the reply by G. Ernest Wright, "The Problem of Archaizing Ourselves," *Interpretation*, III (1949), pp. 450 ff.

25. Th. C. Vriezen, *The Religion of Ancient Israel*, tr. by Rev. Hubert Hoskins (The Westminster Press, 1967); Helmer Ringgren, *Israelite Religion*, tr. by David E. Green (Fortress Press, 1966).

26. *The Interpreter's Bible*, Vol. I, pp. 292 ff.

27. Arthur Darby Nock, *Conversion* (London: Oxford University Press, 1933); *Early Gentile Christianity and Its Hellenistic Background* (Harper & Row, Publishers, Inc., 1964).

28. Erwin Goodenough, *By Light, Light: The Mystic Gospel of Hellenistic Judaism* (Yale University Press, 1935); *An Introduction to Philo Judaeus* (Yale University Press, 1940).

29. Erwin Goodenough, *Jewish Symbols in the Greco-Roman Period*, 12 vols. (Pantheon Books, Inc., 1953–1967).

30. Frank M. Cross, Jr., "Yahweh and the God of the Patri-

archs," *HTR*, LV (1962), pp. 225 ff.; "The Divine Warrior in Israel's Early Cult," in Alexander Altmann (ed.), *Biblical Motifs* (Harvard University Press, 1966), pp. 11 ff.; "The Song of the Sea and Canaanite Myth," in *Journal for Theology and the Church*, Vol. V (Harper & Row, Publishers, Inc., 1968), pp. 1 ff.

31. Frank M. Cross, Jr., and David Noel Freedman, "The Song of Miriam," *JNES*, XIV (1955), pp. 237 ff.

32. *Ibid.*, p. 239.

33. *Ibid.*

34. Cross, "The Song of the Sea and Canaanite Myth," *Journal for Theology and the Church*, Vol. V, p. 16.

35. *Ibid.*, p. 25.

36. Cf. William F. Albright's latest formulation in *Yahweh and the Gods of Canaan* (Doubleday & Company, Inc., 1968).

37. Bertil Albrektson, *History and the Gods* (Lund: Gleerup, 1967), p. 114. Many of the fundamental questions had already been raised by Hartmut Gese, *ZThk*, LV (1958), pp. 127 ff. (translated in Robert W. Funk [ed.], *Journal for Theology and the Church*, Vol. I [1965], pp. 49 ff.). Cf. also J. Coert Rylaarsdam (ed.), *Old Testament Essays in Transition in Biblical Scholarship* (The University of Chicago Press, 1968).

38. Barr, *Old and New in Interpretation*, p. 63.

39. Smart, *The Interpretaton of Scripture*, p. 26.

40. Stendahl, "Biblical Theology, Contemporary," *The Interpreter's Dictionary of the Bible*, pp. 418 ff.

41. Cf. particularly James M. Robinson, "Hermeneutic Since Barth," in James M. Robinson and John B. Cobb (eds.), *New Frontiers in Theology: The New Hermeneutic*, Vol. II (Harper & Row, Publishers, Inc., 1964), pp. 1 ff.

42. "The Significance of the Hermeneutical Problem for the Ecumenical Movement," *Report to the Commission on Faith and Order* (FO/67:37, June, 1967).

43. In my judgment, Gordon D. Kaufman's recent book, *Systematic Theology: A Historicist Perspective* (Charles Scribner's Sons, 1967), in spite of a valiant effort, satisfies neither the demands of the modern Biblical scholar nor those of the

systematic theologian. Cf. the review by David Kelsey, in *Reflection*, LXVI (March, 1969) (Yale Divinity School), pp. 12 f.

44. Langdon Gilkey, "Secularism's Impact on Contemporary Theology," *Christianity and Crisis*, XXV (1965–1966), p. 65.

45. Cf. Peter Berger, *The Noise of Solemn Assemblies* (Doubleday & Company, Inc., 1961).

46. Gilkey, "Secularism's Impact on Contemporary Theology," *Christianity and Crisis*, XXV (1965–1966), pp. 64 ff.; "Dissolution and Reconstruction in Theology," *The Christian Century*, Feb. 3, 1965, pp. 135 ff.; "A New Linguistic Madness," in Martin E. Marty and Dean G. Peerman (eds.), *New Theology*, No. 2 (The Macmillan Company, 1966), pp. 39 ff.

47. Gilkey, "Secularism's Impact on Contemporary Theology," *Christianity and Crisis*, XXV (1965–1966), p. 66.

Chapter 6. *The Shape of a New Biblical Theology*

1. The finest treatment of the theological developments that resulted in canonization is Hans von Campenhausen, *Die Entstehung der christlichen Bibel* (Tübingen: Mohr, 1968). Cf. his footnotes for a comprehensive handling of the secondary literature. Albert C. Sundberg, Jr., *The Old Testament of the Early Church* (Harvard University Press, 1964) is also a significant contribution.

2. George S. Hendry, "The Exposition of Holy Scripture," *Scottish Journal of Theology*, I (1948), p. 41.

3. F. Mildenberger, *Die halbe Wahrheit oder die ganze Schrift* (Munich: Kaiser, 1967), pp. 34 f., cites from Athanasius' letter of 367 to emphasize correctly that the category of norm be understood, first of all, as the "source of salvation." His warning guards against misunderstanding the reformation principle of *sola scriptura*.

4. The approach of Claus Westermann in his recent pamphlet, *Das Alte Testament und Jesus Christ* (Stuttgart: Calwer, 1968), has an emphasis on the continuity of redemptive history that has characterized a generation of European Old

Testament scholars (von Rad, Zimmerli, Wolff, etc.). The stress on the continuity of redemptive history that binds together the two covenants certainly contains an important insight. However, the concept of *Heilsgeschichte* is often used to denigrate the importance of the New Testament's explicit use of the text of the Old Testament, and fails to deal seriously with the early church's understanding of the Old Testament as a sacred *book*.

5. The appeal to the problem of language has become increasingly popular in recent years following the breaking up of the Biblical Theology Movement. The approach can take a variety of forms, such as a commonsense version, or a highly sophisticated philosophical theory which seeks to relate language to ontology. (Cf. Robert W. Funk, *Language, Hermeneutic, and Word of God* [Harper & Row, Publishers, Inc., 1966], for bibliography.) In general, the argument developed is that the function of language has changed from its role in the Biblical narrative that accounts for the chasm separating the ancient record from the modern man. A variety of moves have then been proposed by which to overcome this gap in terms of a hermeneutic of language. However one may judge the soundness of the philosophical underpinnings, the end effect is again to avoid taking seriously the text in its setting within the canon.

6. I am indebted to an unpublished paper of my colleague, Hans Frei, for certain of these formulations and basic insights.

7. Cf. typical formulations from Catholic and Protestant theologians which Barth has collected: *Church Dogmatics*, Vol. I, Part 2 (Edinburgh: T. & T. Clark, 1956), pp. 474 f.

8. Cf. von Campenhausen, *op. cit.*, pp. 123 ff.

9. The correspondence is conveniently collected by J. Schmid, SS. *Eusebii Hieronymi et Aurelii Augustini Epistulae mutuae.* Florilegium Patristicum XXII (Bonn: Hanstein, 1930). Cf. Schmid's excellent introduction and bibliography. I am also indebted to the discussion in H. Karpp, " 'Prophet' oder 'Dolmetscher'?" *Festschrift für Günther Dehn* (Neukirchen: Erziehungsverein, 1957), pp. 110 ff.; F. Stummer, *Einführung in die lateinische Bibel* (Paderborn: Schöningh, 1928), pp.

90 ff.; G. Jouassard, "Réflexions sur la position de Saint Augustine relativement aux Septante dans sa discussion avec Saint Jérôme," *Revue des Études Augustiennes*, II (1956), pp. 93 ff.; P. Benoit, "La Septante est-elle inspirée?" *Exégèse et Théologie*, Vol. I (Paris: Cerf, 1961), pp. 3 ff.

10. Walther Zimmerli, *The Law and the Prophets*, tr. by R. E. Clements (Oxford: Basil Blackwell & Mott, Ltd., 1965), pp. 5 ff.

11. Cf. the excellent treatment of Calvin in H. H. Wolf, *Die Einheit des Bundes* (Neukirchen: Erziehungsverein, 1958).

12. Cf. Barth, *Church Dogmatics*, Vol. III, Part 2 (Edinburgh: T. & T. Clark, 1960), pp. 437 ff.; especially pp. 443 f. Barth's own concept of *Bundesgeschichte* should not be confused with the classic *Heilsgeschichte*.

13. Barr, *Old and New Interpretation*, p. 96.

14. A study of Barth's understanding of the role of the canon needs to focus on far more than his Section § 19 in the *Church Dogmatics*, Vol. I, Part 2, in which he defends the need to have an open-ended canon. Rather, Barth's own method of interpreting Scripture by Scripture throughout the whole of the *Church Dogmatics* is the best indication of his approach to the question of canon and needs a fresh, thorough investigation.

15. Raymond E. Brown, *Catholic Biblical Quarterly*, XXV (1963), pp. 262 ff.; J. Coppens, *Concilium*, 30, pp. 125 ff.

16. The secondary literature on this subject has become very large. The following are representative: C. H. Dodd, *According to the Scriptures* (London: James Nisbet & Co., Ltd., 1952); Krister Stendahl, *The School of Saint Matthew, and Its Use of the Old Testament* (Uppsala: Gleerup, 1954); Birgir Gerhardsson, *Memory and Manuscript* (Uppsala: Gleerup, 1961); Barnabas Lindars, *New Testament Apologetic* (The Westminster Press, 1962); A. Suhl, *Die Funktion der alttestamentlichen Zitate und Anspielungen im Markusevangelium* (Gütersloh: Gerd Mohn, 1965); Robert H. Gundry, *The Use of the Old Testament in Saint Matthew's Gospel* (Leiden: Brill, 1967); T. Holtz, *Untersuchungen über die alttestamentlichen Zitate bei Lukas* (Berlin: Akademie, 1968).

17. Cf. my treatment of Ps. 8 in Part III.

18. Wilhelm Dittmar, *Vetus Testamentum in Novo. Die Alttestamentlichen Parallelen des Neuen Testaments im Wortlaut der Urtexte und der Septuaginta* (Göttingen: Vandenhoeck, 1903).

19. Dodd, *According to the Scriptures*, pp. 28 ff.

20. Robert Rendall, "Quotation in Scripture as an Index of Wider Reference," *Evangelical Quarterly*, XXXVI (1964), pp. 214 ff.

21. Lindars, *op. cit.*, pp. 169 ff.

22. An extreme form of this criticism is found in Ben Zion Bokser, *Judaism and the Christian Predicament* (Alfred A. Knopf, Inc., 1967). Bokser's arguments are generally uninformed by any recent scholarship on the subject of the New Testament quotations.

23. Cf. especially Luther on the Gospels in E. Mülhaupt (ed.), *Luthers Evangelien-Auslegung*, Vol. II (Göttingen: Vandenhoeck, 1935), pp. 503 ff.

24. Cf. my fuller treatment in "Interpretation in Faith," *Interpretation*, XVIII (1964), pp. 444 ff.

Chapter 7. *Biblical Theology's Role in Decision-Making*

1. Fortunately there are some monographs that deal with particular aspects of the field of Biblical ethics. Cf., for example, C. H. Dodd, *Gospel and Law* (Columbia University Press, 1951); Victor P. Furnish, *Theology and Ethics in Paul* (Abingdon Press, 1968). Rudolph Schnackenburg's *The Moral Teaching of the New Testament*, tr. by J. Holland-Smith and W. J. O'Hara from 2d rev. German ed. (London: Burns and Oates, 1965), is somewhat disappointing but has a useful bibliography. In German, cf. N. H. Søe, *Christliche Ethik* (2 Aufl., Munich: Kaiser), and H. van Oyen, *Ethik des Alten Testaments* (Gütersloh: Gerd Mohn, 1967).

2. Cf. G. F. Woods, "The Grounds of Christian Moral Judgments," in Alexander R. Vidler (ed.), *Soundings* (London: Cambridge University Press, 1963), pp. 200 f.

Chapter 8. *Recovering an Exegetical Tradition*

1. Cf. my article "Interpretation in Faith," *Interpretation,* XVIII (1964), pp. 434 ff.
2. John Gray, *I and II Kings: A Commentary* (London: SCM Press, Ltd., 1964), pp. 299 ff. Contrast this to Barth's interpretation of I Kings, ch. 13, in *Church Dogmatics,* Vol. II, Part 2 (Edinburgh: T. & T. Clark, 1957), pp. 393 ff.
3. *The Interpreter's Bible,* Vol. I, p. 754.
4. Cf. Augustine's *Expositions of the Psalms,* on Ps. 103.
5. William Tyndale, in his *Prologue to the Five Books of Moses* (1530).
6. Bengel, preface to his *Gnomen of the New Testament.*
7. Cf. Calvin's preface to his *A Commentary on the Psalms of David* (1557).

Chapter 9. *Psalm 8 in the Context of the Christian Canon*

1. Cf., for example, Mary Turner, "Psalm 8:1-2," *Theology,* LXIX (1966), pp. 493 ff.; and Mitchell Dahood, *Psalms 1-50* (Doubleday & Company, Inc., 1966), pp. 49 ff.
2. Martin Luther, *Works,* Vol. XII, ed. by Jaroslav Pelikan (Concordia Press, 1955), p. 135.

Chapter 10. *Moses' Slaying in the Theology of the Two Testaments*

1. Cf. the parallel vocabulary in I Sam. 21:11 ff.; I Kings 11:17 ff.; Jer. 26:20 ff.; "The Story of Sinuhe," *ANET,*[2] p. 19.
2. Cf. the brilliant essay of Ahad Ha-'am, *Selected Essays* (Jewish Publication Society, 1912), pp. 306 ff.
3. For a discussion of the whole speech, in addition to the standard commentaries, cf. B. W. Bacon, "Stephen's Speech," *Biblical and Semitic Studies* (Yale University Press, 1901), pp. 213 ff.; Martin Dibelius, *Studies in the Acts of the Apostles,* tr. by Mary Ling and Paul Schubert; ed. by Heinrich Greeven (London: SCM Press, Ltd., 1956), pp. 138 ff.; Marcel Simon,

Saint Stephen and the Hellenists in the Primitive Church
(London: Longmans, Green & Company, Ltd., 1958), with
additional bibliography.
    4. See L. Ginsberg, *Legends of the Jews*, Vol. V (Jewish
Publication Society, 1925), p. 404, for the references.
    5. Cf. *ThWNT*, V, pp. 840 ff.
    6. Cf. Peter Katz, *Philo's Bible* (London: Cambridge University Press, 1950), pp. 73 ff.
    7. For a discussion of the formal elements, cf. H. Windisch,
Hebräerbrief, 2 Aufl. (Tübingen: Mohr, 1931), pp. 98 f.
    8. *Ibid.*, p. 98.
    9. Cf. the addition in the Western text of v. 23, which describes the killing of the Egyptian as an act of faith.
    10. Mechilta, Shirata I, 49 f.; Shemoth Rabbah 30.4; cf.
Philo, *De Vita Mosis*, 1.7 f.
    11. Shemoth Rabbah I, 27.
    12. Shemoth Rabbah I, 28; Philo, *De Vita Mosis*, 1.8; cf.
Ginsberg, *op. cit.*, p. 405, for further parallels.
    13. M. Ginsburger (ed.), *Pseudo-Jonathan* (Berlin: S. Calvary & Co., 1903), p. 100. Midrash Haggadol Shemoth, ed.
by Margulies, p. 29, etc.
    14. Cf. Ginsberg, *op. cit.*, p. 405, for references.
    15. Cf. the summary of opinions in Cornelius à Lapide,
Commentarii in Sacram Scripturam, and in M. Poole, *Synopsis
Criticorum*.
    16. H. Frey, *Das Buch der Heimsuchung und des Auszugs*
(Stuttgart: Calwer, 1949), p. 35.

**Chapter 11. *Proverbs, Chapter 7, and a Biblical Approach
to Sex***

    1. The translation "wily" remains uncertain. An interesting
conjecture is to emend the word to "veil" on the basis of the
parallel description in Gen. 38:14.
    2. The Septuagint reads "gently" instead of "suddenly."
    3. The text is very difficult. The MT is retained by few
commentators: "and like a fetter(?) for the discipline of a
fool." Cf. the lengthy discussion in W.O.E. Oesterley, *The*

Book of Proverbs (London: Methuen & Co., Inc., 1929), pp. 53 ff.

4. Roger N. Whybray, *Wisdom in Proverbs* (London: SCM Press, Ltd., 1965), p. 50.

5. Cf. Ecclus. 9:1 ff.; 23:18 ff.; etc.; "The Instruction of Ani," *ANET*, ed. by Pritchard, p. 420.

6. Cf. G. Boström, *Proverbiastudien: Die Weisheit und das fremde Weib in Spr. 1-9* (Lund: Gleerup, 1935).

7. Barr, *The Semantics of Biblical Language*, pp. 263 ff.

8. Ephraim A. Speiser (ed. and tr.), *Genesis* (Doubleday & Company, Inc., 1964), p. 291.

9. Gerhard von Rad, *The Problem of the Hexateuch and Other Essays*, tr. by E. W. T. Dicken (McGraw-Hill Book Company, Inc., 1966), pp. 292 ff.

Chapter 12. *The God of Israel and the Church*

1. Millar Burrows, *An Outline of Biblical Theology*, pp. 54 ff.; Robert C. Dentan, *A First Reader in Biblical Theology* (The Seabury Press, Inc., 1961), pp. 91 ff.

2. T. W. Manson, *The Teaching of Jesus* (Cambridge: University Press, 1931).

3. *Ibid.*, p. 140.

4. Robert C. Dentan, *The Knowledge of God in Ancient Israel* (The Seabury Press, Inc., 1968); James S. Chesnut, *The Old Testament Understanding of God* (The Westminster Press, 1968); Hans Conzelmann, *Grundriss der Theologie des Neuen Testaments* (Munich: Kaiser, 1968), pp. 118 ff.

5. E. Norden, *Agnostos Theos. Untersuchungen zur Formengeschichte religiöser Rede* (Berlin: Teubner, 1913); Martin Dibelius, *Botschaft und Geschichte*, II (Tübingen: Mohr, 1956), pp. 14 ff.

6. The problems connected with the use of the title of "servant" in the New Testament are so controversial that I have avoided the issue.

7. Adolf von Harnack, "Das Alte Testament in den Paulinischen Briefen und in den Paulinischen Gemeinden" (Berlin: Sitzung der phil.-hist. Klasse, 1928), pp. 124-141.

8. H. Braun, "Das Alte Testament im Neuen Testament," *Zeitschrift für Theologie und Kirche*, LIX (1962–1963), pp. 16 ff.

9. Cf. Adolf Schlatter, *Gottes Gerechtigkeit*[5] (Stuttgart: Calwer, 1965), pp. 286 ff.

10. I am indebted to the discussion in N.A. Dahl, *Das Volk Gottes* (Darmstadt: Wissenschaftliche Buchgesellschaft, 1963), pp. 243 ff.

11. For a survey, cf. Frederick Herzog, *Understanding God* (Charles Scribner's Sons, 1966).

Author Index

Subject Index

Scripture Index